THE WILL TO GOVERN WELL

KNOWLEDGE, TRUST, & NIMBLENESS

THE WILL TO GOVERN WELL

KNOWLEDGE, TRUST, & NIMBLENESS

GLENN H. TECKER

JEAN S. FRANKEL

PAUL D. MEYER, CAE

asae | american society of association executives

FOUNDATION

WASHINGTON D.C.

Information in this book is accurate as of the time of publication and consistent with standards of good practice in the general management community. As research and practice advance, however, standards may change. For this reason, it is recommended that readers evaluate the applicability of any recommendation in light of particular situations and changing standards.

American Society of Association Executives
1575 I Street, NW
Washington, DC 20005-1103
Phone: (202) 626-2723; (888) 950-2723 outside the metropolitan Washington, DC area
Fax: (202) 408-9633
E-mail: books@asaenet.org
ASAE's core purpose is to advance the value of voluntary associations to society and to support the professionalism of the individuals who lead them.

Sarah C. Varner, CAE, Executive Vice President and Chief Operating Officer, ASAE Foundation
Michelle Mason, CAE, Vice President, Research Programs, ASAE Foundation

Ann I. Mahoney, CAE, Vice President, Knowledge and Content Management
Anna Nunan, Director of Book Publishing
Glenda Beal, Acquisitions Coordinator
Jennifer Moon, Production Manager
Anthony Conley, Operations Coordinator

Cover design by UDG|DesignWorks and interior design by Black Dot Group.

This book is available at a special discount when ordered in bulk quantities. For information, contact the ASAE Member Service Center at (202) 371-0940.

A complete catalog of titles is available on the ASAE Web site at www.asaenet.org/bookstore

Table of Contents

Foreword

Associations today face a dizzying array of challenges. As the industries, professions, and causes they serve confront rapid and unpredictable change, associations must adapt quickly and flexibly. But how can associations adapt without losing their focus on crucial membership needs?

In a new study supported by the ASAE Foundation, authors Glenn H. Tecker, Jean S. Frankel, and Paul D. Meyer, CAE, uncover the key strengths of associations that best meet those challenges. First, associations must have leaders who exhibit the will to govern well—the strong desire both to create flexible structures and processes of governance and to change governance as needed to meet changing environments. Second, such governance structures must be designed to incorporate three crucial factors: knowledge, trust, and nimbleness. The authors' findings—as presented in *The Will to Govern Well: Knowledge, Trust, and Nimbleness*—should help associations create a knowledge-based governance structure and a process for thinking strategically as a model for good decision-making.

The authors believe that developing and sustaining the will to govern well is truly an imperative for all associations in the future. As they note, "the barriers to successful evolution have more to do with the *willingness* of people to do things differently than with their knowing *what* to do differently." This strong will is the only thing ensuring that associations' unique strengths will not be undermined. It preserves associations' key competitive advantages: the aggregate intellectual capital of their membership, their energy as a community with common purpose, and their credibility as a voluntary institution.

The ASAE Foundation is pleased to present the conclusions of this study to the association community. As the global leader in assisting associations, their executives, and their partners to prepare for the future, the Foundation is dedicated to providing the comprehensive, credible, and current information that associations need to make wise strategic decisions in our constantly changing world. The Foundation's research efforts are designed to ensure that the ASAE Foundation continues to be the source of insight and knowledge that will assist the aspiring association in leading and succeeding in the future.

Sarah J. Sanford, CAE
Executive Director, Society of Actuaries
Schaumburg, IL
Chair, ASAE Foundation 2001–2002

Preface

The purpose of this book is to increase the likelihood that staff and member leaders of associations will come to share a common and rich understanding of what makes their enterprises unique.

Although it is no longer possible to generalize about the association community, this book observes and catalogues the links between knowledge, trust, and nimbleness and how together they contribute to effective governance systems in the 21st century. Qualitative studies and "action lab" experiences with more than 100 associations have affirmed these observations and findings. They represent the cumulative knowledge and insight of a diverse group of more than two dozen experts and practitioners—all with nationally respected reputations and track records for predicting the future.

This book is intended as a handbook for anyone in a position to design, influence, or participate in the governance systems of associations. It is of equal relevance to an association's chief staff executive, chief elected officer, governing board, and staff and member leaders. The authors hope organizations will benefit from its use and make it a primary educational tool for enlightened CEOs to share with their members and staff partners.

The book refers to organizations as "associations," but this label applies to any voluntary organization with a service-oriented mission: foundations; charities; professional, trade, industry, or cause-related societies; certifying boards; academies; and so forth. The voluntary nature of these organizations, not their not-for-profit status, is what defines them. A new model of association is also emerging, called the hybrid, with multiple types of membership and forms of structure (e.g., companies, other organizations, individuals). The hybrid is an "open model" of association structure, has significant implications for membership and competency of the board, and will be discussed in this book.

Study Methods and Sources

The conclusions presented in this book are based on an extensive study of information collected from governance practitioners. The types of information collected include the following:

- One- or two-day in-depth examinations of governance-related practices and issues by several specially constructed panels of experts and practitioners;
- The real experiences in evolving governance of more than two dozen associations that served as "action labs" for studying and documenting changes in structure, process, culture, and strategy;
- In-depth interviews with the executives of several associations identified as positive and negative examples of knowledgeable decision making, trustful cultures, and nimble implementation;

- Case studies of successful, flawed, and failed governance reforms; and
- Questionnaires from approximately 1,000 association staff and member leaders attending ASAE's Symposium for Chief Staff and Chief Elected Officers. These participants from trade, professional, industry, cause-related, or charitable organizations began their learning experience at the symposium by identifying the most significant barriers to the realization of their organization's full potential.

Together, the organizations represented constitute a broad mix across a number of variables: size, industry, and cause representation; general organizational information (membership demographics, budget, staffing, and tax status); organizational structure, including the relationship between national and local units; geographic location; board composition and demographics; board member selection and responsibilities; board meetings; executive and other committees; and governance issues and challenges.

Many case study examples presented in this book are from associations represented in the study. This information appears in formats that include formal case studies, abbreviated examples of case studies, and brief infusions of real-life experiences at key points. Certain case studies also include some detail about the methodologies associations use to develop strategies. The templates in the appendix will be helpful in defining an association's strategic initiatives to build the elements of knowledge, trust, and nimbleness into governance. Some of the templates are tools developed by Tecker Consultants LLC, and others are well-known methodologies with Tecker Consultants' adaptations for use by associations.

The insights and strategies explored in this book are not a panacea for governance maladies or the secret to governance success but are simply observations of common attributes found in a variety of associations that appear to themselves and others as having the will to govern well.

Associations are constantly innovating and evolving as they reexamine their assumptions and refine the governance models on which they operate. While the authors have guaranteed their anonymity, the associations that served as "action laboratories" for our work demonstrated a commitment to developing and testing new alternatives to increase their effectiveness in governance and to developing and sustaining the will to govern well. Those associations involved in our study demonstrated attention, commitment, thoughtfulness, and flexibility that will serve them well as they face the challenges of the future.

Glenn H. Tecker
Jean S. Frankel
Paul D. Meyer, CAE
April 2002

Acknowledgments

Contributing Authors
Elaine Kotell Binder, CAE
Catherine D. Bower, CAE
Heather J. Crossin
Bud E. Crouch
Kermit M. Eide
Patricia Walker Hickmann
Terry Newhard
Irving J. Tecker

Research Team
Elaine Kotell Binder, CAE
Catherine D. Bower, CAE
Heather J. Crossin
Bud E. Crouch
Kermit M. Eide
Patricia Walker Hickmann
Terry Humfeld, CAE
Wells B. Jones, CAE
Pamela A. Kaul
Terry Newhard
Janet G. McCallen, CAE
Michelle Mason, CAE
Judith Shamir, CAE
Irving J. Tecker
Robin M. Wedewer
Sarah C.Varner, CAE
Leigh Wintz, CAE

Introduction

Why Governance Needs to Change

Any look inside an association today suggests there is no shortage of challenges. These challenges include changes in the balance of power, in policy making, and in measures of success. Associations must understand increasingly complex member segments and must create mechanisms to respond to specialized needs.

Past generations of volunteers often committed time and energy selflessly, with duty and loyalty, but today, many members ask, "*What's in it for me?*" Increased demands for tangible benefits and bottom-line outcomes require associations to adjust their ways of thinking—and to alter past mechanisms for measuring success.

With respect to certain industries, professions, and causes—especially those undergoing rapid change—associations are being forced to create or reestablish their reputation for value and relevance among members, customers, and stakeholders. In some cases the very survival of the association and its membership may hinge on the successful establishment of a unique, sustainable reputation. But such a need creates pressures on traditional systems of governance.

Critical to attracting volunteers to active involvement in an organization is the offer of tangible and intangible benefits and outcomes. Tangible benefits are cognitive, relating to time, dollars, and economic returns. Intangible benefits are affective, relating to increased self-esteem, self-worth, and sense of community. Although many associations are successful in providing tangible benefits, it is in the way they meet the needs of members and volunteers with intangible benefits that provides them a competitive advantage over other sources positioned to meet the same need (such as for-profit providers).

In its 1999 publication, *Facing the Future: A Report on the Major Trends and Issues Affecting Associations*, the ASAE Foundation, as part of its ongoing environmental scan research, identified a number of emerging trends. Among them was the need for associations to focus on value—return on investment, as evidenced by the statement, "Associations must have a clearly defined value proposition, carefully choosing whom they will serve and in which products and services they will excel."

As times and markets change, a for-profit entity has the ability to seek out and attract new segments of customers. But if an association does not keep up with the rapidly increasing segmentation of those it serves, and becomes irrelevant in the eyes of its core members, it may experience radical change in the nature and character of its enterprise—a potentially dramatic shift in both mission and identity.

Relevance is an enormous issue for associations. Absent a vision—a sense of direction and an understanding of where the industry and its members are going—an association can exist only in a constantly reactive mode. For a while it may retain its role as a viable information source for its members, but over time it will lose effectiveness as increasingly it learns about changes in the industry, profession, or cause at about the same time that members do. Without a vision and an ongoing sense of relevance, associations may even find themselves competing with members for the role of key provider of information.

How are successful associations meeting these challenges? How is it that some continue to thrive in the face of rapid change? What implications does the need for relevance have for the governance systems of associations? What kinds of systems, structures, processes, and cultures will be required for associations to execute effective governance that yields ongoing relevance and value? What is required for associations to seek and sustain the will to govern well?

The authors of this book believe that what yields success in moving governance systems to evolve to a new level of performance is having the will to do it well. Therefore, the insights, observations, and recommendations presented here are not so much about finding new ways of doing the right things; rather, they show how associations are investing energy in doing things right.

The needed change in association governance lies not in function or role, but in processes for getting work done and in the underlying culture necessary to support more effective mechanisms. **There is no need to "reinvent" association governance**. But there *is* a need to improve governance practices.

Associations are unique because they are like a triple-helix DNA composed of three intertwined threads—members as owners, members as customers, and members as workforce. Associations are different from such organizations as for-profit businesses in that their populations of owners, customers, and workforce are one and the same. Furthermore, there is a constant need to maintain a balance among the three to achieve effective governance. Experience shows that member leaders are willing to alter the balance among the threads only when they are comfortable that their interests are being served by the alteration. Unraveling the DNA balance would put at great risk key competitive advantages associations have in the 21st century—the aggregate intellectual capital of their membership, their energy as a community with common purpose, and their credibility as a voluntary institution. As associations seek to create more effective systems of work and decision making, it will be ever more important to protect this triple-strand balance.

This book, then, is about developing strategies for change in governance. It rejects the notion of wholesale revolution in favor of rapid evolution. When an association talks extensively about reinvention and revolution, members resist. When it talks about evolution, however, they often are more accepting and allow change to occur in a compressed time frame.

Many of the structures, practices, and policies built by successful association leaders were designed to increase predictability of performance, helping to replicate past successful organizational change, or to avoid past mistakes. But associations may need to abandon successful past strategies to be open to the emergent future—a future that may require fewer systems and structures and more attention to and intention by gifted, creative people, both staff and volunteers.

An overview of organizational competencies not-for-profit enterprises need to succeed in the 21st century appeared in the 1997 ASAE Foundation publication, *Building a Knowledge-Based Culture: Using 21st Century Work and Decision-Making Systems in Associations* (by Glenn H. Tecker, Kermit M. Eide, and Jean S. Frankel). The publication outlined an approach to refocusing organizational structures, processes, and culture that has not yet been fully achieved by even the most successful of today's leading associations.

The core of a knowledge-based operational philosophy is a commitment to a different culture and value system, representing the premise that who makes the decision is far less important than the quality of information and insight on which the decision is based.

The knowledge-based operational approach has the following advantages:

- It encourages effective integration of knowledge into governance and decision-making processes.
- It addresses the political realities of associations by endorsing both decision-making based on the quality of the information considered and the development of good business decisions.
- It is useful in examining what pioneer associations have found to be successful strategies.
- It ensures that the association has a means of sustenance through a new way of doing business based not on culture alone but on a culture of strategic thinking.

Knowledge-based decision making requires that any significant decision must both consider information from and satisfy the needs of four basic areas influencing the organization in any significant decision.

1. Sensitivity to members' views will add knowledge and insight relative to members, prospective members, customers, stakeholders, and constituents.
2. Foresight about the industry, profession, or interest area adds an external element of knowledgeableness.
3. Insight into the capacity and strategic position of the organization builds a critical knowledge base about capability and likelihood of success, from both an internal and an external perspective.
4. Awareness of the ethical implications of choices builds a critical and sometimes unconsidered dimension of possible conflicts relative to issues of privacy, competition, and fairness that the association must keep in mind as it develops strategy.

As *Building a Knowledge-Based Culture* suggests, associations that adopt a knowledge-based operational philosophy realize the following benefits:

• It promotes a consultative partnership between staff and elected leaders.
• It institutionalizes decision making based on purpose, policy, strategy, and considered perspective, rather than on politics, power plays, personality, or momentary perceptions.
• It routinely allows the association to use critical information effectively in decision making by individuals and groups at all levels.

Five years later, associations are continuing to move from a political model of decision making to a more businesslike, knowledge-based model and are increasingly responding to a rapidly changing set of member needs by focusing on developing a reputation for value and delivering a set of tangible and intangible benefits to members.

A knowledge-based operational philosophy is enormously important in allowing governance to possess and execute the will to govern well; the authors will therefore use it throughout the book to examine the factors we believe are critical to governance success.

The will to govern well is fundamentally about two things—what governance chooses to focus on and how governance chooses to get its work done. It is not simply what governance does but how it does it.

As we studied associations that view themselves and are viewed by others as having successful governance systems, three critical themes emerged as key to developing the will to govern well—knowledge, trust, and nimbleness.

Knowledge, as defined by *Webster's,* is the fact or condition of knowing something with familiarity gained through experience or association; the sum of what is known; and the body of truth, information, and principles acquired by mankind. Knowledge applies to facts or ideas acquired by study, investigation, observation, or experience, and facilitates the ability to apply facts, to turn ideas into action. In associations, the use of knowledge is critical to effective decision-making.

Trust, in association terms, is the alignment of what is promised by the association to what is ultimately delivered to important stakeholder groups such as members, volunteer leaders, staff, legislators, and the general public. It is often defined in a set of values or expectations and perceived through the willingness to act on those values.

Nimbleness, as used herein, is the ability of the organization to seize opportunities. It is work done in the right amount of time and in the right way; it is not necessarily just about doing things quickly.

In associations, knowledge drives trust and trust drives nimbleness. There is an inextricable relationship between trust and nimbleness that links back to knowledge. Knowledge and trust are important characteristics because there are risks associated with increased nimbleness; this is why the entire association should be vision- and values-based. If vision is clear and values are shared and lived, the activities chosen by the association today or tomorrow will be the best ones it can find at the time to fulfill the vision. The activities themselves should not become the point; rather, their purpose is progress toward the vision.

Nimbleness and trust require a culture that ensures all participants are fully engaged. To be fully engaged, associations need to examine what they think, believe, and feel about successes and joys as well as about failed and flawed initiatives. They need to listen to everyone in the organization and to believe that everyone can be creative and significant in advancing their mission. This process frequently requires slowing down and peeling away the following layers:

- Asking what assumptions lead governance to their conclusions
- Caring for each other beyond the business relationship
- Getting people to tell their personal stories
- Getting people to integrate their personal visions with the organizational vision
- Not assuming that because something was done a certain way in the past it should be done that way again

However, a culture that supports nimbleness and trust may raise some of the following questions:

- Is there a risk that being engaged might be misconstrued as a reason to back away from accountability for outcomes?
- Will focus on discontinuous change create an excuse for member leaders to avoid ensuring clarity and consensus on a vision of what will constitute success?
- Could staff leaders use the new need for nimbleness in assessing the "emerging future" as an excuse to hold themselves accountable only for activity rather than for the delivery of value?
- What structures and systems will be less useful in the future?
- What structures and systems will remain important?
- Is there a need for new structures and systems that might better invite the kind of behavior the future will require?

This book closely examines the elements of knowledge, trust, and nimbleness. It reviews the role played by individual elements as well as how they interrelate with one another. Using a knowledge-based operational philosophy, it identifies what the authors know and believe, what they think is likely to happen, and what associations can do to maximize the elements of knowledge, trust, and nimbleness to achieve effective 21st-century governance systems.

Each of the three themes will be examined in a recursive discussion that reflects the knowledge-based governance process itself. Each theme will be considered in terms of

a. what we know and believe about association members' needs, wants, and preferences relative to governance,
b. what we know and believe about current realities and evolving dynamics of association governance,
c. what we know and believe about the capacity and strategic position of associations relative to governance, and
d. the ethical implications of models and practices emerging as choices for the 21st century.

Part 1.
Changing Governance Systems

Chapter 1

Governance: A Traditional Context

The term "governance" comes from the Greek word meaning to steer, as in steering a ship or a company's strategy. Governance in associations refers to the decision-making units of the organization and the relative powers, authorities, and responsibilities that each possesses, as well as to the composition of each unit and how individuals are selected to participate in each. Governance is about oversight, process, independence, and accountability.

In recent years, as it has become increasingly important to make decisions quickly and with better knowledge, many associations have streamlined their approach to governance, moving toward a more integrated model that focuses not on structure alone but also on systems, processes, and culture. The huge shifts in the nature of associations reflect a new, still-evolving paradigm. This paradigm has significant implications for the structure, process, and culture that will affect an association's ability to develop and sustain the will to govern well.

A review of some of the fundamental functions and roles of governance is useful in understanding the dynamics of governance systems in associations that are viewed by themselves and others as having the will to govern well.

Traditional Functions

The governing boards of not-for-profit voluntary organizations have traditionally had the following three primary functions:

1. The first function is to approve the outcomes the association seeks to accomplish as an enterprise. The board's approval of these outcomes reflects what its member leaders believe will constitute value to members. In associations that sustain the will to govern well, this is not

done by the board alone, absent any involvement by others. Rather, it is done through thoughtful and open dialogue among member and staff leaders, building a collective knowledge base; developing choices of strategy; carefully considering the advantages, disadvantages, risks, and consequences; and articulating in the deliberative process what is to happen and who is to be held accountable for what.

2. The second function is to ensure that resources necessary for achieving the outcomes are available and used efficiently. The board must gain sufficient understanding of the requirements for successful execution of the delineated strategies to ensure that necessary resources are available to deliver to members the promised value and outcomes.

3. The third basic function is to ensure that the desired outcomes are being achieved. Through an effective balance of oversight and accountability, the board must ensure that the promises of value made to members through the articulation of outcomes are delivered effectively and meaningfully.

Traditional Roles

Boards have also traditionally fulfilled three roles. Two of these board roles are still executed in a relatively traditional manner; the third role is historic, but one contemporary associations are finding their boards spending an increasing amount of time on.

1. First is the corporate role. The board engages in this role when it hires a chief staff executive, ensures implementation of a strategic plan, and oversees programs and resources.

2. Second is a legislative role. When the board establishes guidelines, parameters, or directives—within which the operations of the organization must occur—it is setting internal or operational policy as part of its legislative role. When it takes positions on public issues of importance to members or the association's cause, it is engaged in external or public policy, also part of its legislative role.

3. Third is the adjudicator role. It is in this role that many boards find themselves spending an increasing amount of time. When the board finds itself addressing an issue where many responses—or combinations of responses—are possible, it is engaged in adjudication. It must navigate the complexities, sort through the options, and outline a defensible strategic path. Increasingly complex issues consume a growing amount of board time and energy, and traditional models of governance are not well matched to this experience.

The traditional model of association governance tends to parallel the political model of the U. S. Congress constructed more than 200 years ago.

The original purpose of this governance model was to prevent a small group of people from imposing its self-interest on a larger group of people with more diverse self-interests. Although the model still works, it is increasingly ill fitted to the realities of 21st-century association issues. Many associations are therefore looking for more effective tools for executing board governance and new governance approaches that will better accommodate the increasing time and energy most boards must spend in adjudication.

Contemporary Governance's Three-Part Mission

The will to govern well is based on the understanding that contemporary association governance has a three-part mission—operational oversight, direction setting, and cultural oversight. Most boards have significant experience with the operational oversight part of this mission. Direction setting is something most boards mistakenly believe they execute fairly effectively. The third part of the mission—cultural oversight—is a relatively new responsibility and activity for many leadership groups.

Typically, boards spend most of their time in operational oversight, but the nature of how boards execute this responsibility is undergoing significant change. In the past, typical behavior included "snoopervising" the work of the committee structure, meddling in work underway, or requiring permissions to proceed with initiatives. The approach to oversight currently evolving focuses instead on achieving clarity and consensus on the outcomes the association is seeking and then paying attention to the progress being made toward those outcomes. When an association is dissatisfied with progress, the board can intervene in strategy, program, work, or initiatives. If the board has effectively defined outcomes and delegated responsibility for the development and execution of strategy, important work underway no longer requires politically based permission to proceed to the next logical step. This allows them to exercise influential leadership and encourages creative energies throughout the organization in a way that increases its nimbleness. In an association, unlike any other kind of enterprise, governance must use an approach to leadership that relies on influence rather than power. Traditional directive leadership cannot be used. Governance needs to consider this—both in focus and behavior—when leading an important initiative.

Direction setting is the governance responsibility boards often believe they execute more effectively than they actually do. Many associations have for years engaged in strategic planning, but when they review these plans, it sometimes becomes apparent they are merely a set of long-range objectives organized by traditional program or function areas, revealing little about the true nature of the organization's strategy. If the plan has not articulated core purpose or value, it cannot give a clear sense of the organization's identity; if there is no articulation of an envisioned future, an audacious goal, or a description of how the world of the members will be different once the objectives are achieved, there is no clear idea of what the organization seeks to become. The goals in many plans focus on what the organization will do, often overlooking member benefits expected to result from what is done.

Such plans are activity oriented rather than outcome oriented. There is little to communicate the value proposition the organization needs to use to remain indispensable or relevant to its membership. With no strategic objectives to allow an assessment of progress toward goals, leadership has no way of monitoring how well the association is achieving the outcomes it considered worthy of pursuit. There is little connection between the goals and strategies of the organization and the reality of what is occurring on a day-to-day or week-to-week basis within staff or member groups. A plan missing any of these ingredients is not a strategic plan, and without such a plan a board lacks a critical element in its ability to execute its ongoing role of defining and delegating strategy.

The third element of the three-part leadership mission is culture—a relatively new aspect of appreciation and commitment on the part of governance, which has enormous responsibility for behaving in a way that creates the model for culture throughout the organization. There are two critical leverage points for culture in an association.

1. First is the quality of the relationship between the chief staff executive and the chief elected officer. If that relationship is characterized by conflict, withholding of information, political posturing, desire to exercise control over the other, or manipulation, that behavior is transmitted throughout the organization as the expectation for how staff and members relate to each other at all other contact points. If the relationship is characterized by openness; collaboration; an agreement on principles and values; an agreement to disagree without being disagreeable; and a partnership committed to clear, common, and important ends, it becomes the positive model used by the rest of the organization in constructing the working interaction between staff and members. Such a constructive relationship illustrates the will to govern well.

2. The second of the two leverage points for the development of culture is the manner in which the board executes its responsibilities. What the board chooses to focus attention on signals to the rest of the organization what is really important. This involves more than the board's declarations about what is important; it includes indirect contacts (such as through the reading of published board minutes) from which members and others form perceptions about what the board considers important. If the association declares that "x, y, and z" are important but members see no allocation of resources to those points in the annual budget, they will recognize a discrepancy between declaration and action, to the discredit of the board.

If the culture reflects a political model of debate, persuasion, argument, and "deals" cut prior to meetings, or if it shows members of the board coming from particular constituency groups with either a conscious or unconscious directive to vote or decide a particular way, then that is the kind of behavior the rest of the membership will believe the organization values. But if the board addresses substantive issues by using dialogue before deliberation, illuminating the issues, considering what is known, defining the choices, thoughtfully examining the advantages and disadvantages of each of the choices, assessing the risks and consequences, and selecting the path that, at least at the moment, appears to be reasonable, then a culture of open, participative decision making is the one to which members will aspire.

Most organizations have only recently come to appreciate this attention to cultural oversight. If the association is not perceived as the kind of community prospective members would be proud to join, any program benefits it offers will be insufficient to attract them to active engagement and enfranchisement.

In associations that exhibit the will to govern well, the underlying strategy is one of changing the process of governance. By changing the process, the organization is able to change behavior, and by changing behavior, it is able to change the culture. Many associations have achieved dramatic shifts in the effectiveness of governance systems without having to rewrite bylaws or attempt other structural change.

Governance and Information: The Obligations of Leadership

Facilitating the communication of information has traditionally been an important dynamic of governance's role in associations. Taking responsibility and accountability for information dissemination that communicates the intent and actions of governance is critical for those who view themselves and are viewed by others as having the will to govern well. This dynamic addresses three important association variables: information, perception, and, perhaps most important, the relationship between the two. It is a fundamental obligation of governance to attend to these dynamics.

Influencing the behavior of others is a useful working definition of leadership. The principal currency in influencing the behavior of others is information, which frames the perceptions behind the judgments people make and serves as the premise for how they choose to behave.

Because an association is more people-intensive than any other kind of enterprise, perceptions shape realities. Individuals or groups in associations reach judgments, hold opinions, have views, and behave in ways based on their beliefs. Their attitudes are often premised on perceptions they have about what is or is not true, and those perceptions are based on available information—which should not necessarily be construed as "accurate," "comprehensive," "reliable," or "timely."

Our studies of associations have shown that sometimes individuals or groups may hold opinions, reach judgments, make decisions, and adopt behaviors founded on incomplete, inaccurate, out-of-date, untimely, or unreliable information. One reason for this may be the tendency of people to create an assumption to explain what they don't understand, rather than feel out of the loop, unengaged, or not part of the "in" crowd. With respect to governance's decisions, many associations who are not cognizant of this dynamic do not communicate the context around which the board or other leadership group has made a decision. Absent that insight, the membership may interpret governance's actions in a very different way than the actual intent would reveal.

Governance therefore has two significant obligations with respect to the flow of information and the shaping of perception.

1. Governance is obligated to ensure that the decision-making process elicits a continuous stream of information from members, prospective members, customers, and stakeholders. This allows governance to understand what these important groups see as the challenges, opportunities, realities, needs, and expectations about any given situation—and whether their perceptions are mistaken.

2. Governance is obligated to provide a coherent stream of information back to members, prospective members, and other stakeholders, creating synergy between the view of the world held by those whom they seek to lead and their own perspective. In major decisions that involve changing direction or altering pace or path, this synergy of viewpoint enhances comfort to a point where others are more willing to follow. Members understand not only what decisions governance has made on their behalf but the basis of those decisions—in terms of judgment, logic, and rationale. Such an exchange of information creates a balanced worldview between members and leadership.

Because of their governance role, most boards experience a stream of information that is deeper, broader, and more frequently refreshed and future oriented than that experienced by the majority of an association's members. This is why governance must make decisions based on both sensitivity to expressed member needs and its own insight about the foreseeable future and the organization's capacity and strategic position. When those outsider and insider views combine with ethical principles in making a judgment, governance is exercising "informed intuition," which occurs at the confluence of what the board learns about (a) member wants, needs, and preferences; (b) external marketplace dynamics and realities; (c) capacity and strategic position of the organization; and (d) ethical implications of its choices.

A related responsibility of governance is to ensure that all proper questions are asked and answered. If there is ever any question about what the association should be doing, the simplest and most appropriate action is to make sure the question is discussed and answered by the association's governing board.

Governance has the legitimacy and credibility to continuously attend to issues related to strategic direction. This does not mean that other groups cannot come together to think about things in different ways, but such groups must serve the board as sources of insight, ideas, and information. If governance is not actively engaged in considering strategic direction, the association may find that board decisions about policy, program, and budget have little reference or relevance to the significant strategic issues confronting the organization, and instead, priorities will be set in the budgeting process—based on politics, perceptions, and past practice.

Our studies confirm that traditional roles and functions continue to serve as critical frameworks for good governance. The changes beginning to take place in the execution of these roles will be addressed in future chapters.

Chapter 2

Current Governance Practices:
What We Know, Believe, and Predict

Associations and Current Trends

Governance does not operate in a vacuum. The phenomena and dynamics that affect associations often have significant influence on their governance. Much available information explores predicted trends of critical importance to associations, but the following insights highlight dynamics that may be most germane to association governance.

- Increased unpredictability, instability, and uncertainty about the future warrant more open-minded inquiry in governance dialogue.
- Associations are becoming increasingly aware of the need to adapt to changing environments. This will require more flexibility in governance systems.
- Members of many associations will experience significant change in their industry, profession, or cause area, and will view this change as occurring at a faster rate, thus increasing their sense of urgency for the association to focus on tangible outcomes. Governance will still need to articulate long-term vision with sufficient depth to move the association from where it is today to a new and better place, but setting a 10- to 30-year broad vision with no link to shorter-term outcomes and no flexibility to adjust strategy and execution will become a recipe for failure. The long view must balance with a nimble approach to adjusting strategy in the shorter term—through constant and regular dialogue about the issues facing the association and its members, and through setting goals that allow for flexible execution.

- More associations will disappear, merge, or change radically—some will disappear, a few will merge, and in some industries and professions, the pool of membership and therefore leadership will decline.
- The need to associate will remain, as will the need for governance. Although many associations may form, grow, and become obsolete, they will need to be developed, managed, maintained, and hence governed throughout their organizational life cycle.
- There will be a greater need for a sense of community, and the next generation of members will define community differently. Governance will need to recognize that it is leading a community and not simply directing an organization.

Governance Systems

Associations viewed by themselves and others as having the will to govern well have an effective way of defining and changing priorities to ensure relevance to their members' changing marketplaces. The key lies in creating organizations with optimal flexibility, directed by vision and values under the leadership of those who are not overly invested in yesterday's decisions, but who continue to engage in conversation about what should happen tomorrow. The following are key points about how the associations we studied are evolving governance today:

- Most of the associations are either in the process of making, or have recently made, governance changes.
- Changes currently underway are both structural and substantive and are for the most part the result of a board's engaging in the thoughtful process of planning and thinking strategically. A board's need to focus on identifying and responding to the critical issues facing its association is also driving change.
- Board structures have become smaller as many organizations attempt to accommodate quicker decision making. In many associations we studied, this did not mean that fewer people were involved in making or controlling decisions. At the same time that boards are becoming smaller, many are becoming more skilled in facilitating dialogue, employing knowledge-based decision making, and involving others in the process.
- An increasing number of organizations are moving away from geographic representation toward a selection process focusing on the skills and experiences the organization needs to make effective decisions.
- There is a changing role for houses of delegates, large delegate bodies, and meetings of the members. Many associations we studied have

resisted downsizing or eliminating these bodies, instead creating new roles for them as important sources of information and insight on strategic issues facing the organization.

- Associations are placing a higher value on eliminating barriers to communication, both within the board itself and between the board and other segments of the organization. The use of technology increases board efficiency in decision making (in places where the laws allow virtual decision making via teleconference, fax, or e-mail) and enhances board communication as well.

- There is an improvement in board and chief staff executive partnerships, with a greater emphasis on collaboration and consultation to enhance the effectiveness of governance as a system. Many boards, now smaller in size, are operating as executive committees once did, with officers working closely with the chief staff executive on operational issues. The collaborative nature of this working relationship has in many cases even served to blur the traditional lines between what has normally been thought of as the board's and staff's purview or (just as has happened in defining what is for-profit and what is not-for-profit). Dialogue on issues of strategy and implementation has created an important link between governance and management, where previously traditional roles limited the opportunity for clarification and collaboration.

- Board meeting agendas are changing to enable the board to focus on strategic issues and be more knowledge based.

- There seems to be increasing recognition that the process of self-evaluation can assist a board in refining its governing style and in encouraging accountability and performance management across the organization. Few boards currently engage in self-evaluation, although several indicated their intention to do so.

- Issues around leadership succession have surfaced in a number of associations, primarily because of the difficulty of attracting individuals willing to assume time-consuming leadership roles. Attracting strong future leaders who will represent the diversity of the membership on a number of different dimensions and who have the time and interest to serve is a key issue for many associations. A number of organizations we studied had unusually high expectations of board participation, including many days attending board meetings and additional leadership service responsibilities. Several organizations have narrowly limited the time required both of board members and other volunteer leaders and report an increase in individuals interested in these roles. Others have implemented measures to focus limited volunteer time and attention more effectively on strategic issues that have a significant impact on the organization and its members. Several organizations reported having expanded the role of their nominating committees to include ongoing leadership recruitment and development.

- Demographics show that white males continue to dominate governance in many associations. While organizations say they are moving toward increasing diversity on all dimensions, progress seems slow. At-large positions are often used to recruit women and minorities. Some associations are viewing diversity more broadly, looking beyond their existing members to the industry, profession, or cause that the organization represents to determine the makeup of the leadership. Only in the best associations has the level of diversity in the industry or profession been equaled in the association's governance, and few organizations have surpassed it.

- Little attention is being paid to the high cost of governance. Only by carefully costing out both volunteer expenses and staff time can an organization determine the real cost of the function. Additional attention needs to focus on the real costs of maintaining the organization's governance structure—not just direct costs, but the indirect time and attention staff spends on organizing and staffing the multilevel components of governance.

- Associations are creating additional time for boards to focus on strategic direction and mega-issues by delegating increased responsibility to executive committees for operational work. They are also finding new meaning in their governance roles through increased knowledge-based dialogue and deliberation about issues affecting the industry.

Chapter 3

Governance System Changes

The Association Infrastructure

The pressing need to remain responsive to a membership whose world is changing has led in recent years to dramatic shifts in the basic character of associations.

In 1992, the Tecker Consultants' "Model of Association Infrastructure" represented a picture of an association that could be used to help staff and member leaders understand their responsibilities This model (see Figure 1.1) included the following six key structures and four key processes:

1. A membership structure defining who could be a member and who could not and how those who were eligible for membership were clustered into certain groups.
2. A governance structure defining which groups enjoyed what authorities and responsibilities and how people became part of those groups.
3. A program structure defining business lines, programs within business lines, and activities and initiatives within those programs.
4. A workforce structure defining both how the association delineates its committee infrastructure and how it organizes staff, program, and functional structures.
5. A financial structure defining where funds were generally coming from and going to, what proportion of revenue would come from dues and nondues sources of revenue, and judgments about the amount of revenue to be gained from mission-related activities as well as from nonmission-related, nondues sources of revenue.
6. An information infrastructure defining how the association acquires and transfers information and insight from the people and places that have it to the people and places that need it.

Figure 1.1

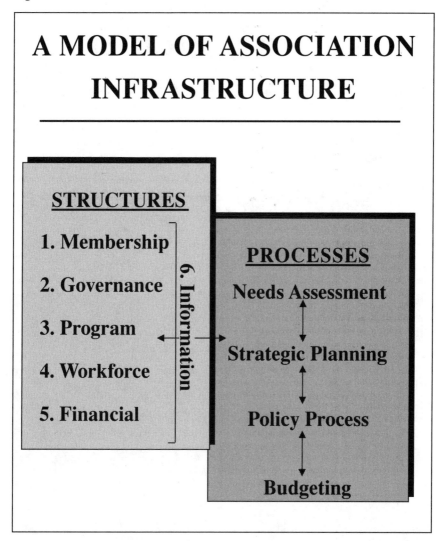

A MODEL OF ASSOCIATION INFRASTRUCTURE

STRUCTURES

1. Membership
2. Governance
3. Program
4. Workforce
5. Financial

6. Information

PROCESSES

Needs Assessment

Strategic Planning

Policy Process

Budgeting

This information infrastructure was primarily driven by the efficacy of an association's four key processes: (1) needs assessment; (2) strategic planning (or what passed for it): how decisions were made about association priorities and the type of work in which it would engage; (3) policy: defining how the association established guidelines for developing public or external policy and operational or internal policy; and (4) the budget process: how decisions were made about the allocation of resources to particular programs, activities, or initiatives.

Over the years, Tecker Consultants has observed that the fundamental nature of this basic infrastructure is changing, and there are implications for

Figure 1.2

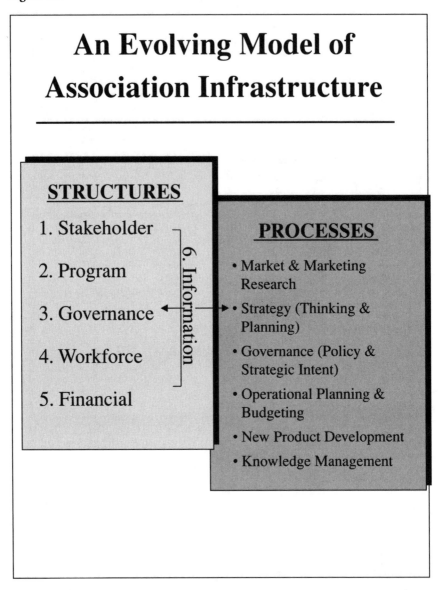

An Evolving Model of Association Infrastructure

STRUCTURES

1. Stakeholder

2. Program

3. Governance

4. Workforce

5. Financial

6. Information

PROCESSES

• Market & Marketing Research

• Strategy (Thinking & Planning)

• Governance (Policy & Strategic Intent)

• Operational Planning & Budgeting

• New Product Development

• Knowledge Management

structure, process, and culture that affect the will to govern well. A new model with six structures and six processes reflects these changes. (See Figure 1.2.) **Associations are moving from a focus solely on members to that of a broad community of stakeholders.** Many associations have begun to ask, given the ready access to community in the Internet age, whether there will continue to be a difference between their members and subscribers or customers of their services. When it is in the best interest of an associa-

Figure 1.2 (continued)

An Evolving Model of Association Infrastructure
By Glenn H. Tecker, Kermit M. Eide & Jean S. Frankel

ELEMENT	KEY COMPONENTS AND ATTRIBUTES
Stakeholder Structure	• Includes members, customers, and stakeholders—all who have an interest in the work of the association. Can be individuals, companies, constituent organizations, and/or industries. Structures define who can be or choose to be a member, how membership groups are classified and organized, and the rights and prerogatives enjoyed by each membership category. May include degree of centrality to identity—understanding who are the organization's core members, members, customers, and key stakeholders. *We are observing that associations have become less concerned with who can be a member; and more concerned with what populations will be attracted to involvement in programs and policy initiatives. Many are rapidly evolving structures to support more customized relationships with the association, whether as individual or organizational members. New structures such as the Open Industry Model, and new categories such as Web-only members, are beginning to emerge and we believe will continue to evolve in the coming years.*
Program Structure	• Business lines, programs, products, and services—the work of the association. *Increased segmentation of membership populations and increasing diversity in member preferences has demanded an increasingly higher degree of competence in planning and program delivery. Associations have become more cognizant of the need to articulate an attractive value proposition which speaks to the stakeholder's definition of value and the nature of the delivery experience expected. The next evolution in association program and service delivery will require a move beyond the ability to develop customized solutions for diverse market and member segments—it will require the capacity to conceptualize and bring to market entirely new types of products and services.*
Governance Structure	• Decision-making units of the organization and the relative powers, authorities, and responsibilities that each possesses. • The composition of each unit and how individuals are selected to participate in them. *We are observing that many associations have already done much to streamline governance systems in a world that requires more decisions to be made more quickly and with better knowledge. We are increasingly seeing associations move toward a more integrated model of governance: knowledge-based strategic governance is becoming a mechanism for consultative leadership that recognizes strategy as the necessary and appropriate link between the board's role for governance and the staff's role for management and implementation.*

tion's core membership to find mechanisms for others who are not members to become engaged in the association's work or when the association determines its importance to accomplishing the organization's goals, others outside the traditional membership structure need to be involved in a meaningful way—and the infrastructure changes from a "membership structure" to a "stakeholder structure."

Figure 1.2 (continued)

An Evolving Model of Association Infrastructure—Processes

ELEMENT	KEY COMPONENTS AND ATTRIBUTES
Workforce Structure	• The human resource pool — both volunteer and employed. • Committee system, staff divisions or departments, relationships with outside experts and contractors, including outsourcing and co-sourcing. *We have observed that many associations have become more responsive, flexible, and fluid in workforce structures—to be able to quickly refocus assets on rapidly evolving and frequently shifting priorities. Volunteer structures have evolved from standing committees to action-oriented, task-based work groups. Staff structures have moved from functional to program and market-based. Communication abilities will continue to be critical to ensure constancy of direction and coherency of program in rapidly changing organizational environments, but increased demand for outcome accountability will require these groups to adopt new systems and processes designed to manage risk, track process, and measure results.*
Financial Structure	• Sources of revenue, relative proportions of revenue from various sources, the allocation and placement of available revenue, the anticipated cost of resources, and opportunities over time. Includes dues structures, investment strategies, and projected estimates of significant costs. • Basic decisions related to fiscal status and selection of tax-exempt status (e.g., 501 c3 vs. 501 c6) are determinations about financial structure with enormous strategic implications. Can apply to the association as a whole and/or to emerging business lines and program and service delivery units. *We are observing an increasingly complex blending of business models and fiscal structures within association structures. They may consistent of 501(c) entities, as well as for-profit subsidiaries, alliances, joint ventures, and other partnerships. Evolving delivery models will have a significant impact on fee structures related to dues as well as more transactional based fee for service models. Not-for-profitness is no longer the defining characteristic of voluntary association.*
Information and Knowledge Structure	• Links the structures of the association to its decision-making processes. Ensures that individuals and groups executing activity have the knowledge they require to make sound decisions and effectively execute work. Includes (a) the decisions that will be needed at each and all levels of the organization; (b) the information that will be required to effectively make those decisions; (c) the sources of that information; (d) the processes for collecting the information from appropriate sources; (e) the methods for tabulation and analysis that aggregate and categorize the information; (f) the technologies, systems, and processes that will be used to interpret the information, integrate it with the appropriate know how, and systematically distribute or provide access to it in useful forms to the person or places that will need to make or coordinate judgments based on it.

This may represent a huge change, particularly for professional associations. For years, many professional societies used exclusivity as a strategy. They would establish some distinguishing characteristic to differentiate those who were their members from those who were not. They created eligibility requirements for membership so they could say their members were superior in "X" ways to those who were not members. Membership structure and eligibility requirements offered a high-level strategy for helping members establish identity and a position within their marketplace. Many associations

Figure 1.2 (continued)

An Evolving Model of Association Infrastructure—Processes

ELEMENT	KEY COMPONENTS AND ATTRIBUTES
Market and Marketing Research	A balanced selection of all the tools of market-directed management: marketing research and assessment (both formal and informal); the development and maintenance of a rational, common database to guide decisions about member wants, needs, and preferences — including demographic, qualitative, and quantitative information about member (and customer) expectations of a product or service's ability to solve a problem or provide a valued benefit; timely delivery of services; value pricing; reliability; and service responsiveness. The ability of developers and decision-makers at all levels to constantly access useful information and consider it in their work.
Strategy (Thinking and Planning)	A continuous process of thoughtfully determining direction, at all levels of the organization, on the basis of careful assessment of clearly defined and desired outcomes representing clarity about what will constitute success; thinking strategically about the changing environment and how the association will respond to evolving influences, factors, and issues.
Governance (Policy and Strategic Intent)	An articulation of philosophy as as well as a system of established and clear processes for effective partnership and rational deliberation guiding oversight of the organization; the intellectual and political steps to producing judgments related to: (a) positions the organization takes on public issues of importance to the membership, or (b) statements of direction, guidelines, or parameters established as frameworks within which initiatives or operations are to be executed.
Operational Planning and Budgeting	A process designed to determine the operational allocation of discretionary resources, driven by a strategic long-range plan, on a short-term, 1-2 year basis. Ensures that the decisions regarding resource allocation are based on strategic considerations, and that there is a balance achieved among three realms of work: (a) transformational work reflecting progress toward each strategic long-range goal, (b) work in support of ongoing programs and services, and (c) resources to support sufficient flexibility for responding to emerging opportunities or challenges. In the annual planning process, action plans, checkpoints, and milestones are developed, and form a basis upon which to measure organizational and individual performance.

were fairly successful in this strategy, but now the needs of their professions, industries, or causes often require engagement and involvement of other populations that are not, traditionally, even eligible for membership. Those associations are therefore looking for new ways to broaden their capture base of who can participate without sacrificing the soul of the organization.

Associations are moving from being power-driven to being value-driven. In the past, membership structure determined an association's governing structure. Governance tended to be constituency-based, with board composition being driven by the makeup of the membership. It was necessary to have an individual on the board representing each of the major

Figure 1.2 (continued)

An Evolving Model of Association Infrastructure—Processes

ELEMENT	KEY COMPONENTS AND ATTRIBUTES
New Product Development	A process that institutionalizes market-focused philosophy in the association's development, design, and delivery of products and services. Creates a mechanism for a) responding to implications of marketing and market research on customer needs and values, b) encouraging innovation, c) improving speed to market, d) managing risk, and e) measuring progress.
Knowledge Management	The process of managing an organization's knowledge assets that enables inventorying, cataloguing, sustaining, and accessing "content" regardless of its original "container." Enables the association to make available to all who are interested the aggregate intellectual assets of an association, and position the association as the unique source of credible knowledge for their industry or professional arena. Creates an opportunity for the association to offer a unique value proposition as a source of instantaneous and easy access to a guaranteed pool of quality knowledge and insight at a reasonable and appropriate cost.
	We anticipate that these these six basic decision-making processes will continue to evolve in the future. They will be at the heart of success or failure for many organizations as they seek to manage through change.

constituency groups, a situation that often represented a power-driven approach to governance.

Today's associations tend increasingly to be driven by what will constitute value to members and by the benefits the organization seeks to provide, both tangible and intangible. Defining what constitutes value determines what kind of work the association will need to do.

More and more, associations find themselves trying to compose governance bodies based on competency—gaining access to the expertise, experience, and interests needed on the board to formulate good judgments about the kinds of things that are critical to the association's success. In associations that are viewed by themselves and others as having the will to govern well, value to members, not representation or constituency, is now driving board composition.

Of course, governance still must be responsive to constituencies. A member must look at the board and see someone like himself or herself to feel that the group is credible and legitimate. But the board also needs to be viewed as appropriately and sufficiently knowledgeable, so that decisions coming from the group are considered credible. Association governance must be *both* legitimate *and* credible. Associations are finding new, innovative mechanisms to reach for both legitimacy and credibility in composing governance structures.

Associations are moving from needs assessment to market research and marketing research. When using the term "needs assessment," questions come to mind such as, "Who are the association's members?" and "What are their needs?" Many associations send members written surveys, which have limitations when used alone.

One limitation is that people can comment only on things they already know about, or about which they are asked to comment. However, because of the changing nature of so many influences on the membership and their needs, the most important concerns and feedback might well be on emerging issues about which the association does not even know enough to ask questions.

Another limitation is that while people can provide opinions, they cannot always articulate why they hold those opinions. This insight is critical to the development of effective strategy.

A third limitation of written surveys is that they often result in a skewed response. The majority of responses come from two groups: people who are already involved (and presumably the association already knows what they think), and people who have an axe to grind.

The fourth limitation of written surveys is that even the best-intentioned member may involuntarily lie. Most members have a sense of what an answer ought to be, and because they do not want to embarrass themselves or others, they respond accordingly. Without an interactive probe, an association cannot really discover whether the member's behavior is different from how he or she describes a preference.

Market research and marketing research are both essential. Market research tells about the demography of membership. It describes how old members are; where they live; their income level; and their role in the profession, industry, or cause. Marketing research provides insight into "psycho-demographic" preferences; it describes values, interests, and inclinations, thereby building an understanding of the kinds of values different groups in the association are seeking. Market research might suggest that a program on "X" would be useful; marketing research describes what language and image should be used to constitute an attractive offer. Hence, both types of research are essential to building knowledge bases in an organization that has the will to govern well.

Associations are moving from policy and parliamentary process to strategic governance. In the search for ways to become more nimble, many associations are abandoning traditional political models in favor of open models that are more knowledge-based and businesslike. Some associations have abandoned parliamentary procedure—at least for half of their conversations in governance.

- One limitation with respect to the traditional functions of parliamentary process is that the board must decide what it is going to consider before it is allowed to talk about it. Conversation must begin with a motion, or a recommendation that comes in the form of a motion. This immediately puts the board into a "react and ratify" mode. In that scenario, the only two choices are to say "yes" or "no" to someone else's idea, a situation that immediately makes the conversation political. Governance in this mode advocates, cajoles, persuades, and argues. It does not illuminate, search, consider, problem-solve, or build ideas. It is not deciding and delegating but reacting and ratifying.

- Another limitation of parliamentary process is that often, as the board talks about a motion, it discovers that the motion does not really reflect what the board wants to have happen or what it needs to decide. In that case, the board must amend the motion. The board chair must call for an amendment to the motion, as well as a second to the amendment, with the permission of those who made and seconded the motion; only then can the board talk about what it really wants to discuss. Now it may happen that the board deliberates a bit more and discovers the amended motion still does not reflect what needs discussion. This problem can only be fixed by calling for an amendment to the amendment, as well as a second to the amendment to the amendment, with the permission of the person who made the amendment, the person who seconded the amendment, the person who made the motion, and the person who seconded the motion. Only then can the board talk about what it wants to talk about. A preferred process might lead the board directly to define first what it needs to decide through a collaborative phase of dialogue. Then it would construct a motion that reflects the collective knowledge and thinking of the group, and finally move to deliberation on the motion created together. At that point, parliamentary process could continue to provide civility to a group where different positions are being advocated.

- Another limitation of parliamentary process relates more to common practice than to the role of the board chair. In parliamentary process, the tendency is to call upon people in the order in which their hands go up. This practice can make dialogue about a complex issue even more complex. Imagine that the board is having a rich dialogue during which a particular member says something especially profound. The group immediately embraces the idea and wants to build on it.

But because of the requirement of calling on members in order, the chair feels constrained to call on someone else who had his or her hand up who wants to talk about something that was in the conversation stream five minutes before. This causes the group to lose its collective train of thought and momentum, and can make the exploration of complex issues almost unintelligible.

Associations are finding new mechanisms in governance processes that create a shift from policy and parliamentary process to strategic governance—where the process of governing is approached in a strategic manner. They are also abandoning the traditional process of strategic planning in favor of an ongoing process for planning and thinking strategically, one that thoroughly integrates strategic thoughtfulness with the ongoing work of the board and senior staff so that every time the board and senior staff gather together, they do so for the purpose of thinking strategically at every level on every decision.

Associations are moving from information distribution to knowledge and insight access. The traditional system of information distribution relies on publications or other paper delivery mechanisms. Associations are moving instead toward more electronically enhanced, instantaneous access. A related shift is from a focus on gathering and disseminating information toward creating knowledge and insight. Associations have the strategic advantage of containing a tremendous amount of intellectual capital about their industries, professions, or causes. They can provide objectivity, perspective, and context as to how information is used in practice and what insights others have relative to the particular knowledge area. They are also often able to position themselves as the best and most reliable source because they have made judicious decisions about the quality and relevance of their information.

Shifts in the Mechanisms of Governance

Many conversations about change in governance tend to focus on such issues as board roles and responsibilities, size and composition, meeting frequency and focus, terms and limitations of office, qualifications and experience, accountability and resources, nomination and election, and membership enfranchisement, involvement, and communication.

These issues, more often than not, reflect mechanisms for organizing and executing the roles of governance. In recent years, associations have made significant improvements to governance by attending to one or another of these mechanisms. However, because most of these mechanisms on their own do not have the breadth and depth to create fundamental change, progress has been slow and incremental, in some cases not outlasting the leadership that brought it to pass, in many of the associations we studied.

What truly needs to change is not the functions and roles of governance, but the processes for accomplishing work and the underlying culture necessary to support more effective mechanisms. An examination of these fundamental mechanisms is important to any consideration of 21st-century governance.

Board Composition: Competency vs. Constituency

Many associations are seeking to move governance to what is referred to as a competency-based board. The goal typically is to ensure that governance is collectively composed of individuals who possess the necessary skills, competencies, and perspectives to effectively govern the industry or profession served by the association.

However, our study has shown that the subject of constituency- vs. competency-based boards—a topic that has become the centerpiece of some evolving governance systems—is, in reality, a false issue. Leaders who aggressively push for this shift in culture may put their careers at risk because the real issue is about legitimacy and credibility in governance. "Legitimacy" means that stakeholders perceive the board to represent all significant interests and perspectives. "Credibility" means that the board is viewed as knowledgeable and fair and that the board process is considered rational. Successful boards enjoy a reputation for being both legitimate and credible. While the right balance may differ from organization to organization, boards must be considered both to be effective.

Some associations have begun to use market research as a replacement for intermediaries (committees) between decision makers (board and senior staff) and the customer (member). For governance to be representative in these environments, it must use defensible data, rather than relying on politically sensitive board composition. Legitimacy, however, involves being perceived as representative, so sometimes board composition also needs to reflect geography in order to earn this reputation.

Members and other key stakeholders want the board to reflect the interests and preferences present in the membership—its constituencies. The key for governance is whether significant segments of the association's membership are able to see their interests and preferences reflected in governance and decision-making processes. "Segments" are subpopulations whose needs and preferences are predictably different from the needs and preferences of other subpopulations. A "significant" segment is a subpopulation of members the organization is unwilling to lose. Variables shared by a segment that differentiates their interests and preferences will be based on explanations of how their world differs from the world of others. These variables likely will include geography, where factors such as marketplace dynamics, licensing, or economic climate differ among areas. They also can include a virtually unlimited pool of variables such as role; educational level; company size; sub-specialization; generational, gender, or cultural experience; beliefs and values; and so forth.

The critical question related to board composition and its representative nature, then, is, "What variables define differences in membership in meaningful ways?" Answering this question can be as complex as it is essential. Significant variables can be demographic or psycho-demographic. For example, many younger members have redefined enfranchisement in a digital world. For these members, being enfranchised no longer means seeing someone like themselves sitting at the table; it means having the opportunity to participate personally in the dialogues from which decisions emerge. This shift appears to be especially pronounced in industry, professional, and charitable organizations with a significant number of members from the "digital generation" who believe that where they are located has little to do with what is important to them.

Boards should be designed so that decisions can be informed by dialogue enriched by a variety of values and perspectives. When the balance *is* adjusted, it is usually accomplished by altering the nominating and/or electoral process or redefining significant segments. Geographic location may be abandoned in favor of some other segment variable, but organizations that move to selecting leaders based on individual skills and competencies alone run the risk of having a smart board composed of experiential clones—who may not have a sufficient connection with the membership. The bottom line may be that association owners want their board to be representative (legitimate) *and* they want their board members to be competent (credible). While they are willing to discuss mechanisms for rebalancing the presence of both conditions on their board, they are seldom satisfied by the abandonment of one element in favor of the other. So a shift from a constituency to competency focus in board composition, if it is not sufficiently sensitive to the perception of representation, will most likely not yield the desired results.

Chapters and Component Organizations

The presence of a chapter structure in an association adds an additional set of complexities to its successful governance. If chapters are geographically based and geography has something to do with differences in the needs and preferences of members, the board, to be legitimate, needs to have representation from those subpopulations whose needs differ. Some proportion of the board should be geographically based. A key question for governance to consider is whether the association will use its chapters as the entities that select those individuals, or whether it will use some other mechanism, such as a nominating committee, to pluck candidates from various regions. That sort of decision depends on the degree to which there is a representative or democratic culture within the organization.

What is good for governance is good for governance, no matter what the level of the organization. Our study reveals that the principles that define good governance in associations apply as well to governance on a component or chapter level. One important difference, however, is that at a chapter level, because there is usually little or no staff, it is expected that governance leaders will be engaged not only in governing the organization but also in actually executing its work. The challenge for member leaders at the chapter level is to remember which hats they are wearing at any given time—those of workforce or of governance.

When chapters are the source from which members of the larger association board are selected or emerge, a board may develop whose members perceive their duties and functions based on the way they worked as board members at the chapter level. It is therefore important for them to have some education or experience outside their roles as chapter board members or in some other development activity if they are to understand the way the larger board must represent more diverse interests (e.g., at the national level) and must execute work in partnership with a full-time expert workforce (a chief staff executive and professional staff). They must realize that the behaviors that brought them success at the chapter level may not bring them success at a national level.

Associations must confront the issue of where board members emerging from a chapter-level experience will derive their new vision of board participation. Associations need to ensure that board orientation serves as the source of this understanding. Association leaders can no longer depend on a lecture on effective board operations and process to influence current and future generations of member leaders to adopt the will to alter their behavior. Rather, those future leaders have to experience success in doing things a different way to create the will to sustain the change.

It is worth noting that the move of some associations from a constituency- to a competency-based board may actually be an attempt to move away from the tradition of taking their leaders from chapter or component leadership because they want to attract leaders with a more sophisticated view of board functions.

Moving from a Management to a Leadership Board

There is a convincing consensus that boards should be spending about 70 to 80 percent of their time on external issues important to the membership and 20 to 30 percent on internal matters. Our study of associations shows, unfortunately, that the percentages are reversed for many boards.

A focus on internal issues suggests a management approach to governance. A focus on external issues, choices of strategic direction, and outcomes rather than implementation issues suggests a leadership approach to governance. A governance body engaging in a knowledge-based dialogue is usually working on issues that focus automatically on external factors; depending on leadership style, this focus can be either stimulating or terrifying.

Governing bodies must ultimately decide whether they wish to play a governance role or a management role. The following case study concerns a national professional society in a medically related field whose board, at the end of a strategic planning process, made a conscious decision to remain a management board. It preferred to continue focusing on management of the association rather than on the leadership necessary to ensure implementation of the association's new strategic plan. The board had not been positioned to lead the planning process, and there was no leadership group overseeing overall progress toward goals. Planning in this association also had not included discussion of significant external factors likely to affect the implementation of strategies on a year-to-year basis. There was no consistent, organization-wide process to review and update the plan annually. The goals and objectives of its previous plans were primarily focused on internal issues, rather than on outcomes or benefits to members.

The board itself was disproportionately composed of individual practitioners: former local leaders who had achieved their positions by successfully navigating the organization's internal political process. Board composition also lacked other critical perspectives and competencies, and, although the association had made some effort toward diversity in composition, one board member was actually heard to describe two "token" board members as "outsiders." The board appeared to be more focused on internal, balance-of-power issues and personal legacies than on an external view of the profession or on delivering value to members in a changing environment.

Despite significant shifts in the world of the association's members and an emerging lack of relevance to its membership, the board did not see a need for change because of the association's long history of success in advocacy issues and membership retention. Some board members believed that a decline in membership was not under their control, while others said, *"Maybe there might be something the membership committee could do about it— let's give it to them to solve."*

The board was often unhappy with work of the committees. Committees brought forward good program ideas, but their work reflected a lack of understanding of the overall direction and purpose of the organization; they expressed frustration about not knowing where the association was heading or how they could help it get there. The board placed the blame for this dynamic on the committees themselves. Some board members suggested the board should be responsible for this, but others argued, "*Our organization's goals are implicit—everyone should know that.*" The board possessed the organizational power to lead but refused the responsibility to do so.

The board also failed to reach agreement on how to define its role. Some board members saw it as "managing the critical issues of the profession," but others admitted they focused most on operational oversight and managing staff and committees.

While engaging in an extensive strategic planning effort and identifying the need to reassess board role and process, the board started reconsidering itself with respect to the role it should play in defining strategic direction and guiding progress of the strategic plan. The following perceptions that arose at that time demonstrate the board's ambivalence about the process of preparing strategically for the future:

- There is no value in planning for more than five years ahead.
- The marketplace is changing too much and too quickly to predict.
- There is no value in making predictions; predictions are uncertain, and we see our role as acting only on the facts.
- Thinking about mega-issues is a waste of our time.
- The issues are long term, and they do not relate to us.
- There will be a new board five years from now; it will be its job, not ours, to answer these questions.

The board continued to wrestle with the idea of change, and when it reached consensus on the need for change, it allowed disagreement over how to start stand in its way. Good governance has discovered that implementation of change in process and role must start incrementally and be accomplished gradually. This group appeared to expect results overnight, so it could not agree on when or where to begin.

As key starting points, the association was counseled by its consultants to put into place the following approaches to move the board to a more strategic role:

- Reconstruct the board of directors to be a strategic governance group composed of the best thinkers and most influential members of the profession and its industry.
- Ensure that the composition of the board represents the most appropriate range of industry perspectives, which may involve including state organization leadership and giving due consideration to regions, size, and so forth.
- Review and improve the board process—ensure that board meetings become a platform for dialogue and deliberation on issues of strategic importance to the organization, rather than an opportunity to review information already provided, redo work already completed by others,

or set administrative and/or operational program policy without sufficient study of context, alternatives, consequences, or likely implementation realities. Allocate sufficient time for these discussions.

- Abandon political controls that waste time and do not add value to decisions by increasing trust levels throughout the organization through (a) maintaining clarity and consensus on what will constitute success, (b) providing for open and easy access to common information, and (c) building confidence in the competence of others by composing staff and board of the best talent possible.

The board ultimately adopted few of these recommendations. It remains a management board today. The association has experienced significant membership loss. Retaining student members once they enter the profession has been especially difficult. The emerging generation of members does not view the association as representing its interests or as providing sufficient value. The profession itself has experienced significant encroachment from both higher-level practitioners and entry-level technicians—neither of which segments the association has made any attempt to attract or embrace. Yet the association is successful—if success is measured by its continued existence. Had it chosen the role of leadership over that of management, governance in this association might have been able to navigate these issues more successfully and deliver greater value to members.

Nominating Committees

Among the governance innovations observed in our study is the reconstruction of the role of the nominating committee. Such committees continue to have responsibility for identifying a prospective slate of officers or groups to fill vacancies on the board, but, more and more frequently, they are being asked to assume responsibility for leadership development in their organizations as well. In many associations, the nominating committee is being asked to define a leadership development strategy similar to a career-role strategy that might be seen in a corporate enterprise or business. It is also asked to implement and execute that leadership development strategy, find new and promising talent, and offer candidates significant opportunities for involvement—thereby essentially growing the next generation of member leaders.

Taking on this new role has had a remarkable effect on the types of issues nominating committees focus on when they execute their responsibility for nominations. Not only do they follow the traditional notions of rewarding loyalty to the organization, activity over time, and certain experiences in their selection of a slate of nominees, but also, because of their involvement in the leadership-development program, they are able to reflect on the emotional, intellectual, and behavioral competencies critical for leadership success. Our study suggests that as a result of these kinds of innovations in the roles of nominating committees, better balance is being achieved between the political correctness of selecting legitimate candidates and the newer emphasis on finding those whose knowledge base will enhance their effectiveness.

Delegate Bodies

Traditionally, governance in associations with large delegate bodies (e.g., houses of delegates, assemblies, meetings of the members) has resulted in a less intellectually stimulating agenda and frustration with balance-of-power and oversight issues. Some associations, especially professional societies, have begun to clarify the role of these bodies, underscoring that the role of the board is to govern the association and the role of the house is to govern the profession. The clarification of these roles, coupled with the use of innovative strategies for dialogue and deliberation, has energized more than a few houses of delegates and has helped these groups make a meaningful contribution to governance and decision making.

In one association, a governance study commission recommended discontinuance of the house of delegates (HOD) because it believed its function as a communication agent between chapters and the national organization had been replaced by other elements of a proposed restructuring. After spirited discussion of this recommendation with the HOD and other national members at the annual meeting, the board decided not to accept the commission's recommendation to abolish the HOD. Because of that dialogue, the HOD's role and communication lines have been better delineated, resulting in improved understanding. Now that its role is clearer, the HOD is more proactive and serves as an effective link with the grass roots and as a critical source of knowledge and insight from a broad perspective of members.

Committees and Task Forces

Our study revealed an interesting shift in the role and work of committees in associations that use a knowledge-based governance strategy. They are not just executing their traditional role of researching an issue and making recommendations for someone else to approve. In these organizations, committees are being asked to serve as both "thought forces" and "workforces." In many associations, these committees also have identified significant issues that require board attention. They continue to fulfill the role of researching issues for the board but in a very targeted and focused way.

In these associations, committees serve as the authors (or co-authors with staff) of background papers on significant issues. The papers are framed around the following four critical knowledge bases:

1. What is known about member and stakeholder wants, needs, and preferences

2. The capacity and strategic position of the association
3. The dynamics of the profession, industry, or cause
4. The illumination of ethical considerations related to choices of strategy

In another new role, such committees also participate, when feasible, with the board and senior staff in dialogue on whatever issue is being explored. Background papers prepared by a committee may not only provide illumination of the four knowledge bases but may also identify a number of possible choices of action. Rather than preparing one recommendation and hoping it will be approved, committees are framing the board's consideration of the issues by defining possible choices and perhaps even offering insight on the advantages and disadvantages of each choice. Instead of suggesting a recommendation for which the board does not have sufficient background and context, the committee provides relevant information coupled with thoughtful possibilities of strategic choice. When a committee functions in this way, it is often invited to be a part of the dialogue and develop strategy along with the board.

This change has obvious advantages for both committees and boards. The committee becomes an active partner in the development of strategy, and the board has more time and energy to address important issues because the committee did the work of illuminating choices and logical outcomes. With this kind of committee assistance, the board can now address issues that might otherwise have had to wait until a future board meeting because the board had run out of time and energy. Because the committee is asked to play an active part in the dialogue, regardless of whether its choice is ultimately selected by the board, it has a much better sense of the deliberative process. With knowledge of the board's discussion and action on the issue as well as its intent, the committee can build an action plan for implementing the strategy the board selected. The committee infrastructure (whether ad hoc or standing) illuminates, participates in, and then assumes responsibility, along with staff, for action planning and implementing.

This change in governance allows meaningful opportunity for members themselves to participate in the work of the organization. Because members are often pressed for time, many associations have moved to the efficiency of having staff rather than members execute work. Some factors an association must take into consideration in deciding whether staff or volunteers should execute a particular piece of work follow:

- Information and Expertise—Who has the knowledge, information, and expertise needed? Work related to the profession or industry might be most appropriately executed by a volunteer, while work related to association management functions such as meeting management or membership development might best be executed by staff.

- Time—How much will be required and when? When either staff or volunteers are in equal possession of information and expertise, work that requires a significant time investment may best be executed by staff rather than volunteers.

- Legitimacy—Functions and issues of a political nature usually require volunteer participation. Volunteers may need to be involved because decisions by a staff member would not be respected or given legitimacy by the membership. An example would be speaking on industry issues in advocacy-related activities.

- Resources Required—What will be most efficient? Associations must compare the financial cost of internal or contracted staff with the cost of volunteer involvement.

- Shared Activities—The extent to which the activities required are similar to responsibilities of existing staff or committees. If there are opportunities to leverage existing resources engaged in similar activities, then work might go to either a staff group or volunteer committee as appropriate.

- Nature of the Work—Whether the work is appropriate for a group or is a one-person responsibility. Most one-person responsibilities lend themselves more effectively to staff than to volunteers.

- Culture and History—How have similar responsibilities been handled in the past? What expectations do members and leaders have, based on past practice, experience, and so forth? Although the association may purposefully choose to execute something differently this time, it should be aware of the culture of the organization in making the decision.

All of these criteria should be considered in deciding how governance can take the fullest advantage of its committee infrastructure. But regardless of the choices made in any of the preceding variables, an association must always maintain a fundamental sense among the volunteer workforce that the membership is meaningfully involved in the organization's work. If an association is not able to do this, it loses enfranchisement and may ultimately sacrifice its unique sense of volunteerism. The heart of the association lies in people doing things together that they could not do alone. Indeed, what distinguishes any association from other enterprises is the active involvement of members in its work. Volunteers must have an emotional attachment to the organization; it is more valuable than the efficiency of paying others to accomplish a task.

Further, the historical notion that all committees and task forces should have the same structure, composition, work processes, and reporting rela-

tionships is no longer applicable, nor is the traditional notion that same-
ness somehow equals fairness. The most effective committees are those
whose composition, work process, and accountabilities are custom-
designed for their assignments. Governance must therefore redefine fairness as a commitment to ensuring optimal organization and execution of
its work.

Special Governance Issues Unique to Associations with Related Foundations

Some special governance issues unique to associations with foundations
include the degree of crossover between the association's board of directors
and the foundation; the role of the association's chief staff executive; to
whom foundation staff reports; whether the foundation has a separate strategic plan and planning process; and governance structure, bylaws, policies,
and procedures. These issues are among the most important and often most
difficult areas of governance in an association with a related foundation.

Our study shows that in the early years of a foundation's existence, it often
makes sense to create a structure with overlapping boards between the association and the foundation. The association board is committed to whatever
has driven it to create the foundation, and board members usually believe
they are best prepared to carry out that mission.

Over time, as board members change and commitment to the dual board
role decreases, the foundation will begin to bring in outside directors for its
board.

The last thing either organization needs is competition between the association and the foundation, but competition does often arise for volunteers,
donated dollars, attention of members, and so forth.

The best practice in associations we studied included having two separate
boards, with some overlap of leadership. At one leading association, for
example, the chairman-elect of the association is a voting member of the
foundation board, and the foundation chair is a voting member of the association's board. In addition, a majority of foundation directors are elected by
the association's board, but one nominating committee (comprised of members of the association board and the foundation board) proposes a slate to
each of the two electing groups. This structure enables the association to have
a say in who serves on the foundation board and thus to affect the direction
of the foundation.

It is also important for the staffs of both the association and the foundation to commit to meeting the goals of both groups. At one leading association, the chief staff executive is president and CEO of the association and of
its two subsidiaries, including the foundation. In the foundation, the chief
staff executive is executive vice president/COO and has day-to-day management responsibility for the foundation. Although the COO works more

closely with the foundation board, she always has access to the CEO. The CEO has ultimate hiring responsibility, but the board is involved in performance evaluations.

Most state laws require that a foundation (which is almost always a separately incorporated entity) have its own bylaws and articles of incorporation to ensure that its unique needs are met (e.g., bylaws addressing elections, gift-acceptance policies, etc.), although at times it makes sense to have them mirror the association's policies (e.g., when determining the foundation's fiscal year). The strategic plans of the two organizations are compatible but not necessarily overlapping. The foundation's plan is about achieving the purpose for which it was created; the association is initially involved in determining that purpose and, in the long term, ensuring that the foundation continues to support the industry or profession served by the association.

For-Profit Subsidiaries

Because some of the differences in governance between for-profit and not-for-profit boards are major, not-for-profit associations seeking to establish and sustain for-profit subsidiaries must be cognizant of them. In either type of organization, a board member's fiduciary duties of care, loyalty, and obedience apply equally. Fiduciary duties always mandate that the board member act in the best interests of the organization. As a practical matter, that will usually mean that a board member of a for-profit should be primarily concerned with increasing shareholder value, while a board member of a nonprofit association usually will be concerned about acting in a way that benefits the members. However, these should not be the board members' sole concerns. For instance, 501(c)(6) associations are charged by virtue of their tax-exempt status to benefit an entire line of business or profession. As such, tax law would frown on a 501(c)(6) board voting to offer benefits only to members while denying them to nonmembers.

Thus, board members' responsibilities are to act in the best interests of the organizations they represent. On a for-profit board, then, fiduciary responsibility suggests that a board member will be acting in the best interests of shareholders. Success is measured by increased value of the share. A good board is also concerned about what is right for its workforce and its customers, but only to the extent that these concerns produce profitability for the enterprise.

The primary focus of fiduciary responsibility on an association board is to the member. However, measures of success are more amorphous. Because of the associations' unique "triple-helix DNA"—the overlapping of members as owners, customers, and workforce—fiduciary responsibility is to the member from all three of those perspectives. Members, when they serve on a board, function in the same way as do owners, but, at the same time, they serve also as customers and the workforce.

This is very different from corporations, whose boards function only as owners of stock. Corporate boards are expected to maintain some distance from the work of the corporation, and the model of governance is based on the objectivity created by that distance. In fact, some would argue that bad corporate governance occurs when those who govern are too close to the work of the corporation and are therefore interested in their own personal reward and remuneration, rather than in the reward and remuneration of a broad class of owners. Conversely, in associations, board members tend to be selected *because* they are close to the work of the organization. The board of an association is more like a partnership or a family business than a corporation. Regardless of differences or similarities in size, marketplace, or complexity of the organization itself, the mission and the definition of success are different. In the for-profit, the mission is increasing value for the shareholder; success is reckoned in dollars. For the not-for-profit, the mission is about increasing value, and success is reflected in ensuring satisfaction to the organization's owners/workforce/customers, all of whom are the braided membership.

An association considering a for-profit subsidiary should construct a board similar to a corporate board, with composition, processes, and culture well matched to what the board is being held accountable for, which is profitability. Otherwise, the organization's governance process would put it at a significant competitive disadvantage. Most corporate boards have two kinds of board members. Internal board members represent both the major stockholder groups and senior staff management. External board members represent individual objective outsiders who possess expertise in areas important to the business.

The following case study illustrates the dynamics of for-profit subsidiaries. Ten years ago, the National Association of Realtors (NAR) created a for-profit subsidiary that sought to give Realtors and the public instant and easy access to Multiple Listing Service (MLS) listings that had previously been either electronically or manually collected, posted, and distributed by hundreds of independent MLS systems. The board structure was controversial, because many older members were concerned that if a single MLS, particularly one with public access, were created, customers would no longer need to seek Realtors as providers of this service. Local Realtor boards were also concerned that NAR's proposed subsidiary might destroy a major revenue source for Realtor organizations. As a result of these internal political dynamics, NAR put together a board for its new Internet initiative composed of well-respected leaders of the Realtor community. Private vendors and some state Realtor organizations and local boards immediately went into direct competition with this for-profit subsidiary. Staff of this venture developed a proprietary technology delivery model, which, by the time it was implemented, had already been replaced by a superior, subsequent generation of technology.

The for-profit subsidiary had spent several million dollars before NAR staff discovered it had developed a model that a board knowledgeable about the Internet business would never have permitted. NAR paid off the debt and reconstructed the enterprise conceptually as REALTOR.COM. It created a board for this for-profit subsidiary consisting of some representatives of NAR as the major stockholder group but primarily composed of experts in technology, marketing, banking, and law—arenas germane to an Internet business.

The board of a for-profit subsidiary should view itself as the top shareholder in the enterprise rather than the manager. A sense of distance is critical. A traditional association governance model will not work in a for-profit enterprise; rather, an association starting a for-profit subsidiary should have governance well matched to its for-profit mission, with representation from its association owners as well as from business professionals of the for-profit subsidiary's business area. This assumes that the board has the objectivity to replace board members if the for-profit subsidiary doesn't meet financial or quality-of-service objectives. An association that has a for-profit subsidiary and is being held accountable for the income it generates and the quality of service it provides ideally should be in a position to make decisions about new products based on business considerations, not political ones. Otherwise, the organization will be at a serious competitive disadvantage with other for-profit enterprises.

Balancing Authority, Responsibility, and Capacity

It is important to maintain the appropriate balance between authority, responsibility, and capacity, regardless of the choices an association makes in restructuring its governance. Authority refers to governance commitments made on behalf of the organization. Responsibility refers to performance obligations of governance to the organization. Capacity has to do with composition, frequency of meeting, and the amount of time available to work together. Adjustments to the mechanisms and structures of governance without consideration of the critical balance of these three elements will result in misalignment and incongruence.

A classic example of an imbalance of the three would be giving accountability for approval of all external communication to a board of 200 who meet for one day every six months. The authority is at too high a level—the chief staff executive should be accountable for external communication. Responsibility is misaligned—the board of 200 may not have the operational context in which to make appropriate decisions in this area. Also, the capacity to execute is not present in that the governing body meets with too seldom to keep communication flowing on a timely basis.

If these three factors are not balanced, dysfunctional governance bodies and dysfunctional organizations result. In each of the governance structures and mechanisms described in this section, organizations should not undertake change without considering and understanding the interaction of these elements. The traditional political association model does not provide for appropriate balance. As a result, governance systems become dysfunctional and less and less attractive to potential volunteer leaders.

Chapter 4
Twelve Key Findings: Implications for Change

What is clear from this discussion is that a new paradigm of governance is in the process of emerging in the associations we undertook to study. Many elements are responsible for the shift—new trends in membership needs and demographics, new emphasis on values, knowledge, and strategy, and, of course, the technological revolution. And as the infrastructure of an association changes, so must the governance system that leads it. The questions are: What must change in an association to develop and sustain the will to govern well and what are the implications are of that change?

In the course of our study, we identified several key findings with extraordinary implications for the future of voluntary organizations. These findings confront myths, fantasies, and false promises about governance.

1. Because of the unique makeup of associations, governance cannot be reinvented but must evolve. Many experts and association leaders speak of reinventing governance with activities that focus on changes to the balance of power. However, it is not advisable to reinvent governance, because the very nature of what makes associations unique enterprises would be put at risk.

The DNA metaphor illustrates this concept. Human DNA has two strands, but the organizational DNA of an association can be thought of as having three strands, representing each of the three overlapping populations and the unique relationship that distinguishes associations—owners, customers, and workforce. Unraveling this organizational DNA would put at risk key competitive advantages associations have in the 21st century—the aggregate intellectual capital of their memberships, their energy as communities with common purpose, and their credibility as voluntary institutions. Reinventing governance would require abandoning this unique relationship.

However, it is essential for the association community to contribute to an evolving governance practice, process, culture, and behavior to establish the will to govern well and to sustain success in increasingly complex environments.

It is currently popular to suggest that associations should become more businesslike. Although this may be a good direction, associations must be mindful that they cannot be run exactly like businesses because of their organizational DNA. They need to preserve their sense of association culture. A greater focus on community is increasingly the strategy of successful associations.

2. Associations will increasingly understand governance as a process, and will move to alter key governance processes rather than organizational structure. Governance itself is as much about process as it is about structure. In fact, because so many key practices are linked to it, governance may be the most essential process of the association. Unfortunately, many organizations do not look at governance in this light—they think about it as a series of structures. When asked to draw a picture of governance, many leaders draw an organization chart, not a flow chart. They view governance in terms of unmovable roles and responsibilities, focusing on the balance of power. Too few understand it as a link between work and the decision-making processes.

When associations alter governance structure without attending to necessary adjustments in process, they merely change the players, not the productivity. The experiences of many associations that have achieved significant change in structure with little gain in their ability to deliver value bear this out. Altering structure may change the balance of power but not the quality of what is produced. Altering board process, on the other hand, has an enormous impact. What the board talks about has to do with responsibility and role, but how the board talks about it has to do with the issues of process and culture.

The will to govern well is not just about what governance does but the way it does it. Governance agendas focused on issues of strategic direction and high-level policy enable the board to lead. Background materials and conversations designed to illuminate an issue and identify potential choices rather than support a predetermined decision promote a process of knowledge-based decision making and a culture of commitment and confidence.

The best change strategy to improve governance involves changing the process of governance, thereby changing the behavior that changes the culture that sustained the original process.

3. Board process is becoming a more important issue than composition or structure. Both large and small boards have been observed to be either effective or ineffective. Both constituency-based boards and competency-based boards have been observed to be either satisfied or unsatisfied with their performance. Issues of size and composition cannot be viewed independently from the issues of authority, responsibility, capacity, and process. Therefore, board process is becoming a more important issue than board composition or size because, increasingly, process is viewed as the leverage point for creating the desired balance among the variables on any given board.

There is a two-way relationship between composition and process. For many years, common wisdom held that who was on the board determined how the board worked. Increasingly, however, how a board works determines who is willing to serve on it. Good process enables governance to earn credibility by being competency based and to maintain legitimacy by being constituency based.

There is also a movement from geographically based constituency representation to constituency representation based on specialty or interest area. Roles or personal demographics are moving boards to embrace multiple variables in composition. Increased diversity is driving the development of new methods for board work that take fuller advantage of the variety of perspectives available in decision making. Knowledge-based governance strategy and modern communication technologies are enabling smaller boards to engage in decision making while increasing participation in the process. They are also allowing larger governance bodies to execute their responsibilities more effectively.

Changes in process—what the board talks about and how it talks about it—are improving the quality of decisions as well as the enjoyment of the leadership experience. Boards focused on issues of strategic direction and high-level policy that use a knowledge-based governance strategy to identify alternatives and assess potential solutions are succeeding in attracting talented individuals to positions of leadership.

The nature of the leadership experience has as much to do with the sophistication level of individuals attracted to participate as their sophistication level does with their quality of governance. How does an association develop the kind of collegial and honest exchange necessary to attract talented members and staff to participate? The traditional belief was that who was on the board determined its culture. But it is just as true that the culture of governance determines who is interested in participating. As reported earlier, our study revealed that when process changes in association governance, behavior changes, and when behavior changes, culture changes. If an association successfully changes what the board spends its time on, it is likely governance in that association will become attractive to individuals who were not attracted to previous board cultures.

The next generation of members will not define enfranchisement merely as having a person with similar demography in a seat on the board. Many volunteer organizations struggle periodically with issues related to board composition in the belief that minority voices growing to majority position desire participation in the traditional mechanisms of governance. But for some associations, slotted board seats may move them in the opposite direction of future member preferences. Younger members seem to prefer a knowledge-based approach to governance that allows them to participate in the dialogue on substantive issues confronting the industry and the association. Hence, the notion of enfranchisement as having someone on the board who resembles oneself is being superseded by the expectation of active participation in the conversations of an association from which choices and decisions emerge. The next generation of leaders and members expect technology to enable them to participate in the work of the organization without having to travel to a certain place at a certain time to contribute. This has significant implications for governance and will be discussed later as one of four specific expectations related to association use of technology.

4. Good governance sees its mission as having three dimensions, and the allocation of its time among those dimensions is shifting. As identified in Chapter 1 (the three-part mission of governance), the three facets of the board's purpose are direction setting, oversight of operational effectiveness, and attention to the culture of the organization.

Direction Setting

Strategic thinking is as much about partnership and trust as it is about knowledge and good decision theory. Increasingly, governance is evolving from a retreat-driven, product-oriented, traditional process of strategic planning to a process of ongoing strategic thinking. Direction is being defined as a vision of preferred conditions. Strategic principles that enable decision making, resource allocation, and program implementation to be more nimble allow for direction that provides coherency over time while still maintaining the fluidity and flexibility necessary to remain relevant during change.

Oversight

As members have more choices about where to belong and less time and money to give, attention to whether programs are achieving their desired outcomes consumes an increasing amount of board time. Oversight involves refocusing on whether things are working as opposed to how much is being done.

How governance chooses to approach accountability will have an impact on achieving and sustaining the necessary culture for trust. The trust essential for nimbleness to keep pace with change and for an enjoyable experience to attract participation is supported by accountability that is shared and formative rather than imposed and summative. The strategic planning process, when effectively integrated into governance's ongoing role, provides continuous opportunities for governance and management to share accountability. This enables both assessment of whether desired outcomes are in fact being achieved and the sharing of ideas for changing strategies, programs, or activities to improve the potential for success.

New methods of accountability and performance appraisal are emerging that are more difficult to sustain but more rational in judgment. *Summative evaluation,* in its simplest form, is about catching someone doing something wrong, documenting it, and imposing a penalty. *Formative evaluation* is about assessing progress toward a declared end so as to be able to adjust course to improve the probability of success. A summative philosophy inhibits trust. A formative philosophy promotes it. Without a culture of trust, an enterprise is likely to achieve neither the nimbleness required in the 21st century nor the enjoyable participation experience required to attract talented volunteers and staff.

Attention to Culture

As strategic community building becomes increasingly important in differentiating associations from other kinds of service providers, culture is receiving added attention. Boards that try to understand their impact on the association's culture (whether manifested in behavior consistent with the association's stated core values or in the way board members behave among their peers) enhance their leadership and exhibit the will to govern well.

Traditionally, members who volunteer a disproportionate share of time to working in organizations been rewarded for their energy and dedication. Their rewards have usually included an enjoyable experience that fed a perceived desire for elite or special status. Sometimes the nature of involvement experiences created for top leaders became so differentiated from that created for others that both members and leaders perceived a "them vs. us" dimension to the culture. Contemporary volunteer leaders still seek that personal reward and distinguishing experience. However, their interest is in access to insight and acknowledgement of their contribution while they participate in an enjoyable activity with colleagues whom they respect. Regal trappings of power are insufficient to satisfy these redefined demands for reward. Successful boards recognize that their values and behavior set the tone for the rest of the enterprise.

5. Governance is moving from the traditional political model of debating the ideas of others to a more knowledge-based model of defin-

ing desired outcomes and establishing goals for those who will be accountable for action plans and implementation.

The history of voluntary organizations in the Americas may provide intriguing insight into the relative advantages and disadvantages of our traditional governance models. The contemporary voluntary association experience has been heavily influenced by the model of American trade guilds, which first appeared in the 1700s when the American colonies were engaged in a dispute with King George over taxation and representation. A prototype of public governance evolved during this period, the primary purpose of which was to prevent the self-interests of a small elite from subordinating the conflicting interests of the larger majority. Successful governance was envisioned as that which imposed the least.

Naturally, and often unconsciously, the trade, professional, and cause-related organizations that evolved subsequent to this period assumed this historic philosophy of governance and built structure systems and rules modeled on it. For example, an elaborate committee system reporting to a house of delegates is a congressional model. A strong elected president with powers separate from a board of directors represents a distribution of power modeled on the constitutional separation of powers. A board of governors composed of members selected from each of the states is modeled on traditional American notions of representative democracy.

The philosophies, systems, and rules of this approach do fulfill their function in terms of inhibiting elitist actions. Contemporary associations, however, are seeking to preserve participation and democratic ideals while avoiding the institutionalized barriers to significant change embedded in the historic American political model. Perhaps a better illustration for contemporary governance is to be found in the constitutional convention of 1787. Each colony was represented in drafting what might be considered the ultimate set of bylaws. The formal process the founders employed created sufficient sensitivity to the confluence of political, economic, and personal interests that were in play among the framers. And it was this process—not the size of the group, not the structure of the group, and not the furnishings of its meeting space—that enabled successful navigation through constellations of complex interests. The process both captured and liberated the designers' will to govern well.

Differences in the intensity of commitment to the political ideals of participation and democracy are among the distinguishing characteristics in governance cultures associated with trade; large and small professional organizations; and philanthropic, charitable, and cause-related organizations. It is not the commitment to participation per se that is important so much as what constitutes a satisfactory level and type of participation. Governance is moving from the traditional political model of debating the ideas of others to a more knowledge-based model of defining the outcomes desired and establishing outlines for the work of those who will be accountable for action plans and implementation. This shift increases the nimbleness of the organization by removing unnecessary permissions to proceed and promotes a culture of trust based on clarity and consensus about what will constitute success. A culture of trust decreases the need for detailed supervision, increases the pace of innovation, and enhances the enjoyment of those involved.

There is also a link to the issue of competency- vs. constituency-based boards. If an association moves to a knowledge-based culture and addresses these issues in a productive and rewarding way at an organizational and individual level, the pool of competent individuals will very likely grow. To the extent that governance must still be mindful of constituent representation, it is even more likely that those individuals will also prefer to participate in a board with a knowledge-based culture where competency—not interest and acumen in politics—is prized.

6. The needs and preferences of members related to time and expertise are causing the fiduciary responsibility of boards and the role of the chief staff executive to evolve. Historically, boards sensitive to role differentiation have believed the old bromide, "It is not the board's job to run the association but to see that the association is well run." While seeing that the association is well run and actually running it are definably different jobs, both tend to focus on operations rather than direction, on management rather than leadership, and on efficiency rather than value. Good leaders have less discretionary time to give and are more aware of the limitations of their own experience and knowledge of contemporary association operations. Hence, the old adage is morphing as more and more boards are holding the chief staff executive accountable for seeing that the association is well run.

The board's role is evolving to define what will constitute value and to ensure that value is delivered. This trend is moving effective boards further away from issues of management and operations and closer to issues of governance and leadership. In the 21st century, this trend will elevate the chief staff executive and the association management profession to the next plateau of accountability and contribution. A knowledge-based governance strategy will enable the board and the chief staff executive to coordinate and execute their evolving roles more effectively.

7. Significant dimensions of the governance cultures of different types of organizations are becoming less alike. An increasing number of for-profit and not-for-profit organizations are providing a range of generic tools designed to address the dynamics of voluntary organizations, as if they were identical. This mind-set ignores the unique dynamics of different types of organizations and the implications of their peculiarities for the execution of leadership within them. For example, the corporate culture of trade association members is moving trade association governance closer to a corporate board model that ensures delivery of value to stakeholders. Demands for increased accountability in the use of funds and board-member involvement in fundraising is moving charitable governance closer to management and implementation. The governance culture of professional, charitable, and cause-related organizations is distributed across a continuum that spans these two directions—with location on the continuum primarily determined by the complexity of the organization and the degree of confidence governance has in the competence of the executive. Executives who transfer strategies or tools from one type of voluntary organization to another with insufficient sensitivity to key differences in their dynamics run the risk of assaulting their organizations' cultural values and beliefs.

Our study shows that two significant forces tend to drive the governance cultures and activities of philanthropic, charitable, and cause-related organizations to different places. First, the traditional notion of the threefold role of the board member of a philanthropic organization as bringing two of three *W*s—work, wisdom, or wealth—is coupled with the often unspoken but accepted norm that bringing the third *W* can relieve one of responsibility for the others. When members of governance are asked to roll up their sleeves and become personally involved in the activities of fundraising, they are engaging in their role as workforce in a way that may make it difficult for them to refocus their attention on the policy-maker role when they revert to members of the body politic. Our study shows that philanthropic, charitable, and cause-related organizations that have successfully navigated this natural dichotomy have employed a board process that formally announces and acknowledges when the volunteer leader is being asked to play one role or another. Because a knowledge-based governance strategy declares the employment of dialogue and the requirement for deliberation, it enhances the ability of board members with dual roles of policy maker and worker to understand which role is required at the moment. Similarly, in trade and professional associations, where board members serve as chairs, liaisons, or members of committees, a knowledge-based governance strategy can assist them in subordinating their natural allegiance to that committee's work to the greater good of the larger organization.

Second, the absence of shared background among the board members of many philanthropic, charitable, or cause-related organizations often poses difficulty in sustaining trust among board members, between board members and senior staff, and between the board and the constituency served. Structural solutions such as slotted seats or game-like solutions such as color-coded tent cards or multicolored hats will not be sufficient to address the potential for conflict inherent in these natural dynamics. Good board process that acknowledges differences and uses them as a source for varied perspectives to increase confidence in decisions can support strength and trust building rather than paralysis and mistrust among the partnership.

Another observation from our study is that philanthropic organizations themselves are becoming less like each other as the age of specialization emerges in associations. We observe four distinct types of philanthropic organizations. First is the truly philanthropic—an organization with an endowment that it gives away. Second is the charitable—an organization involved in raising money and distributing it to a very good cause. Third is the foundation—an organization attached to an association that raises money for research and education related to the knowledge areas represented by the association. Fourth is the cause-related organization, which spends and dispenses money for the purpose of advocating a particular issue.

Governance culture in trade, professional, cause-related, and philanthropic organizations may also be getting less, rather than more, similar relative to the respective roles of the chief staff executive. The role of evolution noted earlier (regarding the chief staff executive and the fiduciary responsibility of boards) is moving boards further away from management and administrative concerns. This change will eventually take the traditional partnership between a board and its chief staff executive to a very different place than it is today, and we observe significant differences among the types of voluntary organizations in terms of how that partnership may manifest. Philanthropic boards are being asked to participate more actively in the fundraising work of the organization, moving them closer to operations and activity. Professional and trade association boards are more diverse in their beliefs and leadership cultures, with size and complexity of the organization and the talent and competence of the chief staff executive determining the norms of role expectation and execution.

Member companies of trade associations tend to be more comfortable using market and marketing research to guide decisions about value and allocation of resources. Such an association should attempt to fill seats on the board with the right people rather than the right constituencies. In a trade association, a competent nominating process—guided by board-approved criteria—can ensure board competence. Trade associations practicing a knowledge-based governance strategy often find the combination of a competency-based board, a competent nominating process, and good use of market and marketing research to be a practical combination for improved decisions—one that does not require continuous bylaws change. Because constituency-based board selection can encourage a political governance culture, in a trade association where member companies are more interested in improved return on investment for their businesses than in the internal politics in their association, this can engender a reputation that is unattractive to the best, brightest, and most influential in the industry.

These dynamics are real—they cannot be ignored; and they are natural—they cannot be re-engineered. Each set of interactions is peculiar to one or another of the three basic kinds of voluntary organizations—and solutions employed in one cannot easily be transferred to another without significant and sensitive adaptation.

8. Governance desires a higher level of partnership and shared accountability with staff, so clearly defined roles are less valued. For many years, association staff and member leaders have been counseled to define clearly their respective roles and responsibilities. Some associations directed as much energy to protecting these distinctions as to providing value. But all this is changing.

Boards increasingly want staff to provide information and insight and to participate with member leaders in decision making about desired outcomes and potential strategy. The traditional walls between governance and management are becoming porous, with strategy as the common ground. Successful relationships share information about what works and what doesn't. Modern communication technology makes membership aware more quickly of decision-making deficiencies. And the pace of change makes involved association members less patient with staff behavior that doesn't focus on their needs or provide perceived value.

More than ever before, governance expects staff to be conversant with the dynamics of industrial, professional, or cause-related issues. They want staff to offer insightful, specific advice about how the association can work to meet their needs. Many associations have eliminated the concepts of "staff-driven" and "volunteer-driven" and have moved toward a true partnership that defines "leader" and "support" roles for both staff and volunteers. This requires constant re-education as volunteers rotate and staff changes.

9. As expertise and honesty increase in value, governance is less tolerant of inexpert or manipulative behavior. Leaders of volunteer organizations have access to more information about associations and their operations through conversations on the Internet and an increasing number of publications directed specifically toward their concerns. A concomitant result has been more informed volunteers with higher expectations and demands. Additionally, as volunteer discretionary time continues to become subordinated to personal and professional demands, a larger number of volunteer leaders are participating in the leadership pool of multiple organizations.

Exposure to successful practices in one organization is often transferred as an expectation of improved performance in another. Therefore, association governance is becoming less tolerant of inexpert or manipulative behavior on the part of staff or volunteers. The term "manipulative" refers to a heightened understanding of how knowledge is used as power. Historically, the association withheld knowledge to gain power (leadership). Now, knowledge is used as power through its distribution: The wider the distribution, the greater the number of information dependencies created; and the greater this number, the greater the influence. In this context, then, manipulation can be defined as the act of selectively providing managed information to achieve a preconceived goal (e.g., a chief staff executive who knows something but doesn't share it is being manipulative).

To avoid the perception of manipulation, it is important to understand how board members want to view their work before selecting an instructional or developmental strategy or tool. Some boards have expressed concern about the use of "climate-setting" videos in orientation retreats. They perceive that videos have been used to get them to feel the way "the staff" wanted them to feel about the board's work rather than to arrive at their own conclusions.

Where change is needed, the challenge is to craft an open strategy that creates an informed environment where the board can decide honestly that it wants to change its assumptions, beliefs, and values. If a tool such as a video is to be used to help shape perspective, it may be useful to have the tool introduced by a member leader prepared to speak about the reason for its use and its relevance to the organization's values.

Manipulation is dysfunctional, regardless of who—staff, leaders, or volunteers—is employing it. With increased access to knowledge, everyone in the information stream has become less tolerant of its use, regardless of where it originates.

10. Managing risk effectively requires that governance be more knowledgeable. Risks tend to occur every two to three years in the association world, but every 30 to 60 days in the corporate world. Members, therefore, are accustomed to much quicker decision processes. To remain relevant, associations will need to manage a higher level of risk. To become comfortable with risk, governance will demand information that helps it manage risk more effectively. Systems for prudent innovation are emerging, and boards are expecting their staff to design and operate such systems effectively. Attention to these systems and the judgments they produce is replacing traditional committee status reports on board agendas. Boards are becoming increasingly less tolerant of large volumes of information designed to demonstrate how successful the organization is and how busy the staff and committees are. What interests boards is information that allows them to determine or anticipate whether value is being delivered. In many associations, risk will require the association to increase the percentage of the program portfolio that addresses new or emerging products. With mechanisms for appraisal in place early on, governance will be able to change or abandon an initiative before summative appraisal announces its demise.

11. Governance must focus on policy rather than politics. Governance that exhibits the will to govern well enables board members to distinguish between being a *representative for* a constituency and being a *representative of* a constituency. The difference is manifested in the reasons that individuals have for participating in governance. The *representative for* argues and votes on behalf of a defined population. The *representative of* ensures that the interests, beliefs, and values of a population are reflected in the decision process and votes according to the best interests of the enterprise as a whole.

The shift from a closed political model to a more open, rational model appears to be best achieved by a change strategy that first alters the governance process. It is the declared culture of governance that either supports or inhibits the respective behaviors. By changing process, the organization changes behavior, and by changing behavior, it can make sustainable changes in culture. Where the evolution of governance has been successful, it has been catalyzed by a competent executive who knows how to enlist more than one generation of member and staff leaders as champions of the change.

12. Governance must develop the will to govern well. Good governance makes conscious choices, not just about what will be accomplished but also about how it will lead. The will to govern well is fundamentally about two things: (1) what governance chooses to focus its attention on, and (2) how governance chooses to get its work done. Boards no longer wish to be viewed as elite bastions of atypical intelligence or special influence. Governance that sacrifices the necessary critical mass of being representative in favor of a disproportionate commitment to some defined set of "competencies" is more vulnerable to perceptions of elitism, detachment, and irrelevant agendas. Ultimately, this perception destroys the culture of trust.

In many associations, when leadership groups consciously make choices about how they can be most successful in leading, they sustain the will to govern well. Those choices must be made continually and on a case-by-case basis to promote (a) the knowledge necessary for strategic thoughtfulness, (b) a common commitment to earning the trust necessary for others to agree to follow, and (c) a disciplined flexibility consistent with nimbleness.

These twelve findings and their implications are the basis for the discussion that follows of specific strategies that successful associations will employ in seeking to evolve governance systems, structures, and processes, and to achieve and institutionalize the will to govern well. In the next section of this book, we will explore how the mechanisms of knowledge, trust, and nimbleness can nurture this evolution.

Part 2
The Role of Knowledge in Governance Systems

Chapter 5
Knowledge: A Definition

Becoming more knowledgeable is one key to developing and sustaining the will to govern well. Webster's defines knowledge as "the fact or condition of knowing something with familiarity gained through experience or association; as the sum of what is known: the body of truth, information, and principles acquired by mankind. Knowledge applies to facts or ideas acquired by study, investigation, observation, or experience."

With respect to association governance as it is considered in this book, the ability both to *create* and *effectively use* knowledge will distinguish successful associations in the future and encourage the will to govern well. Knowledge creation is the act of taking relatively random data from a broad spectrum and translating it into a meaningful, insightful context through study, investigation, observation, and experience.

Associations with the will to govern well focus on knowledge creation in two contexts related to the leadership obligations of managing information. One is to ensure sufficient access in the decision-making process to a continuous stream of information from members, prospective members, customers, and stakeholders that allows governance to understand their views of the world. The other is to provide sufficient information to members to help shape their perceptions of the association.

Knowledge is what effective associations use to make decisions, expand their relevance, and govern themselves. It is not opinion. This is an important value-added distinction because the collection of needed data cannot be accomplished either inexpensively or quickly. If it is not leveraged appropriately, boards used to basing their decisions on personal intuition may view knowledge acquisition as too costly and potentially unnecessary. The intent of knowledge acquisition is to broaden the context upon which decisions are based, shifting the focus away from individual opinion and personal power toward good data and collective wisdom.

Recognizing the importance of both collecting and using knowledge in work and decision-making systems is essential to the success of associations and the new models of governance discussed in this book. Without good data, associations cannot establish themselves as the knowledge leaders in their respective fields or achieve and maintain a position of value to members or to the larger community.

Chapter 6

Knowledge in Current Governance Practices: What We Know, Believe, and Predict

The following questions will frame our discussion in this chapter: "How can governance (systems, structures, role, process, and culture) use knowledge to ensure an effective system?" and "What will be the nature of decision making, and what behaviors will sustain increased knowledge in governance?"

Knowledge Is Built Through Community

Valuing knowledge is critical to good governance. In associations that have the will to govern well, knowledge and insight inform dialogue and decision making with a constant stream of relevant insight about member needs, wants, and preferences; capacity and strategic position of the organization; dynamics of the industry, profession, or cause; and ethical implications of strategic choices.

Knowledge in associations is built through community. The unique knowledge associations possess resides in the intellectual capital of their members—their experiences, knowledge, insights, and wisdom—all of which are shared through members' participation in communities of interest.

The ASAE Foundation has been engaged in a multiyear research effort designed to explore the dimensions of community as a strategy for associations. The following is from the Foundation's 2000 report, "Community as Strategy: Creating the 'Stickiness' of Community—Ten Fundamentals."

> *Associations have always been in the community business, building the networks that draw together and support their members. For associations, community is strategy. But*

> *information technology is a dislocating force, offering new ways to communicate and new ways to sustain community. As members' needs shift, associations are finding it harder and harder to know how to provide community. Meanwhile, competitors— and potential competitors—are jumping in where associations were once the only game in town.*

The foundation's work defines community as social glue—providing "stickiness" or connection: "Community is what people do for each other; community is the creation of a web of social relationships. It is the social machinery that holds groups together. Both these definitions point to the bedrock fact that community takes work; it must be accomplished anew every day."

The existence of community encourages the use of knowledge in governance systems. Community encourages dialogue, generates insights, and creates new knowledge. Good governance requires a constant stream of knowledge and insight to successfully lead an association toward its vision.

Three Paths to Greater Knowledge

In governance theory, some suggest that the path to better governance is universal suffrage and ubiquitous dialogue. Others suggest that the path to being more knowledgeable in governance lies in smaller groups of more competent people. However, though these two paths are based on the work of identified thought leaders in the field of governance, uncompromising commitment to either path by itself has been marked by a number of failed or flawed governance reform initiatives.

A common attribute of organizations viewed by themselves and others as having successfully evolved their governance systems is that they have navigated a third path between these extremes by taking advantage of both, though specifics differ markedly from organization to organization.

The first path to becoming knowledgeable is articulated by Peter Senge, author of *The Fifth Discipline* (1990). Senge eloquently argues for process change and broad-based dialogue in concert with the democratic ideals of association culture as keys to organizational improvement.

> *Organizations are products of the ways that people in them think and interact. To change organizations for the better, you must give people the opportunity to change the ways they think and interact. No one person, including a highly charismatic . . . CEO, can train or command someone else to alter their attitudes, beliefs, skills, capabilities, perceptions, or level of commitment. Instead, the practice of organizational learning involves developing and taking part in tangible activities*

that will change the way people conduct their work. Through these new governing ideas, innovations in infrastructure, and new management methods and tools, people will develop an enduring capability for change. The process will pay back the organization with a far greater diversity and intensity of commitment, innovation, and talent.

Senge's notions from *The Fifth Discipline Fieldbook* (1994), as applied to knowledge in associations, would argue for broad-based participation in work and decision-making systems.

The second path relates to the work of Jim Collins, who, in *Good to Great* (2001), argues that transitioning to great doesn't require "a high-profile CEO, the latest technology, innovative change management, or even a fine-tuned business strategy." A key change strategy he argues for is to "get the right people on the bus" before pursuing change. He advocates use of a mechanism called, " 'the Council,' which consists of a group of the right people who participate in dialogue and debate . . . [repetitively] and over time . . . about vital issues and decisions facing the organization." This concept argues that more efficient governance can be found in a smaller group of people and suggests a movement toward meritocracy, a representative democracy, with sensitivity to the information coming from the broader whole.

Many associations we have observed are creating a third path by harnessing the best attributes of both visions. This middle way builds broad-based participative dialogue processes where members feel a link to their association's work and decision-making systems; at the same time, it builds a small board of sufficient representation and reputation to engender confidence in its abilities among the membership at large.

Which path members will select tends to be based upon which has characteristics congruent with their beliefs and preferences as shaped by their sociosphere outside the association. How members link to their world differs among trade, professional, and philanthropic or cause-related organizations. Trade associations, which value efficiency, tend toward Collins, while smaller professional societies and cause-related organizations, which value a high degree of participation, lean toward Senge.

In the future, associations may select among these paths based on business lines. Technology has increased the availability of open information, created faster knowledge transfer, and improved efficiency while preserving broad participation.

Question 1

What do we know, believe, or predict about association members' needs, wants, and preferences relative to increasing the use of knowledge in governance?

Members' environments will continue to become increasingly complex. They will seek organizations that can simplify their lives, requiring demonstrated value for their involvement. As the business world grows and becomes more global, members need knowledge to navigate industry issues. Governance will need to clarify emerging issues, as well as take a defensible stand on them.

Members need not only knowledge, but also new and efficient sources of it. The confusion between knowledge and information hinders the work of associations in gathering relevant data for members. The traditional approach has been to inundate members with as much information as the association could produce. With the advent of the Internet and e-mail, random information is even easier and less costly to pass on. But how can members be expected to discern which data are meaningful? Time limitations make them less tolerant of being inundated. Governance, in its obligation to shape the perceptions of members, can direct where they should focus their attention.

Successful governance is able to access all relevant insights of strategic importance to its members. Governance that has the will to govern well is able to access timely and intelligent insights from all perspectives that have strategic relevance to members and customers. It is able to create the space for alternative views in dialogue, while still protecting the ability of the association's core membership to make decisions about direction, program, and policy. This is often accomplished by separating the membership structure from the governance structure—creating a situation where various segments of members can participate in the thinking and programs of the organization without jeopardizing the critical mass of decision power of the actual owners of the enterprise—the core members.

The strategy of seeking to access a broader set of insights in governance dialogue will challenge some assumptions about who should sit at the board table, and may suggest two possible organizational strategies. Both argue for more diverse boards.

One strategy is for the association to "focus down"—to decide to concentrate its efforts on serving a discrete population of people or issues and not try to be everything to everyone. In a traditional political governance model, that choice would likely lead to a board composed of a group of individuals representative of a smaller array of more common interests. However, in terms of knowledge and insight, the risk is that such a board may become so insulated from broader perspectives that it will lack the information or expertise needed to make effective decisions on behalf of its defined membership population.

A second organizational strategy is to "focus out"—to choose to encompass and represent the views and interests of multiple segments of an industry, profession, or interest area. Should an organization choose this strategy, it is likely that a wider variety of segments and perspectives represented in the membership would be represented on the board, and thus access to broader knowledge would be easier. The danger with this approach can be the potential disenfranchisement of a variety of membership segments in the decision-making process and the inability to reach consensus on common issues across the organization's interest areas.

In either case, we observe that successful governance finds a way to have timely and intelligent access to the insights of all perspectives that have strategic relevance to their members and customers without jeopardizing the enfranchisement and decision power of the core membership.

Members will increasingly look to their associations to develop relevant knowledge for them, and governance will need to be accountable for delivering this value. The expectation that information will be directly applicable to members' professional roles is growing. Associations have a potential competitive advantage in that as a community they have access to advice on how to use information, counsel as to why it is important, and ideas about how to apply the insights it provides.

Because they exist as communities of interest, they can access not only data and information, but also knowledge, insight, and wisdom uniquely relevant to the industry, profession, or cause and filtered through the experiences of their members.

In the ASAE Foundation's 2000 report, "Community as Strategy: Creating the 'Stickiness' of Community—Ten Fundamentals," this phenomenon is referred to as "learning to be an accountant."

> *Learning to be a member of a profession or trade—whether accounting, electrical, contracting or anything else—has as much to do with social strategies as it does with facts and techniques. In learning how to talk, act, and be recognized as an accountant, you have to tap into the vast reservoir of knowledge that exists below the surface, where it is hard for people to talk about or even to know they know. This tacit knowledge is transferred not through books but in everyday interaction with others.*
> (ASAE Foundation 2000, p. 7).

This knowledge transfer will also permeate the governance systems of associations that have the will to govern well. Work and decision making will become an opportunity to share tacit knowledge and insight, and members will realize that getting involved is well worth their time and effort.

Members will hold governance increasingly accountable. Member expectations of governance are limited and do not always serve as the drivers to active involvement. In most associations members have little understanding of the inner workings of governance or of what is required for leadership involvement, expecting that people voted onto the board simply "know" how to be board members. Seldom do they see governance in action and automatically want to be involved. But as far removed as members may feel from governance currently, in the future, they will begin to hold governance increasingly accountable for behavior, actions, and results. They will develop greater understanding of the context and content of governance's decision-making processes, and if decisions of governance fail to ensure sufficient value, members will hold them accountable.

Becoming knowledgeable regarding association practices and leadership issues will be critical to governance. New board members in any organization need comprehensive orientation concerning their new roles and responsibilities, as well as to whom they are accountable and for what. Governance is not about hands-on, committee-style work; it is about leadership. The average member coming into a leadership position has little or no context for understanding this.

Successful associations consider it a necessity, not a nicety, to orient their boards to the mechanics of leadership in a voluntary environment. These associations recognize that most board members do not like feeling as though they are being "trained" or "developed." Associations seeking to instill the will to govern well hold orientations to offer new board members opportunities to experience successful governance by doing real work the right way—working on a real issue in a manner consistent with the organization's expressed governance philosophy. In these task-oriented training sessions, a facilitator explains the rationale and value of the approach being employed while guiding the group through the work itself. This is very different from the kind of association orientation that focuses on distributing information to new board members about staff, programs, budgets, and expense reimbursement. It also differs markedly from orientation programs that promulgate a set of universal do's and don'ts about board roles and responsibilities without providing an opportunity for the board to experience a work process reflecting those rules.

Members expect their leaders to communicate, through language and behavior, three things:

1. A clear, common, and positive vision of an achievable future. Each of these adjectives is critically important because they reflect the essential mission and function of the board. People do not want to follow negative leadership. They may listen at first, but after a while they will clearly recognize that the leader is damaging himself or herself. People do not want to feel bad about things that are important to them.

2. Appreciation of the values, expectations, needs, and anxieties of the members. When a board fires a chief staff executive, it is often because the board, or an important part of it, begins to perceive that the executive is no longer concerned about the values, expectations, needs, and

anxieties of the members. Something else appears to be more important to the executive than what the organization is supposed to be doing for its membership. It is irrelevant whether this perception is true; if the group perceives a lack of concern, it will act accordingly.

3. Optimism that ability, good plans, and hard work will lead to success. Several associations have embedded this statement in their job description for board members. Others use it in developing criteria that nominating committees can use to make more rationally based, systematic judgments about who they should recommend for leadership positions.

Additionally, members want governance to empower people to deliberate effectively through astute management of the dynamics of group process. In an association, more than almost anywhere else, groups are the decision makers, and one of the most frustrating conditions for association executives is that often no individual in the organization is empowered to make a decision alone. However, in an association, a good executive must always be willing to sacrifice speed for involvement, unless—and this is a judgment call—the autocratic style is essential at the moment because there is only a limited time to accomplish an objective.

In a good working partnership, partners have both mutual and separate responsibilities. Although most things are done by mutual consent after proper deliberation, occasionally one partner must make a decision on his or her own initiative because of a lack of time for consultation or the existence of emergent conditions. In such instances, the partner must be sure to inform other partners as promptly as possible and explain the conditions and the rationale for the solo decision. This situation has implications for trust as much as it does for knowledgeable decision making.

Question 2

What do we know, believe, or predict about current realities and evolving dynamics of associations relative to knowledge in governance?

The pace of evolution of association programs will need to be at least equivalent to the pace of change in the world of members, and knowledge transfer will need to occur rapidly. The implication is that governance will need to increase the rate at which knowledge and insight are exchanged among those who require it. Governance should anticipate how to lead the organization in developing the things necessary to meet the needs of those it seeks to serve, and to do so in an appropriate timeframe. Governance must learn how to determine what is right more quickly, and to commit to that decision. It will also need a process for constant assessment and adjustment, as these things become necessary. This suggests that knowledge transfer among all involved will need to accelerate significantly.

International activities of associations will continue to add a level of complexity in gathering and using knowledge. An illustration of this observation is the experience of a newly arrived executive director in a large international professional society. She tells how during her first day on the job she sent an e-mail to all members. She closed by saying she hoped everyone would have a good summer. Soon afterward, she received a reply from Australia reminding her it was winter in the southern hemisphere.

Governance has a responsibility to provide value. Different economies, standards, and cultures will render more complex the process of knowledge creation that informs governance in associations seeking to operate in international arenas. The governance dimension of an association's transnational strategy also differs markedly among trade, professional, and charitable or cause-related organizations. What value they will deliver to members should drive strategies in this area.

Many associations question whether to consider themselves as "international" or "global." Adopting an international strategy suggests the structuring of membership and governance based on geopolitical boundaries. A global strategy, on the other hand, ignores geopolitical boundaries but might create sections based on variables other than geography. Trade associations tend to go international because of market-share issues. Professional and scientific societies tend to go global, making all members from anywhere equal. They may have chapters as part of program delivery, but the chapters would not be connected to governance structure.

Many U.S.-based associations also struggle with whether to remain focused on the United States or North America but to allow access or membership to anyone from anywhere. Possible transnational structural choices that have implications for governance are:

- International with chapters that are smaller than nations;
- International as a federation of national or regional groups;
- Global with no subcommunities;
- Global with subcommunities formed around variables other than geography, such as size, having a role in industry, being a multinational company, having a subspecialty or topical interest area, functionality, etc.

These basic choices have an unlimited number of permutations.

Regardless of whether an association chooses the international or the global route, operating outside U.S. borders has complex implications for knowledge creation in support of governance. A relevant example involved an organization we studied—a professional society in an engineering-related field with more than 50,000 members in 110 countries spanning virtually all regions of the world. Global growth for this association has swelled in recent years; the association is still trying to reposition itself to take full advantage of this growth and to provide value and benefit to a global membership. During a recent strategic planning session, the board and senior staff were building a set of assumptions about the relevant 5- to 10-year future of the association and its members. Small groups constructed assumptions in the areas of social and demographic focus, industry structure, science and technology, regulation and legislation, and global business climate. As the groups began to share their assumptions with the board, it became apparent that global perspectives within each small group were narrower than in the full board. For example, two subgroups came up with the same assumption but described different conditions based on the part of the world they were from. Sometimes knowledge creation is a matter of viewing things from where you sit—wherever it may be on the globe. The challenge to this association will be to create a broad enough set of assumptions to reflect the global environment from which it will be operating while meeting member needs around the world. It may happen that the differences identified in global permutations of similar issues will be among the strategic considerations governance will have to deal with in this association.

Governance will need to have a high tolerance for ambiguity and uncertainty. Recognizing unknown factors should not be used as an excuse for not acting. Ambiguity and uncertainty require a greater commitment to managing risk knowledgeably—they should not become an excuse for paralysis of decision making. Most significant issues that come before boards today are sufficiently complex that it is likely some important aspect will not be known or understood. In fact, if a board finds itself with an agenda loaded with issues that are completely understood, that agenda may be focused on issues of specificity and detail inappropriate for the board's attention. Increasingly, the decision not to decide must be a purposeful decision and not a temporary patch for a failure to have developed an adequate knowledge base.

Question 3

What do we know, believe, or predict about the capacity and strategic position of associations relative to knowledge in governance?

There is little real assessment of capacity and strategic position going on in associations today. Many associations understand capacity from an internal resource perspective but have little understanding of the external dimensions of strategic position within the marketplace they seek to serve. Other associations have just the opposite problem, with a clearer conception of their market than of their internal resources. A fundamental lack of understanding on the part of governance of what is needed to do the work of the organization creates a knowledge gap around one or more of the four critical knowledge bases: member needs, wants, and preferences; capacity and strategic position of the organization; dynamics of the industry, profession, or cause; and ethical implications of strategic choices.

Because of a continuing need for understanding markets and marketing, effective associations of the 21st century will be committed to research. Associations using knowledge to improve governance must have a commitment to research. A core competency essential to decision making will be in market and marketing research executed with enough specialized expertise to allow users to have faith in the objectivity and lucidity of the information. In a knowledge-based association, sufficient investment is made in sustaining a stream of such information, and this investment is considered no less important than the cost of committee meetings, board retreats, or lobbyist expenses. Associations will either need to build this core competency in-house or retain it from external sources with which they establish a long-term relationship. In any case, it must be viewed as an ongoing functional line item and budgeted accordingly rather than as a special project or ad hoc activity.

Associations will need to create more effective ways to gather knowledge, including reassessing the role of an intermediary as knowledge provider. Regarding the capacity to gather knowledge, many associations do not have it, some do not know they do not have it, others do not know who to get it from, and all desperately need it. Traditional models for validating information will become more critical. Reliable sources of information may not be immediately apparent, and this suggests that using intermediaries as sources of information or insight about the needs, wants, and preferences of others is likely to become less comfortable. Rather than depending on committees, task forces, or advisory groups, an increasing number of associations seek market and marketing research directly from those whose behavior they are trying to influence—the individuals to be served. Intermediary groups provide an advisory capacity to (a) help interpret what the data may suggest and (b) provide advice about the attractiveness of alternative responses. The cost of reliable knowledge will rise and then plateau, after which people will become more accepting of the expenditure.

A core competency for successful 21st-century associations will be the ability to collect and analyze information on a continuous basis—to establish and maintain effective internal and external scanning mechanisms. An organization should constantly be answering the following questions: Whom do we serve? What needs is the association best positioned to meet? How will the association meet those needs? Where the competency for this scanning resides (internal staff or external outsourcing) is less important than that the organization recognizes such a mechanism as central to future success and therefore commits the necessary funds for it.

Governance systems and mechanisms for communication and management of knowledge should become more porous. Governance will require internally focused knowledge that draws insight from the external world into the knowledge base it uses to make informed decisions. A knowledge-based governance strategy is often employed as the template for understanding and organizing external knowledge essential to satisfactory resolution of a particular issue. Simultaneously, governance, as a provider of value, will need to ensure that the association collects relevant information from the external environment, subjects it to analysis and interpretation by the aggregate intellectual capital of the organization, and returns it to its members in relevant and usable forms. It is this notion of knowledge management that again demonstrates association uniqueness.

Knowledge management in associations differs from that in the private sector, where it is internally focused and concerns identifying, capturing, organizing, and then distributing insight about how the company can best do what it does. In an association, knowledge management is externally focused—identifying, capturing, organizing, and distributing information about how members can do what they do well—not about how the association operates. Most corporate tools of knowledge management are not directly applicable to the needs of an association. In associations, the four essential knowledge bases—of member needs, wants, and preferences; capacity and strategic position of the organization; dynamics of the industry, profession, or cause; and ethical implications of strategic choices—serve as a template for identifying the kinds of information an association needs in order for governance to make intelligent and defensible decisions.

New staff skills will be necessary relative to governance. Staff will need to play a more active leadership role when governance delegates responsibility for development and execution of strategy. Staff must be willing to take risks and offer suggestions. These changes in relationship will occur at all levels: board to board, board to staff, staff to staff. Long-time staffers with organizational memory may leave, and new staff may have trouble keeping up. Competencies, skill sets, salary, and structures will need to change. Building a staff with the necessary skills may be difficult as associations continue to support current programs while also taking on new responsibilities. One association we studied gave itself a year either to assist current staff members with the acquisition of good business practices (e.g., in product development, marketing, business plan development) or to define and fill new staff positions.

Staff will bear significant responsibility for the development of knowledge for members and for governance. Association staff of the 21st century will need new skills to be knowledgeable in association management and conversant with the dynamics of the industry, profession, or cause associated with the organization. They will need to know where to find relevant information and how to transform it into the meaningful insight members and governance will expect. These skills may not be easy to develop, since it is difficult to reward those who exhibit them using traditional models for evaluating staff leadership.

Without meaningful and insightful information, boards cannot make effective decisions. In successful governance, senior staff acts on its understanding that if boards do not have the knowledge they need to exercise control by oversight, they have no choice but to control by supervision. Boards tend to talk about the information they are given. If the reports before them focus their attention on how things are being done, they will talk about how the association does things. If the reports focus their attention on whether things are working, they will talk about whether the association is doing the right things.

Many association staffs do not understand how much responsibility they have for why boards meddle and micromanage when they do. If they are given supervisory information, boards will supervise. Staff that does not understand this dynamic will not realize why the board is telling them how to execute work. But the information staff gives the board about the execution of strategy and the questions staff asks them to consider will affect the level of decisions they make.

One trade association we studied offers an example of this dynamic. In this construction industry organization, board and staff were executing an annual review of the strategic plan and setting targets for the next year on indicators that would demonstrate progress. The association's goals were a mix of external value and benefit to members and internal metrics of program and process activity. The objectives were primarily focused on incremental progress in program areas that reflected quantity, not quality. For example, one goal area sought to "pursue aggressive programs to promote chapter growth and development as well as membership recruitment and retention." In most associations, these metrics represent basic functions and are usually the purview of staff. Governance is concerned with overall results but typically is not involved in tactical implementation or in setting targets for ongoing functional areas. In this particular association's strategic plan review, a long and contentious dialogue emerged between staff and member leaders on the percentage the association should target for increasing new memberships in the coming year. Herein lay the issue that frustrated both staff and member leaders. Staff thought the board was "meddling" in operational space, and the board couldn't understand why it was being asked to consider a relatively routine metric.

Governance will meddle in programs and operation when the information it receives from staff describes organizational success in terms of internally focused measures. *Governance will direct* when the information it receives from staff describes organizational success in terms of externally focused measures.

The right definition of oversight will ensure sufficient knowledge, trust, and nimbleness to govern strategically. Governance is now spending face-to-face time in a more compressed fashion. Governing bodies used to need more time because they executed oversight by direct management and review of the budget and programs. Governance that defines oversight at the appropriate level will ensure sufficient knowledge to govern strategically, and associations are creating new mechanisms for informing the oversight process. More and more associations are designing key indicator, Balanced Scorecard-type methodologies to provide knowledge of operational performance. However, if the association uses a benchmarking system and the key measures are internally focused, the board must focus on organizational issues. A key question becomes whether the measures of success should be internally or externally focused. External outcomes are defined as things beneficial to members (e.g., do members report being more successful?). Internal metrics are important to the association and its operations but not necessarily to the members (e.g., how many more education programs should be developed?). The appropriate balance of external and internal knowledge will ensure governance's ability to monitor operational performance as well as the level of value delivered to members.

Governance knowledge should focus on effectiveness of programs (outcomes) rather than on efficiency of operations (activities) to enable a board to evolve from a management status to a governance/leadership model. Association leaders often engage in decision making about effectiveness and efficiency, but they are not the same thing. *Effectiveness* answers the question, "Am I doing the right thing?" *Efficiency* answers the question, "Am I doing things right?"

Governance's special responsibility in an association is to focus on issues of effectiveness to ensure that the organization is doing the right thing. Unfortunately, many highly efficient organizations are not at all effective. Of course, good governance should observe both effectiveness and efficiency, but the special obligation of governance is to ensure that the boat is being steered in the right direction so that those who are rowing know where to put the pressure.

The most successful associations are those in which a culture of trust allows leadership to focus on effectiveness. They use other expert, and less preoccupied, sources to focus on issues of efficiency and how to get things done right. A culture of trust allows an association to eliminate unnecessary controls, thus increasing nimbleness. (*Unnecessary* is defined here as adding no value to the quality of the decision. *Necessary* is defined as being essential to ensure that an uncorrectable abuse or error does not occur; these controls decrease the risk of irreparable harm to the organization.)

The resource pool available to support governance efforts will shrink, and there is potential for regression in governance reform efforts if fewer dollars are available. It is likely that there will be less money to fund participation in governance and greater difficulty in reimbursing travel. There will be increasing concern about the proportional cost of governance, and non-participants may misconstrue that cost as an inappropriate reward for the "in crowd." The pool of those willing to participate in governance may become limited to those who can afford to lose income or time and to pay for travel. As a result, there may be fewer board meetings of shorter duration at less attractive sites. The time the board does have together will become increasingly precious; therefore, it will need to focus on decision making, not on information collection. This situation will likely drive increased use of virtual technology and Web-based work systems to enable the board to exchange information and discuss issues between meetings.

Effective governance will need processes for issues management and policy development. The concept of issues management, which first surfaced in the 1980s in corporate America, should be revisited and refreshed to ensure that knowledge of emerging realities is factored into the organization's decision making. An effective policy process will provide responsiveness and sensitivity to evolving association and member needs. It will allow for broad membership involvement and representative decision making in addressing public policy issues, as well as in formulating governance/operational policy related to the association's mission, goals, objectives, and identified needs. It requires clearly defined roles and responsibilities for each level of governance.

The policy process should define primary policy-making authority for both public policy matters and internal governance/operational issues. The implementation of a policy process also requires consideration of financial and staff resources needed to manage and operate it effectively. Policy processes need to be executed at a pace reflective of the speed of change in the members' world; they also need to be assertive and less reactive. The for-profit sector already uses this methodology, and the nonprofit sector is increasingly favoring it.

There will be increased reliance on technology for dialogue. Boards that are wrestling with the most important issues confronting their fields tend not to be comfortable making decisions outside of a face-to-face environment. High-level issues require significant levels of trust, which are difficult to sustain in a virtual environment. However, these same boards are demonstrating increasing comfort dealing with information bases that can illuminate both the dynamics of their issues and the dimensions of their choices. Technology will enable boards to spend their precious time together effectively, using information, not collecting it. Similarly, good governance expects information germane to the real experience of the organization in implementing strategy and executing programs. Because time is becoming increasingly precious, governance is less tolerant of information designed primarily to demonstrate how busy staff or committees have been.

The people closest to an activity who have responsibility for making decisions about direction need to be able to exchange information and insight instantaneously. When they have this ability, the following two positive effects occur:

- First, there is an increase in the depth, breadth, and frequency of information available about specific initiatives.
- Second, it precludes the maintenance of secrecy. For example, if committees or task forces are using listservers, board members may either "eyesdrop" on those conversations, participate in them directly if they are open, or receive digests of them.

Some associations have abandoned traditional committee reports as part of the board meeting in favor of periodic e-mail progress reports from committee chairs, which summarize problems, progress, and next steps and are automatically distributed to board members, other committee chairs, and key staff. This practice allows boards to reclaim some time and be more fully informed. The paradox is that participation in dialogue and decision making is more efficient and timely while simultaneously becoming more democratic and open. In this environment, a secret has been redefined as a broadcast e-mail that is read by one person at a time. Attorneys are also redefining traditional notions of confidentiality, executive privilege, and conflict of interest at the request of boards trying new operational strategies in this more open environment.

Governance will need to cultivate a culture of strategic thinking. In addition to creating and distributing knowledge about its member base and its relevant future environment, the organization needs a baseline of knowledge about itself and where it is headed. Clarity and consensus on what constitutes success is the result of an institutionalized process of planning strategically. Such a process forms the foundation for the kind of governance shifts we are observing and provides a lens through which to view relevant information and knowledge. That process includes creation of a solid strategic plan, which guides staff and volunteer actions and activities, links into board discussion, and includes a clear definition of purpose, an envisioned future, and goals.

Boards will need to be more nurturing and less political. Successful nurturing occurs in a positive climate of enjoyment, humor, and mutual respect. However, efforts to nurture in a climate characterized by unhappiness, bitterness, and mistrust may be perceived as arrogant and destructive criticism. There is an interdependent relationship between trust and nurturing—boards can best nurture in a trusting culture, and a trusting culture creates more opportunity for boards to nurture. Nurturance leads to more openness in dialogue, and when dialogue is used to discover, capture, and transfer insight of value to those accountable for acting on it, the exchange of knowledge that occurs can be thought of as the currency of the exchange.

Question 4

What are the ethical implications of increased use of knowledge in governance models and practices emerging as choices for the 21st century?

Transparency and Knowledge

In the post-Enron era of corporate governance, many corporations are questioning whether their leaders have (a) sufficient access to relevant company knowledge to execute their oversight role, (b) sufficient understanding of the implications of that information for the future of the organizations they govern, and (c) sufficient will to use the information in a responsible manner. Because of the unique triple helix of associations, association governance is tied even more closely to the work of the organization. In some cases this will encourage greater accountably, because governance has a deeper understanding of the organization's work, but in other cases it may manifest as the same kind of tunnel vision that has affected the boards of many unfortunate organizations.

To promote the highest levels of ethical behavior, good governance will need to use its increased knowledge to promote and sustain a culture of transparency in decision-making systems. The ASAE Foundation's *Exploring the Future: Seven Strategic Conversations That Could Transform Your Association* (2001) identified transparency as a key issue all associations should discuss; as it observes, "Transparency involves operating in an open, accountable manner and providing the public with information it can use to evaluate performance."

Among other factors, the need for transparency is driven by increased demand for greater openness and accountability. To sustain trust in their ability to govern well, associations must operate in full view of the public. Their governance will therefore need to determine what information should be kept confidential and what should be shared. Leaders must be cognizant of how their decisions support or detract from members' understanding of what the association is and what it stands for. How much information should be made available? When and to whom? Is the association being managed responsibly, and can people tell how to be involved in what they care about? There will continue to be questions about ensuring the "correctness" of data and its ethicalness. Governance will need mechanisms to judge the efficacy and appropriateness of the data and information it receives. Privacy and access to personal information about members will lead to ethical conflicts about how and whether such information may be used in governance. There may be a head-on collision with privacy and security issues. Further, the use of technology will raise an entirely new set of concerns, especially in terms of evolving knowledge and implications that may add to or compromise competitive advantage.

There may also be conflicts with legitimate confidentiality concerns and business strategies. Some governance knowledge may not be appropriate to share with the membership.

Overall, the ethical implications of enhancing knowledge in governance are significant. Gone are the days when members knew decisions were made when they saw a puff of smoke arise from whatever domicile governance was housed in during its deliberations. Associations that are viewed by themselves and others as having the will to govern well will need to balance ethical issues of information disclosure to members and stakeholders; sufficient access to and analysis of relevant knowledge; and the will to act according to what is righteous, ethical, and in the best interests of the association—and not of governance—for any given decision.

Associations should be mindful of the renewed interest in the governance structure of corporate America and the questions of ethics, transparency, conflict of interest, and oversight. Like company owners, managers, or corporate board members, many volunteer leaders are raising issues concerning their responsibilities. Whether forced because of circumstances or encouraged as a response to corporate trends, associations need to consider the ethical implications of all governance models emerging as their future choices.

Fairness in Decision Making

In terms of association governance, an ethical issue is that of fairness, or the idea that decisions made by volunteer leaders and staff may benefit one group of members over another. For example, "What are the fairness issues associated with a proposed dues increase?" "Will this decision significantly disenfranchise one group of members for the benefit of others?" A dues increase usually benefits the active members—those who take advantage of the products and services of the association—but what if active members represented only a small percentage of the associations' total membership?

The answers to these questions and others like them is less important than the willingness of the association to ask them seriously and to contemplate the consequences of the final answer.

A knowledge-based approach to governance thoughtfully considers the advantages and disadvantages of choices along with background information to illuminate them. This approach not only assists the association in making an appropriate choice but also records the thoughtful and thorough dialogue the volunteer leaders have engaged in. Members, who now expect more transparent organizations and decision-making processes, will be more satisfied recognizing that all choices were considered in the decision.

Transparency Affects Member Expectations

Ethics is also about transparency. As we noted earlier, this is a characteristic of a culture committed to the will to govern well. As corporate governance structures continue to reform and require additional transparency, association members at all levels of the organization will also expect transparency in decision making. Not only are current changes in corporate governance influencing expectations in associations, so is the Internet. Many members now expect instant access to information and decisions. For example, they expect to find past board meeting minutes online. Gone are the days when associations could avoid sending out minutes because they are too expensive to mail and provide them only on request. The majority of members will never read the minutes, but if minutes and other documents are not easily accessible, members will perceive the association's leaders as secretive and, ultimately, not to be trusted. As associations strive to govern well, they will make their decisions and the rationale behind those decisions more accessible to their members.

Transparency Between Organizations

Research is also identifying the importance of increased transparency between organizations. Research professionals agree that today competitive data are usually free and accessible online. Companies can no longer easily conceal information about product sales, new product launches, real estate transactions, or mounting debt. As the world and all of its knowledge, information, and data continue to become more and more accessible to everyone, associations need to view relationships with other organizations—both non-competitors and competitors—differently.

Governance needs to assume and encourage transparency with and among other organizations, and to create opportunities to bring together the volunteer leaders of likely and unlikely organizational partners. This creates a higher level of transparency within whole industries, professions, or special-interest groups. Governance should identify opportunities for association leaders to collaborate on projects, share information, merge meetings, and, ultimately, share in the future success of such endeavors.

Transparency in Leadership

In addition to information and process, governance needs to be more open and accessible to the membership. Gone is the myth of the primary volunteer leader as a figure sitting on a throne in a distant castle. New leaders and members will expect increased access to those at the top and increased communication from the association's leaders. Our study indicates that associations are moving toward more horizontal leadership structures rather than traditional hierarchical or vertical structures. In creating a horizontal structure of volunteer leadership, associations are not necessarily abandoning titles or leadership ladders. But they are abandoning processes and channels that require movement up and down the ladder for decisions to be made and communicated. They are establishing a culture of trust so that appropriate decisions can be made at the proper decision-making point rather than at the top of a convoluted and misunderstood hierarchical chain of command. When a horizontal leadership structure is operative, members and new leaders in all positions within the organization will gain a greater sense of value in being involved and a greater trust in those who lead the association.

Chapter 7

Knowledge-Based Governance:
Strategy Through Knowledge

In many associations, efforts to improve governance have resulted in recommendations for significant structural change, which often represents major shifts in the balance of power among an association's governing bodies. These efforts may encounter resistance, and therefore, ultimately, are not implemented. For associations seeking to become more nimble, and for boards seeking to become more effective in deliberations and decision making, what are the possible solutions? How is good governance spending its time at the board table today?

Associations have begun to make vast improvements in governance not through radical structural change, but often by merely changing a board's process of work and decision making. By creating "space" for dialogue to occur within a board's traditional but often-restrictive process of deliberation under parliamentary procedure, many associations have been able to increase both the quality and the speed of decision making, without sacrificing participation or enfranchisement.

Knowledge-based governance is a philosophy of deliberation, decision making, and board process. It is a mechanism for consultative leadership that recognizes strategy as the necessary and appropriate link between the board's role of governance and the staff's role of management and implementation.

Knowledge-based governance embraces the following basic and long-standing concepts of effective leadership that allow boards to govern strategically:

- Effective leadership focuses on the outcomes desired rather than on the activity required.

- Strategic leadership focuses on what should happen next, rather than on what has already been done.
- Good boards spend their valuable and limited time together using information, not collecting it.
- Effective boards routinely consider issues of capacity, core capability, and strategic position in deciding what to do.
- Boards can exercise fiduciary responsibility by defining desired outcomes consistent with strategic intent and core values, rather then detailing how an outcome is to be achieved or remanaging work after it has been accomplished.

A knowledge-based governance strategy provides the tools and mechanisms needed for a board to lead rather than manage. It focuses on issues of strategic direction and high-level policy, purposefully developing strategy through partnership and dialogue with staff and volunteers. Through knowledge-based governance strategy, both the staff and the volunteer workforces can participate in board dialogue as full partners, bringing richness of insight and increased ownership to the ultimate decision.

The knowledge-based governance approach clarifies the distinction between policy and implementation. It creates a way for the board to spend more time in dialogue, provides context for actions, and defines what those actions will do for the association. It helps a board execute its role of guiding the organization through the development of strategy and makes greater use of the intellectual capital resident on the board.

In associations exhibiting the will to govern well, sufficient knowledge is present in the dialogue and decision-making processes that governance employs. Commitment to a knowledge-based governance strategy and operational philosophy ensures the development and use of a constant stream of relevant information and insight throughout the association.

Four Elements of a Knowledge-Based Governance Strategy

A knowledge-based governance strategy is the seamless integration of four parts. Each of these parts has its own track record of success. After years of experience with hundreds of associations moving in this direction, we are finally prepared to observe that the *integration* of the four parts also has its own track record.

Knowledge-based governance strategy rests on the following four fundamental elements:

1. adoption of a knowledge-based approach to decision making,
2. commitment to a process of planning and thinking strategically,

3. implementation of dialogue before deliberation, and
4. selected principles of policy governance.

Element 1. A Knowledge-Based Approach to Decision Making

Associations are moving from a political model of decision making to a more information-based or rational model that uses knowledge and insight. The core of the knowledge-based operational philosophy is a commitment to a different culture and value system representing the premise that who makes the decision is far less important than the quality of information and insight on which the decision is based.

The knowledge-based operational approach encourages effective integration of knowledge into decision-making processes. It seeks to address political realities of associations by endorsing a model for decision making based on the quality of the information considered and the development of defensible business decisions. The knowledge-based association model puts this thinking into the context of what pioneer associations have found to be successful strategies. It ensures that the association has a way to sustain itself based on a culture of strategic thinking.

A knowledge-based operational model involves building and sustaining an organization throughout which individuals and groups routinely use information in decision making. Knowledge-based decision making considers the four knowledge bases and the kind of information needed to satisfy the considerations they engender before making any significant decision; it is attention to these four areas of information that inspires confidence in decisions, and confidence is important at every level of the organization.

The first consideration is sensitivity to members' views. This will add knowledge and insight relative to members, prospective members, customers, stakeholders, and constituents. The second consideration is foresight about the industry, the profession, or the issue area. This adds an external element to knowledge acquisition. The third consideration is insight into the capacity and strategic position of the organization. This builds a critical knowledge base about capability and likelihood of success from both an internal and an external perspective. The fourth consideration has to do with the ethical implications of choices. This builds a critical and, in many cases, otherwise unconsidered dimension of possible conflicts relative to issues of privacy, competition, or other potential conflicts the association must be mindful of as it develops strategy.

Relative to these four knowledge bases, gathering information and insight and employing effective mechanisms for dialogue and deliberation help governance to be knowledgeable. The four knowledge bases can be thought of as the answers to the following four key questions:

1. What do we know about the needs, wants, and expectations of our members, prospective members, key stakeholders, and customers that is relevant to this decision?
2. What do we know about the capacity and strategic position of the organization that is relevant to this decision?
3. What do we know about the current realities and evolving dynamics of the members' marketplace, the industry or profession, or the issue area that is relevant to this decision?
4. What are the ethical implications of these choices?

In many organizations studied, we observed that the richer and deeper the answers to these questions, the more effective governance has been in developing and executing strategy.

How is a knowledge-based model different from a traditional political model? The diagram of a knowledge-based organization (Figure 7.1) illustrates this dynamic. The diagram can be thought of as a process model, although it is not meant to be linear or chronological. Rather, it is intended to illustrate the critical elements that governance must pay attention to in a knowledge-based enterprise.

Figure 7.1

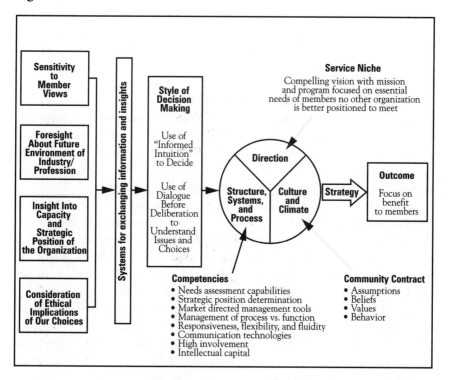

Over the last 10 years at CEO symposia, Glenn Tecker has described the process of integrating knowledge into the enterprise as follows:

> *Some stuff comes in, you do some stuff with the stuff that comes in, and some stuff comes out. Now, it's not always that simple. If you have no stuff coming out, not enough stuff coming out, or the wrong stuff coming out, you tend to get less stuff coming in and, with less stuff coming in, you have less stuff to get stuff done on that your members think that stuff needs to be done about. On the other hand, if you have the right stuff coming out at the right time in the right way, then you attract more stuff coming in. With more stuff coming in, you have more stuff that you need to get stuff done on that your members think needs to have stuff done about. Now, as a leader, you have to understand this stuff. This is also known as the George Carlin School of Organizational Analysis.*

The difference between the knowledge-based philosophy and the traditional political model is that in the latter, the "stuff coming in" is constituency power; in the knowledge-based model, the "stuff coming in" is knowledge and insight. A knowledge-based operational philosophy suggests that who makes the decision is less important than the quality of the information and insight upon which it is based. The knowledge-based model characterizes the knowledge and insight into four categories that match the four knowledge bases.

Members' Needs, Wants, and Preferences

The first of the four knowledge bases has to do with sensitivity to members' views. Good governance does not include in this category opinions, unfounded beliefs, personal prejudices, whims, or delusions. It concentrates on gathering rational, verifiable information about the needs, wants, and preferences of members, prospective members, and other relevant stakeholders.

To gather relevant knowledge in this area, an association may look to its track record of interaction with members. For example, who plans to attend the conventions and, when they go, what are they going for? Another source of interactive information involves the products the association offers and who is buying what. Qualitative research and telephone interviews— conducted either on a specific issue or routinely over time—are also good sources of member insight. Regular membership satisfaction surveys may also be available.

Associations that inform an issue relative to member needs, wants, and preferences usually have routine mechanisms for collecting information related to issues, ongoing market and marketing research, and ad hoc mechanisms that can be instantaneously executed on a particular issue. If, for example, an association has adopted the practice that whenever it deals with a contentious issue, it gathers key stakeholders' views on the issue, it might conduct a series of telephone interviews (not with a stratified sampling, not using quantitative research) with individuals who reasonably reflect the views and experiences of the concerned stakeholder groups. The enhanced knowledge this contributes to governance is especially valuable in communicating the rationale of a decision on the issue to members and in gaining critical buy-in. If the association can demonstrate that it has executed a defensible process of considering the needs, wants, and preferences of all relevant stakeholder groups, there is a much greater chance that each of the groups consulted will have a stake in the final decision.

Evolving Dynamics of the Environment

The second knowledge base involves an external view of the current and evolving dynamics of the industry, profession, or issue area relevant to the question before the board. The purpose of examining this knowledge base is to ensure that governance makes decisions about what to do today with sufficient attention to the implications of those decisions for tomorrow.

If an association has implemented a process for planning and thinking strategically, it has articulated an envisioned future for the organization. It has goals that represent outcomes it seeks to achieve. It has articulated these goals in the context of assumptions about the relevant future environment of its profession, industry, or interest area. Assumptions about the future are not trends; they are speculations or projections of how the world of members will be different. When considering any given issue, governance would likely turn to these assumptions as the first step in seeking answers.

In the associations we studied, making assumptions about the future is part of thinking strategically about the future. For example, one group, in looking at external environment and resources, made the assumption that changes in technology would increasingly be involved in all aspects of services. Another group, looking at consumers, made the assumption that clients and consumers would be increasingly involved, as well as much more knowledgeable and demanding, in their choices and rights, and looking for better value at no increase in price. This group also assumed that the structure of service delivery, while difficult to predict, would likely be different from what is in place today. It foresaw possible consolidation, takeovers by larger organizations, and more alliances, some of which might be with former competitors or current suppliers.

This last example of an assumption is unusual because it represents a critical uncertainty. Even though the outcome might not be known today, it is likely to have an impact on the association's strategy no matter which way it evolves. For governance, the implications of critical uncertainties are essential to consider. If the board is pondering an issue, and there is a relevant assumption suggesting uncertainty about how things will turn out, the implications for strategy might suggest that long-term commitment to an initiative in that area would be unwise. At the very least, any significant initiative in that area should be carefully benchmarked at the front end, because it may be necessary to ascertain quickly whether it is still responsive to the environment as changes occur.

What this does for associations is to enable nimbleness and agility. Externally in programs and internally in operations, nimbleness suggests that the association must be able to shift, to turn on a dime, if necessary.

When an organization does not sufficiently understand the future, it frequently does nothing. This could be worse than doing something wrong. For an association, this is especially apt to be true because the consequence of doing nothing is that membership, looking for something to happen, will get impatient and migrate elsewhere. By the time the association has determined what it is comfortable doing, it may have lost the critical mass needed to do anything well.

Implications for governance's development of strategy are critical. Building a sufficient knowledge base of assumptions allows an association to manage risk more effectively as it moves forward.

Capacity and Strategic Position

Among the most frequent errors an association can make is failure to pay adequate attention to issues of capacity, core capability, and strategic position. Governance should never raise expectations to a point beyond what the organization can deliver. If that were to become a pattern, both prospective and current membership would migrate to other places with a better track record for delivering value.

A critical knowledge base for governance is to determine what is known about the capacity and strategic position of the association relevant to any given decision. Capacity and strategic position are different. *Capacity* asks the association to look internally. Does it have sufficient internal resources to execute the organization's desired outcomes? Does it have the right staff and volunteer competencies? Does it have the assets required for effective execution? Does it have the dollars, the time, the expertise, the technology, and the experience—whatever is necessary given the nature of the issue? *Strategic position* asks the association to look externally. What are the external marketplace factors and variables operating in the environment? Are other enterprises offering similar services? Would the association likely be seen as a logical and desirable source of the product, service, or benefit? What other variables and factors are operating in the environment relevant to this issue that might influence its outcome? And of those other variables, are any so powerful that they will determine how this issue turns out no matter what the association does?

One trade association we studied had to reach a decision on a public policy issue. To create success in a public policy initiative, an association must demonstrate that the interests of its members or stakeholders are congruent with the public's interest. It must also demonstrate that its stakeholders' interests are consistent with the interests of the policy makers. This particular association conducted a competitive analysis and discovered that while the association's position on this issue was righteous, another group was making a stronger case. The reality was that the public's interest would not be best served by the association's position. It therefore had two choices. It could consume enormous amounts of tangible and intangible assets on a campaign it knew was not going to produce a reasonable outcome, or it could invest those assets in another campaign on an issue whose likelihood of success would be much higher. The association chose the latter option.

Suppose governance discovers that the association's members have a real need, thus providing a program opportunity for the association. Then governance discovers that another group—maybe a competitor, maybe not—is already providing a more than satisfactory response to the identified need. In fact, on closer examination, governance discovers that the other organization would be able to provide a better response to the need, much more affordably, with easier access, and with a superior marketing position.

There is a choice. The association could proceed with a program initiative because it is attractive and doable, or it could conclude that it would better meet members' needs by enhancing their access to what the other group is already providing and viewing that group as a potential collaborator. This second choice allows the association to concentrate its resources on those things it can do better than anyone else. Both of these choices are illuminated and discovered only when governance takes the time to consider the issues of capacity and strategic position.

There are many questions governance needs to ask and answer concerning this base. Where does knowledge about capacity and strategic position come from? In associations that exhibit the will to govern well, knowledge about capacity regularly comes from an objective and knowledge-based assessment of the association's program and service portfolio, which provides insight into what the association is positioned to do effectively and what it should cede to others.

Core competencies are not the same as staff competencies. Every organization has a set of core competencies—things it does especially well as an organization. If an association's strategic planning process has been truly strategic, one of its elements would have been to identify and discover core competencies. The association might also have sought to discover what competencies will be needed in the future that are not present today, because good strategy always builds from strength.

The most frequent and egregious error in associations' strategic thinking in operational planning is the failure to give sufficient attention to this knowledge base. Failure to carefully address capacity and strategic position is what causes organizations to make promises they cannot keep. It is what causes governance to create expectations it cannot meet. And sometimes it also creates the vulnerability that leads governance back into the political model. If governance does not consciously consider capacity and strategic position, it tends to take a political approach to distribution of resources. When the philosophy is that the association will try to keep everyone happy by doing a little bit for everyone, the reality, of course, is that it will end up not doing enough for anyone, thereby pleasing no one.

No matter how politically or emotionally attractive a commitment might be, the will to govern well suggests that an association should realistically evaluate its chance of success. That may not necessarily mean abandoning commitments to things an association may not be able to do successfully. It may simply mean the association will have to take the time to build capacity and strategic position while it amasses a record of wins in other areas where it can make a more immediate and tangible difference.

Ethical Implications

The last of the knowledge bases addresses the ethical implications of choices of strategy or action. The expected question is, "How in the world can governance determine the ethical implications of its choices, when it hasn't figured out the choices yet?" Another way to consider this is to ask, "Are there ethical dimensions to this issue that require sensitivity in governance dialogue and action?"

For instance, what ethical issues should the association be sensitive to as it builds choices of strategy? What are the issues that may not pass the "smell test"—and, important, whose nose is being used? Are there issues of fairness? Are there issues of rightness and wrongness?

Any time governance is dealing with an issue where resource allocation is part of the judgment, issues of fairness almost automatically move the discussion to an ethical dimension. In a political enterprise such as an association, the issue of fairness of resource allocation to positions attached to particular constituencies will become critical.

Informed Intuition

In governance, knowledge-based decision making is not the same as data-based decision making. When governance is engaged in its most important role, it is considering what needs to happen next. By definition, these discussions involve thoughtfulness about the future—the one thing that can never be known for sure. Paradoxically, at the very moment when governance is engaged in its most important work, it is most vulnerable to uncertainty. Successful governance therefore uses informed intuition, which can be a source of insight of equal importance to hard data about current conditions or past performance.

Informed intuition occurs at the confluence of what the board learns about the four knowledge bases: (a) member wants, needs, and preferences; (b) external marketplace dynamics and realities; (c) capacity and strategic position of the organization; and (d) ethical implications of its choices. To have confidence in and understanding of any significant decision, governance needs insight into the four knowledge bases relative to any issue. This approach represents a new balance between being politically correct and being appropriately and sufficiently knowledgeable.

In a subtle but real way, the collaborative development of informed intuition with shared group ownership creates a powerful common bond that promotes understanding and commitment and helps engender trust. The act of developing informed intuition as a group experience makes a board meeting not unlike a petri dish for the growth of trust. Establishing and sustaining trust in governance involves not just what is done but how it is done. And the will to govern well means making a commitment to process, behavior, and culture that nourishes and sustains trust.

A commitment to a knowledge-based culture is as much a value statement as it is a definition. If it is not compatible with the culture and stated values of the association, then a knowledge-based governance strategy will not be an effective solution. In order to develop and sustain the will to govern well, this commitment must encompass not just how the board does its work but how each committee does its work, how chapter leadership at the state or local level does its work, and how the staff does its work when it gathers together.

In a knowledge-based governance strategy, prior to the actual dialogue, a group of staff, volunteers, or some other source requesting action from the board provides the board with background material that addresses the four knowledge bases. When an association board moves to the dialogue process, the background paper is a starting point for dialogue. The strategy is powerful because the group then illuminates and, in many cases, builds on the information, drawing from the collective experience of the board members.

Equally powerful is that the dialogue identifies important information gaps. By considering the question, "What is not known but needs to be?" governance identifies key gaps that either suggest the need for more study or that the board will be making a decision without a significant piece of information, in which case at least it has identified the risks of moving forward.

As critical as the four knowledge bases are, no board will ever have all the answers to the possible permutations of the questions they generate. Hence, informed intuition in a knowledge-based operational philosophy is an important part of decision making. It blends carefully considered, defensible information with best instincts about the future. In the absence of all possible answers, informed intuition can be most effective when it follows a constructive dialogue designed to illuminate options, leading to the second element of the knowledge-based governance process.

Element 2. A Process of Planning and Thinking Strategically

The second element of a knowledge-based governance strategy involves approaching the process of strategic planning and thinking in a way that integrates it with the ongoing work of governance. This means strategic planning is not something to be viewed as a task or function with a defined beginning or end, but is what organization leadership spends its time doing (i.e., its role and function).

In assisting associations in constructing strategic long-range plans, we have found a framework of four planning "horizons" to be a powerful tool both for the creation of effective strategy and for ensuring relevance of an association's long-range direction over time. (See Figure 7.2)

Figure 7.2

Four Planning Horizons

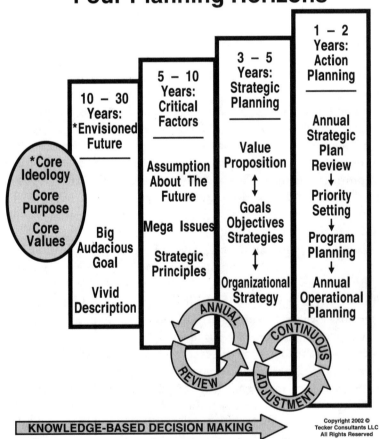

*Adapted from *Built to Last*, Collins and Porras, 1994

In general, the "four planning horizons" concept crafts a comprehensive strategic direction based on the balance between **what doesn't change**—the *core ideology*, or timeless principles of the organization's purpose and values—and **the vision that drives change**—what the organization seeks to become within a 10- to 30-year horizon. The *envisioned future* consists of an audacious goal and a vivid description of what it will be like to achieve the goal. (Note: The concepts of core ideology and envisioned future are based on the work of Jim Collins and Jerry Porras in *Built to Last*, 1993).

The articulation of an envisioned future guides the organization in considering the next set of factors that will affect the 5- to 10-year horizon—a set of preliminary judgments about future conditions affecting the association and its members. Elements of the strategic plan in this horizon include **assumptions about the relevant future environment** that provide an underlying set of factors, both likely and uncertain, upon which the association will define its three- to five-year goals. When conditions change, strategy should be adjusted. These assumptions provide a basis upon with the association can annually update its strategic plan and ensure the ongoing relevance of its strategy.

Within the three- to five-year context, governance in many organizations finds that clarifying its projected relationship with members/stakeholders is important in defining its service niche and recognizing the core capabilities it needs to serve that niche successfully. This is a critical determination for governance in any organization to make. Four models for excellence, adapted from those employed by for-profit service organizations, are useful tools for considering the core competencies required for an association to earn a reputation for excellence.

The models for excellence are adapted from Michael Treacy's and Fred Wiersema's 1995 book, *The Discipline of Market Leaders: Choose Your Customers, Narrow Your Focus, Dominate Your Market.* Treacey and Wiersema reference two critical concepts needed for an organization to determine how it wishes to earn its reputation for value—concepts that are just as relevant for associations. The value proposition defines the programs and services the association will offer and the nature of the delivery experience, based on the relevant dimensions of perceived value of members and customers. The value discipline reflects the behaviors and actions associations must execute as an organization to ensure delivery of the value propositions they offer. An association must determine what dimensions of value will be most important to its members (value proposition) and decide where and how it will stake its claim in the marketplace in order to deliver that value and to earn an identity of excellence. The choice of a value discipline enables an association to deliver on the value proposition most likely to satisfy member and customer expectations. Selecting a value discipline is not just a choice about what to do —it is a choice about what not to do.

The four models of excellence represent choices of direction and related competencies that an organization needs to relate to and serve its members and stakeholders successfully. Three of the models (operational excellence, product or program leadership, and customer/member intimacy) are based on Treacey and Wiersema's work and involve the interaction between the organization and its members and stakeholders. The fourth model, eminent influence, focuses on what an association must do to earn a reputation of influence. It has less to do with the relationship that individual members want with the organization and more to do with the reputation the organization seeks to achieve with those it influences. In associations where advocacy is a primary business line, the eminent influence model provides a useful profile of the core competencies needed to earn a reputation for excellence where representation is the organization's primary mission.

Operational Excellence Model
Value Proposition
(What the association offers in terms of relationship and experience)

- Delivery of a combination of quality, price, and ease of purchase that no one else in the market can match.
- Basic cost-effective, no-frills products—associations following this model do not attempt to be product or service innovators.
- Similar relationships with the entire marketplace—does not cultivate one-to-one relationships with customers.
- Extraordinary execution and delivery.

Value Discipline
(What the association must do well in order to deliver on the value proposition)

- Maintain cost efficiencies.
- Offer programs in large volumes that reduce costs.
- Provide quality customer service.
- Demonstrate rapid, responsive fulfillment capabilities.

Product or Program Leadership Model
Value Proposition
(What the association offers in terms of relationship and experience)

- Leading-edge programs that expand existing performance boundaries.
- Seen as a "thought leader" of its profession, industry, or interest area.
- The source of useful new applications of existing programs and services.
- Demonstrated commitment to offering the best products/programs.

Value Discipline
(What the association must do well in order to deliver on the value proposition)

- Support organizational processes of innovation and creativity.
- Have an entrepreneurial organizational culture that rewards risk.
- Develop scanning mechanisms to identify potential new programs before they become apparent to others.
- Execute effective program development; business and management processes supporting nimbleness.
- Be willing to "leapfrog" its own latest programs and services with something new.

Customer/Member Intimacy Model
Value Proposition
(What the association offers in terms of relationship and experience)

- Long-term bonds and relationships with members and customers.
- Delivery of what a specific customer wants rather than what "the market wants."
- Knowledge of its members/customers and the products and services they need.
- Constant upgrades of what it offers to stay one step ahead of its customers in terms of anticipating needs, wants, and expectations.
- Cultivation of customer loyalty, which is its greatest asset.
- Commitment to taking care of member and customer needs.

Value Discipline
(What the association must do well in order to deliver on the value proposition)

- Have knowledge and understanding of the needs and expectations of members and other stakeholders (needs assessment).
- Maintain a member database supporting relationship building and individual response and/or customization when possible/appropriate.
- Engage in relationship building and maintenance through relationship management.
- Delegate authority to those closest to the member/customer.

Eminent Influence Model
Value Proposition
(What the association offers in terms of relationship and experience)

- Successful advocacy, representation, and voice for the interests of a cause, industry, or profession.
- Advancement of a cause, industry, or profession through public relations, media relations, marketing, communication, lobbying and

government relations, influencing regulations, coalition building, and strategic partnerships.

- Personalized relationships with powerful decision makers and other nonprofit, governmental, and for-profit organizations.
- Strong strategic positioning with key targeted audiences and stakeholders.
- Positions on key issues of importance to members, stakeholders, or the organization's core purpose, cause, industry, or profession
- Awareness and recognition for being a powerful advocate or representative for the cause, industry, or profession that is viewed as a significant source of benefit and value by members, stakeholders, and others.

Value Discipline
(What the association must do well in order to deliver on the value proposition)

- Be creative in representative and advocacy efforts, which will require new activities, processes, and behavior that support innovation and new ways of doing things.
- Build recognition as a credible resource of valuable information to decision makers concerning the importance of the cause, industry, or profession.
- Position the organization as the authoritative source for the projected future of the cause, industry, or profession.
- Develop strong research- and data-gathering capabilities to ensure that issues can be anticipated and predicted.
- Understand on a timely basis the proposals, positions, opinions, and worldviews of other key constituents.
- Structure the organization's infrastructure to support its new advocacy activities and efforts.

The linkage continues into the three- to five-year horizon through the development of a formal long-range strategic plan, in which governance articulates the outcomes it seeks to achieve for its stakeholders. How will the world be different as a result of what the organization does? Who will benefit, and what will be the likely results? This articulation of strategies will bring focus to the association's annual operational allocation of discretionary resources.

A one- to two-year operational planning process, which includes action plans, checkpoints, and milestones, allows governance to assess progress toward each goal in every planning year. Operational planning is a repeatable, systematic approach with key process points reflecting strategic judgment as well as measurability. It links the long-range strategic plan with annual budgeting, evaluation, and resource allocation, and assesses the plan and progress being made even while it is happening.

Associations that are viewed by themselves and others as having the will to govern well do not focus their operational planning primarily on the budget process. Instead, they view it as an annual process designed to determine the operational allocation of discretionary resources, but driven by a strategic long-range plan on a short-term, one- to two-year basis. An effective operational planning process ensures that decisions regarding resource allocation are based on strategic considerations, and that there is a balance achieved among three realms of work—(a) transformational work reflecting progress toward each strategic long-range goal, (b) work in support of ongoing programs and services, and (c) development of resources to support flexible responses to emerging opportunities or challenges. It is not one process, but an integrated and interlocking set of processes. Key subprocesses include governance, budgeting, strategic plan review, prioritization, program planning, and reporting cycles that together make up the association's annual program of work.

A strategic long-range plan is not intended as a substitute for an annual program or operating plan. It does not detail all the initiatives, programs, and activities the organization will undertake in the course of serving its stakeholders and the community, nor can it foresee changes to the underlying assumptions on which the organization bases its key strategic choices.

Instead, the strategic plan identifies what the association is not doing today but must be doing in the future to be successful. Consequently, the strategic plan implies change—doing new things or doing more or less of current activities to ensure successful outcomes.

In associations exhibiting the will to govern well, strategic planning becomes the methodology for the organization's operations. If it is successful, the process yields not just a document, but serves as a catalyst for the process of planning strategically at all times and levels throughout the organization. To achieve its vision, governance must not look at strategic long-range planning as a one-time project that produces a milestone document of its best thinking at the moment. Instead, governance must adopt strategic planning as an operational philosophy of ongoing reevaluation of the critical knowledge bases that form the framework of its world, including

- sensitivity to member needs,
- insight into the future environment of the industry,
- understanding the capacity and strategic position of the organization, and
- effective analysis of the ethical implications of policy and program choices.

In a knowledge-based culture, the vision evolves from conversations in which (a) members and staff participate as partners, and (b) the discussion is informed by market research about current and future conditions. The board ultimately approves the vision as part of a well-constructed process for strategic planning. A useful vision communicates identity and direction.

Knowledge-based governance strategy works best when there is a clearly articulated, outcome-focused strategic plan in place, as well as an underlying process of strategic thinking. Recalling the three basic functions of any board—to set direction, provide sufficient resources to accomplish the direction, and ensure that desired outcomes are achieved—it is the third item that becomes most problematic and causes boards to fail, primarily because they have no measures in place to know whether they have succeeded. The outcome-focused goals and objectives in a plan form the baseline for this measure, and within this context the board can comfortably delegate authority for strategy to staff and volunteer workgroups. This delegation of authority for the development and implementation of strategy to staff enables governance to focus on the longer-term issues—to answer the question, "What's next?"

As suggested earlier, governance is evolving from retreat-driven, product-oriented traditional strategic planning to a process of ongoing strategic thinking. Associations are increasingly defining direction as a vision of preferred conditions. Dialogue about issues affecting the association's ability to achieve the vision provide coherency over time while maintaining the fluidity and flexibility necessary to remain indispensably relevant in changing times.

A process of planning and thinking strategically is critical to knowledge-based governance because ongoing dialogue about issues affecting the envisioned future yields a constant stream of critical uncertainties and key questions. Mega-issues are overriding issues of strategic importance that cut across multiple goal or outcome areas. They address key strategic questions, illuminating choices and challenges the organization must face in moving toward an envisioned future.

Mega-issues articulate the questions the association will need to answer in the next 5 to 10 years. Here are a few examples from associations we studied:

- *How should we respond to changes occurring in the industry? What are the implications for our role and focus in the future?*
- *How will we continue to obtain company support in light of mergers and reduced expenses? How can we better meet the needs of employer organizations?*
- *How will we balance our desire for quantity of membership against the quality of membership? Should we have a growth plan when the industry workforce is shrinking? Should we be an inclusive or exclusive organization?*
- *How can we best elevate the stature of our designation within the industry so that it is recognized and accepted as a premiere achievement? How*

can we most effectively educate the public about our members' capabilities and assist them in achieving the level of recognition of any other major professional designation?

- *How can we best serve the evolving global industry that is emerging and still continue to serve professionals within the United States?*

Associations viewed by themselves and others as having the will to govern well include a list of mega-issues as part of the strategic plan. Once a year, usually during the annual formal review of the strategic plan and often as a result of insights gained from revisiting the 5- to 10-year assumptions, the board prioritizes these questions and selects several for its consideration during the coming year. This allows sufficient time to task (and even to construct, if necessary) the appropriate workgroups within the organization to gather background information concerning a given issue that is framed around the four knowledge bases. Often, those groups or representative subsets of them attend board meetings to consider the issues and participate as full partners in the dialogue portion of the board's discussion of the issues.

Element 3. Dialogue before Deliberation

Dialogue before deliberation is a way of promoting trust, nimbleness, and increased knowledge by enhancing understanding of different perspectives on the matter at hand. It separates discussion and its purposes into two parts. Dialogue purposefully creates open discussion among board, staff, and other knowledgeable parties to illuminate the issue. It uses an inquiry process to establish the basis of opinions, clarify choices, examine advantages and disadvantages, and consider risks and consequences before the board moves to deliberation and debate to render a decision.

Peter Senge, in *The Fifth Discipline* and *The Fifth Discipline Fieldbook*, articulates a number of seminal concepts about dialogue. Key to the success of the knowledge-based approach to governance is the use of dialogue for (a) creating understanding of the perspective present within the group, and (b) finding areas of commonality across the discussion. This approach draws from the strength of the group in exploring a wide range of possibilities before narrowing down and eventually deciding upon a single option. Dialogue strives for understanding to create the best possible strategy.

Dialogue requires discussion, which involves listening, not just speaking. In *The Fifth Discipline Fieldbook*, Senge offers a number of keys to engaging in skillful dialogue.

- **Stop talking.** One cannot listen if one is talking.
- **Imagine the other person's viewpoint.** It is not enough for governance to know the opinions of everyone in the group. It needs to know

why each person holds his or her opinion. What experience, what expertise, what values, and what perspectives are behind the views?

- **Look, act, and be interested.** Interest must be genuine. Sometimes in groups or one-on-one conversations, individuals unknowingly communicate attitudes with body language. One particular manifestation, called "steepling," is when a listener holds his hands in front of him or her with palms facing each other and fingertips touching. Steepling, regardless of intent, will almost always be perceived as saying, "I know far more about this than you will ever understand." Or if someone at a meeting has turned to the side and has crossed his or her legs and arms, the body language communicates disinterest, which is only a step away from really poor behavior, such as reading a newspaper during a discussion, doing other work from the office, or working on a laptop while the board is engaged in conversation on issues.

- **Observe nonverbal behavior.** To engage in skillful dialogue, governance must learn to engage in body language reflective of the kind of conversation it wants to have. Physical presence should be an intellectual and emotional reflection of what is happening—being open, accepting, listening, leaning in, and lifting the eyebrows up, not down. Facial expressions are critical for leadership and good governance. Sometimes individuals fail to pay attention to facial expression. If one says, "I think the job you did is the most superior performance we ever experienced in this organization," but the facial expression resembles what happens when one tastes a lemon, what does it really signal? If a board member says, "We're so disappointed in what you've done we are terminating your position immediately," but is wearing a wide smile while saying it, what does that signal? Some say that striking a pose like Rodin's "The Thinker" literally sends a signal to the body that allows for better listening and says, "I'm inviting the ideas in."

- **Do not interrupt.** When someone interrupts a speaker, what will the speaker perceive about that person's view of the speaker's idea? Clearly, that whatever the one who interrupted had to say was far more important and valuable than whatever the speaker was saying. And what behavior does this earn back when the one who interrupted has something to share? The same thing—disinterest.

- **Listen between the lines.** This is where one searches for meaning, just as in the expressions about reading "between the lines" or "behind the lines." Part of effective dialogue is an agreement between parties to ask questions about both what people think and what they feel. In the future, governance must agree to seek answers about the latter.

- **Rephrase to ensure understanding.** Communication does not occur just when one says something. Communication doesn't even occur when something someone has said has been heard. Communication occurs when what one intends to have understood was, in fact, understood by the person who heard it. This reality operates at the level of the association communicating with its members and stakeholders. It occurs at the level of the board communicating as a body. It occurs at the level of the chief staff executive and chief elected officer communicating to each other. It occurs any time a group of individuals comes together to think or work together. Communication occurs not just when one speaks, and not just when one is heard, but when one has a sense that what one intended to be understood was, in fact, what was understood. A way to test for understanding is to rephrase what one has just heard to ensure that one's understanding is an adequate reflection of what was said.

The skillful use of dialogue has significant implications for governance because, in a knowledge-based governance strategy, conversation is facilitated, not chaired. How governance exercises leadership during conversation is different from the way it exercises it by wielding the gavel during deliberation. As boards become more skilled in these techniques, they actually begin to facilitate all communication from whatever quarter.

Element 4. Selected Principles of Policy Governance
The fourth component of a knowledge-based strategy embraces two selected elements of John Carver's 25-year-old model of governance. Although this model predates the advent and integration of strategy into how associations make decisions, it still represents, in our judgment, the most eloquent job description of a board. The following two elements of Carver's model relevant to a knowledge-based governance strategy are:

1. Good boards decide and delegate; they do not react and ratify.
2. A board's primary responsibility is to declare the ends to be achieved and the outcomes to be accomplished.

If the declaration of what will constitute success, or in other words, of the outcomes the association seeks to achieve, represents what will be of value to a member, then the officers must share responsibility to ensure that the organization's assets are invested in things that produce value for the members. In its deliberations, the board then focuses on the ends it is trying to achieve, not on how those ends will be accomplished. It stays focused on dealing at the strategic level of what and not how. It uses motions constructed with attention to the difference between ends and means, articulating its decisions in a fashion that appropriately distinguishes between policy and management.

Chapter 8

What Change Strategies Will Promote Knowledge in Governance?

Key Change Strategies

Associations that are viewed by themselves and others as having the will to govern well develop a knowledge-based governance strategy to enhance the quality of knowledge in the governance process. In Part 5 of this work we will detail some of the mechanisms associations employing this strategy have put into action. Below is a case study of one association's process for developing such a strategy to increase its knowledge base.

Case Study—One Association's Strategy to Strengthen Its Knowledge Base

A professional society in the financial services profession had a strong and active chapter network, successfully attracting both well-established and newer practitioners. Members' professional environment was subject to constant change, and in its recent strategic planning process, the society had gathered a wealth of data with a broad set of insights from the member community by engaging large groups of chapter leaders in regional input sessions. The society sought to institutionalize this process to take advantage of the aggregate intellectual capital of its members both in the society's planning process and its externally available knowledge products. A task force determined that the society needed an initiative to achieve broader chapter involvement. The task force used a strategic tool of Tecker Consultants known as the Competencies of Collaborative Strategic Thinking. (See Figure 8.1) A full template of the tool can be found in the appendix.) The task force used this tool to execute several steps and built an initiative for expanding its knowledge base to encompass the views of its grassroots communities.

Figure 8.1

Using the Competencies of Collaborative Strategic Thinking

A "Real-Time" Mini Case Study

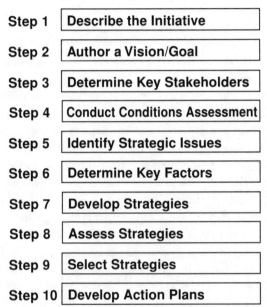

Step 1	Describe the Initiative
Step 2	Author a Vision/Goal
Step 3	Determine Key Stakeholders
Step 4	Conduct Conditions Assessment
Step 5	Identify Strategic Issues
Step 6	Determine Key Factors
Step 7	Develop Strategies
Step 8	Assess Strategies
Step 9	Select Strategies
Step 10	Develop Action Plans

"Strategic thinking is a cognitive discipline that can be learned. Competency can increase with practice over time. Application will improve as insight is gleaned from experience."
—Glenn H. Tecker
Address to The Planning Forum, 1991

Step 1—Describe the initiative

- *What is the goal?* To develop a process for involving chapters across North America to gather input on issues, changes, and trends occurring in their regions. This information will be used both for updating the society's strategic plan and for input into its marketplace knowledge products.

- *Generally, how do you intend to accomplish this goal?* By developing mechanisms to encourage involvement and collect relevant data that institutionalize some of the processes used in the strategic planning initiative.

Step 2—Author a vision/goal

- *Who will benefit and how?* Members and members' businesses will benefit from the society's ability to develop a comprehensive and relevant knowledge base of industry issues, changes, and trends. Chapter organizations will benefit from an increased sense of involvement among chapter members as well as from having access to the consolidated knowledge base that the society's efforts will build.

Step 3—Determine key stakeholders

- *Who are the key stakeholders, what are their interests and concerns, and what are the implications for this effort?* **Chapter leaders'** interests include retaining members and encouraging greater involvement in the work of the society. Concerns include competition from the national society in a variety of program and activity areas. Implications for the initiative suggest a need to ensure that this effort becomes a true partnership with obvious benefit for both sides. **Members'** interests include a return on their investment of time and attention to the association and the desire to have access to useful tools to enhance business success. Concerns include a sense of "What's in it for me," and there may also be issues of members not wanting to share proprietary information. Many members are small businesses that compete with each other within a confined geographic area. The financial services industry is becoming extremely competitive; issues may arise concerning how much or what kind of information members are willing to share. The society needs to position this effort as an opportunity for members to build a rich knowledge base they can access and use in their own businesses. It has to be seen as more than just providing information to the national office for its planning efforts.

Step 4—Conduct conditions assessment

- *Strengths/internal:* The society has established a precedent for knowledge-gathering mechanisms. During its recent planning processes at several of its regular chapter leader conferences, it held input sessions on emerging elements of the strategic plan, including assumptions about the future. Chapter leaders' input in these areas helped the board and the strategic planning committee to create a strategic plan document that considered a wide variety of perspectives.
- *Strengths/external:* Its previous strategic plans have successfully positioned the society in the marketplace as the product and program

leader—the place to go to obtain the latest and greatest information about certain parts of the industry.

- *Weaknesses/internal:* Chapter members do not universally have a perception of value in contributing to a national knowledge base of industry information and trends. The society has limited resources for managing and collating input. Some see the effort as proprietary and don't want to share.
- *Weaknesses/external:* Other competing sources exist for industry knowledge and insight.
- *Opportunities:* The industry is changing quickly, and there is a need to gather accurate, relevant knowledge and insight. The use of a broad base of such input will help the society position itself to serve a wider segment of the financial services industry.
- *Threats:* Other societies seeking to serve the same marketplace may build better knowledge bases of deeper insight faster and more effectively, threatening the society's membership base.

Step 5—Identify strategic issues
- *Using the following criteria, what are the most important issues to be addressed in this initiative?*
  - **Impact**—a measure of "breadth" of importance, related to relationships. How basic is the factor? How many other things depend on it or are related to it?
  - **Consequence**—a measure of "depth" of importance, related to intensity. How bad or good will it be?
  - **Immediacy**—a measure of the importance of opportunity and sequence, related to time. How much time is available? Is there a chronological order? Chapter members' desire to develop a national knowledge base of industry information and trends is basic. If the society cannot communicate the value and benefit of engaging members in building a collective knowledge base, the initiative will fail, and the association can take no other steps. The society has limited resources to manage and collate input. If it cannot dedicate sufficient resources to the effort to develop capability, the society will not be able to use the data or deliver value to members by communicating knowledge and insight.

Step 6—Determine key factors
- *What are the most important factors/forces that will need to be considered in addressing each strategic issue?* How chapter members perceive the value of contributing information is critical.

  Driving factors include the need for information, desire to enhance their society experience and make a difference in the planning and future direction of the organization, and recognition of the broad industry knowledge that exists among chapter members.

Restraining factors include lack of understanding about how to be involved; lack of opportunities available; concern about sharing proprietary information; possible lack of knowledge about the society's core values, which include respect for and understanding of proprietary and competitive boundaries; and lack of accountability to participate.

Step 7—Develop Strategies

- *What actions will be required to address the strategic issues? How can the existing capabilities of the organization (assets, skills, technologies, relationships, expertise, etc.) be used most effectively? What other capabilities will be required for success?*
  1. Encourage chapters to integrate regular discussion of issues, changes, and trends into their meetings.
  2. Encourage chapters to hold joint venture meetings with chapters of other groups to acquire an expanded perspective on current industry issues.
  3. Use chapter-training sessions to promote such a program.
  4. Convene a specific meeting for this purpose on an annual basis.
  5. Create competition and offer recognition, making each chapter responsible for one idea per quarter.
  6. Use chapter chairs to form a chapter relations committee; maintain regular contact (by phone, e-mail, etc.) with the committee to assess progress.
  7. Expand beyond chapter structure; include members from society interest groups, and invite them to share their insights.

Step 8—Assess strategies

- *Using the following criteria, make a list of all potential strategies. Is each strategy: **necessary**—responsive to an area of strategic importance; **feasible**—able to make some progress toward achieving the initiative; **appropriate**—related to the mission of the society; and **sufficient**—inclusive of all areas of strategic importance?*
  1. Encouraging chapters to integrate into their meetings regular discussion of issues, changes, and trends is necessary, feasible, and appropriate.
  2. Encouraging chapters to hold joint venture meetings with chapters of other groups to acquire expanded perspective on current industry issues is not necessary—there may be other ways to gather data—and it may not be feasible given that some groups may choose not to participate, but it is certainly appropriate to the society and the initiative.

3. Using chapter-training sessions to encourage such a program is necessary so that members will know how to be involved, it is feasible because national can provide modules for chapters to use, and it is appropriate to the society's mission and this initiative.
4. Convening a specific annual meeting for this purpose may not be necessary or feasible, but it is appropriate.
5. Creating competition, offering recognition, and making each chapter responsible for one idea per quarter is feasible and appropriate, but may not be necessary.
6. Using chapter chairs to form a chapter relations committee and maintaining regular contact (phone, e-mail, etc.) is an effort that must be managed and coordinated at the chapter level, and chapter leaders must be involved. It is feasible and appropriate.
7. Expanding beyond the chapter structure to include members from other society interest groups and inviting them to share their insights is not necessary, but it is feasible and appropriate.
8. Continuing to be positioned successfully as an industry knowledge source will require a broad set of input and the utilization of the society's aggregate intellectual capital wherever possible.

Step 9—Select strategies

- *How do you want to (a) add to, (b) delete from, or (c) modify the potential strategies list?*
  1. Encouraging chapters to hold joint venture meetings with chapters of other groups to acquire expanded perspective on current industry issues is not necessary, so it should be eliminated at this time as an active strategy.
  2. Convening a specific annual meeting for this purpose may not be necessary or feasible given current resource levels, so it should be eliminated at this time.

Step 10—Develop action plans

- *For each strategy, what are the key events, who has responsibility for them, what are the target dates, and what resources will be required?*

  Example: An action plan for using chapter-training sessions to promote such a program would include the following key events:

  1. Society staff will enlist a small task force of chapter leaders in reviewing current curriculum by first quarter (1Q) 2003.
  2. Society staff will determine current schedules for chapter training by 1Q 2003.
  3. Society staff, in partnership with chapter leaders, will build training modules for data-gathering processes by 2Q 2003.

4. Society staff will train all chapter leaders on the modules by 3Q 2003.
5. Chapter leaders will deliver the training at their chapters by 4Q 2003.
6. Society staff and the task force of chapter leaders will evaluate results and adjust process by 1Q 2004.

The task force completed an action plan like the one above for the two strategies it selected (Step 9) and built a master action plan for monitoring progress on the initiative as a whole. By using a process of collaborative strategic thinking, this organization was able to develop an effective, timely methodology for increasing its knowledge base, thereby providing governance with a valuable tool for adjusting and refining the society's future direction.

Part 3
The Role of Trust in Governance Systems

Chapter 9
Trust: A Definition

Trust in a voluntary organization is about reliability, focus, and constancy. Reliability is dependability as defined by focus and constancy. Focus means that what governance declares as being important is what it attends to. Constancy is about sustaining that commitment over time. When members see the work of the organization related to goals they perceive as valuable, they experience trust in the organization.

A useful definition of trust in terms of associations is that even when governance is not available to oversee what happens, the organization keeps its promises. If a person or group holds this belief, then the relationship can be a trusting one. If not, then the relationship cannot be a trusting one until the organization discovers the source of discomfort. This often requires the use of sensitive dialogue, diplomacy, and a positive approach to problem solving, driven by a commitment to discover what is right rather than a compulsion to uncover what is wrong.

Creating and sustaining a culture of trust becomes an imperative for success as an association develops strategies for a more responsive and effective governance structure. Trust can be considered the alignment of what an association has promised with what it ultimately delivers to important stakeholder groups such as members, volunteer leaders, staff, legislators, and the general public. It is often delineated in a set of values or expectations and perceived through the willingness to act on those values. Trust is more than forming values; it is honestly acting on those values. In other words, it is "practicing what is preached."

Trust and association nimbleness are inextricably linked. Nimbleness and the ability to make the right decisions efficiently in response to marketplace challenges will separate associations that provide significant member value from those that do not. An underlying culture of trust must support the open sharing and valuing of relevant information as part of the decision-making process. A trusting environment respects the qualifications, expertise, and accomplishments of the individuals it represents. Quite honestly, who wants to spend valuable time with an organization characterized by the absence of trust and the type of behavior that emerges when trust is not present?

The result of creating a trusting environment is an enjoyable culture—based on trust and communication. What is unique about an association is not its "not for profit-ness," but its "voluntary-ness." An enjoyable culture attracts people to become involved and to make a difference. Members will not involve themselves in an organization that is not enjoyable and does not create meaning for them. If associations do not attract people to choose to belong and participate voluntarily, with trust and a high degree of communication, then they may end up throwing a party that no one chooses to attend.

People yearn for honest and trustworthy relationships with other individuals and groups. Followers want to trust their leaders to make the right decisions; leaders want to trust their followers to accomplish things. Members want to trust their associations to meet their unique needs.

Now more than ever, members will make decisions to participate in associations that have commitments to open access to information and communication, leadership with integrity, the chance for quality relationships, and volunteer opportunities that will make a difference. All of these characteristics have trust at their root.

Chapter 10

Trust in Current Governance Practices:
What We Know, Believe, and Predict

Question 1

What do we know, believe, and predict about association members' needs, wants, and preferences relative to trust in governance?

For a culture of trust to exist in an association, there must be

1. clarity and consensus about what will constitute success,
2. open access to common information, and
3. confidence in the competence of partners.

An association must answer the four knowledge-based questions, as discussed in previous chapters, to determine how its governing body can establish and sustain a culture of trust.

1. What do members and leaders want and need?
2. What are the current realities and dynamics around trust?
3. What is going on in the association related to trust?
4. Are there any ethical implications to consider that affect a culture of trust?

After answering these questions, governance can begin to determine what systems, structures, roles, processes, and cultures can establish and sustain trust. They can plan governance's role in achieving trust and the behaviors that will contribute to sustaining it.

Member Demand

Member demand will drive trust. Expectations by association members for increased value drive the demand for a culture of trust. As the diversity of members' needs, wants, and preferences continues to increase, it will become more critical for associations to focus on creating a trusting environment. A culture of trust creates a satisfying and enjoyable environment that encourages involvement, open access to information, community building, support for grassroots lobbying efforts, and a general sense that the association is at the center of relevant activity within the industry, cause, or profession it represents. Trust allows the association to eliminate unnecessary controls and create increased value for members through an increase in nimbleness and responsiveness.

Members' Insights

Governance should trust members' insights. In a culture of trust, governance asks members to provide insights and direction to the decision-making processes. The leaders then must be willing to listen and trust the insights of members. Traditionally, members have viewed governance as their representative surrogates; therefore, they trusted the leaders to know their needs. But as organizations have grown and members' needs and preferences have become more diverse, it has become more difficult for volunteers to represent their distinct and diverse needs. As a result, many associations have now instituted mechanisms to seek insights directly from members. To sustain a culture of trust, it is imperative that governance and staff act on these insights and sustain clear lines of communication with members.

Risk and Expectations

Governance must manage risk and expectations. Reducing an association's traditional aversion to risk is critical to building a culture of trust in governance. If there is not common agreement on what taking the risk should accomplish, the association will be even less tolerant of uncertainty. In a knowledge-based environment, associations can begin to take informed risk. Sometimes the potential window of opportunity suggests that the organization must take risks, and even though governance puts in place mechanisms to inform the issue, there is still no such thing as a reliable risk. Understanding the elements of risk does not occur in a vacuum—it builds from knowledge of what members have done and what other associations have done. If an association has evaluated new opportunities that include the ability to test ideas while expending minimal resources, to assess potential risks, and to evaluate progress and pull back if conditions change, it will become less risk averse. There should also be a common definition of what will constitute success. In any particular initiative, there may be a variety of outcomes, such as informative failure, outstanding or marginally good response from stakeholders, and so forth. Governance and the association's workforce must define acceptable outcomes, constantly focus on what they define as success, and allow for mistakes.

Effective leaders, as Warren Bennis says,

> . . . *have a faculty one might think of as the Wallenda Factor, the ability to accept risk. One CEO said that if she had a knack for leadership, it was the capacity to make as many mistakes as she could as soon as possible, and thus get them out of the way. Another said that a mistake is simply "another way of doing things." These leaders learn from and use something that doesn't go well; it is not a failure but simply the next step.*
> (Warren Bennis. 1994. *"The Four Competencies of Leadership," in* An Invented Life: Reflections on Leadership and Change. *Boston: Addison-Wesley. World Wide Web page http://www.cio.com/executive/edit/chapter5.html [accessed July 24, 2002])*

Using Time Wisely

Time is precious. Members want their association to be respectful of their time considerations and constraints. They want to be part of a governance system that has shared values. However, younger generations have needs that may affect their continued involvement in the association. Many want flexibility in their leadership experience—to engage and disengage as their personal needs change, without having their motives or loyalty questioned.

Question 2

What do we know, believe, or predict about the current realties and dynamics of associations relative to trust in governance?

External Forces

As a general observation, trust between individuals and communities in the United States is on the decline. Most indicators of mistrust are on the rise— violent crime, civil litigation, changes in the family unit, personal isolation, and decentralization of communities. These indicators suggest that people today approach personal or group relationships through a lens of mistrust or, at the very least, question an individual's or group's values before entering into a relationship.

This overall lack of trust in society follows individuals from their personal lives to their involvement in groups—most notably their work with associations. The lack of trust is also evident in the workplace, and the association's staff is not immune to common workplace issues. Most organizations today face the challenge of moving from a reputation of mistrust—or at least an environment lacking in trust—to one of mutual admiration, respect, and ultimately, trust.

People find it easier to trust in an environment in which they are comfortable. They also find it easier to trust others who are like minded. Traditionally, an association has represented a group of people coming together around common interests and goals. The homogeneity of membership has made this kind of community a naturally trusting environment.

Differences in generational, ethnic, and gender-related experiences create different preferences for organizational cultures. Over time, as member populations have become more diverse in both goal and interest areas, trust levels have begun to decrease. In a heterogeneous culture, where the goals of some are not known or shared by others in the organization, there is no immediate clarity around what will constitute success, because trust is difficult to sustain.

In associations viewed by themselves and others as having the will to govern well, a knowledge-based governance strategy creates a mechanism for converting the potential discomfort of diversity and heterogeneity of interest and goal to a more attractive appreciation for inclusion. It allows for the legitimate disclosure of diverse thought and opinion in a non-threatening environment where dialogue moves into deliberation with full understanding. As groups work together and create strategy, trust is strengthened.

Trust and Competition

Highly competitive professions or industries may stifle openness and the communication of ideas and information—the very qualities that contribute to trust. Despite the movement toward open access to information, competitive forces will continue to drive some organizations to hoard information and maintain control over their secrets. Coca-Cola is not any closer to sharing information with Pepsi than it was 25 years ago. There is no trust between traditional rivals; if these groups serve in the association's leadership, their tendency to mistrust others in the room will affect the association's ability to change the culture. The association is therefore challenged to create a "safe haven" for competitors that allows them to dialogue freely about the issues that will mutually benefit the industry, profession, or cause the organization represents.

Splintering Organizations

The trend toward specialization, or even splintering of associations into subsets or communities of interests—some of which may be based on ethnicity, age, or geography—can fracture trust. Another factor affecting the level of trust within an association is also related to geography. International members may not have the same level of trust as those in the United States because it is more difficult for them to meet with one another.

Societal expectations of organizations and institutions are different today than they once were. Members value organizational leadership that will listen—one that is open and communicative; acts ethically; is respected by the profession or group that it represents; has a vision and a sense of "we"; understands issues; and is charismatic, inspirational, and effective. Thus, the credibility of an organization's leadership is crucial to building trust.

Question 3

What do we know, believe, or predict about the capacity and strategic position of associations relative to trust in governance?
It is critical to examine the capacity and strategic position of the association itself in the context of member and leader needs and factors that influence how associations operate. An organization can best achieve this by responding to a series of questions such as the following:

- How much of a sense of community exists within the association?
- Are the members similar enough to form community?
- What existing organizational and procedural constructs promote open communication?

At the staff level these issues relate to the degree of trust the staff has in the volunteer leadership, the adequacy of resources, and whether the staff is committed to the organization's mission or views its involvement as just a job.

Governance Structures and Role Clarity

Changes in association governance systems have affected the ability of an association to create a culture of trust. For example, there are those who believe the delegate assembly is archaic and has outlived its usefulness. Many consider it ripe for mistrust in that it may polarize segments of the governance structure itself. Multiple governing structures within an organization can have an adverse impact on trust if turf battles take control of decision making and organizational finances.

A clear delineation of roles and responsibilities among the various governance structures is critical to creating a culture of trust, but increasingly, those roles may shift in particular contexts on a given issue. In the past, associations defined the relative roles and responsibilities of members and staff leaders as rules, applicable at all times. In the 21st century, associations must redefine the roles and responsibilities of members as leaders/workers within the context of any given initiative. Rather than rules, consensus on desired outcomes and agreement on the evaluation of behavior will serve as the framework for trust. The response to this shift may be higher tolerance of organizational ambiguity, but it will present difficulty for those who crave order and simplicity. In this changing environment, organizations will achieve success by working well together, not merely working by the rules.

It is important for all decision-making parties to know their capabilities and roles in moving the association forward. When an organization establishes and communicates roles, individuals and groups become accountable for what they do and do not do; therefore, the organization can delegate responsibilities to those best suited to carry out the tasks.

Good governance is about balance. Either extreme in the continuum of role relationships between member and staff leaders can cause dysfunction in governance. There is a caution to remember, however. As trust builds between volunteer leaders and the chief staff executive, there is a tendency for volunteers to rely more and more on staff to do the association's work. As a result, the board begins to depend too heavily on staff competencies to lead, disengages from the work, and withdraws. Volunteer leaders start sensing that staff has too much power and try to dominate decision making. Boards that are too satisfied with staff competency create a ticking time bomb that may explode at any moment. This situation could eventually lead not only to mistrust and conflict between the staff and volunteer leaders, but also to termination of the chief staff executive.

To prevent association cultures from forming "unhealthy" trust, chief staff executives need to communicate the board's role continually and bring issues and problems to the board to keep it actively engaged in the association. This maintains the proper level of trust.

The trend has been to downsize boards to facilitate decision making. But board size can be either a contributing or an inhibiting factor to creating a culture of trust. Tokenism can generate lack of trust when individuals are appointed to governance positions because they represent certain membership segments. Some other trends that affect trust concern governance processes—whether boards discuss and make decisions about issues relevant to the future of the members; the level of board participation, with small-group dialogues taking place and filtering information back to the larger group; and the need for committees to take action within the constraints of the association's strategic direction.

Communication as an Essential Factor

The essential underpinning of a culture of trust is a communication system and process that is open and that spans all segments of the organization. Members and leaders both want to participate without consequences in an environment that is accepting of individuals from different backgrounds and with different perspectives. They want a heightened level of quality communication both to and from the organization and its constituents. Under those conditions, both members and leaders will be willing to be open, take risks, and trust the process. Members and leaders want a governance system that is clearly defined, with policies that are developed out of a commonality of goals and made public. When the organization operates in a principled fashion under a system that is policy rather than control oriented, hidden agendas or manipulation are absent.

Both leaders and members know that politics can play a role in organizational life. Members want organizational leadership based on competence rather than on politics and endurance (i.e., bestowed as a reward for those who stay around the longest). Leaders want to move ahead based on their ability rather than on tenure; at the same time, they also want to be rewarded for tenure. These two perspectives can lead to organizational and individual stress, to which governance systems and structure must be sensitive.

We cannot overemphasize the importance of having member leaders as visible co-champions of change efforts—especially if the issues involved have to do with defining value to members, distribution of power, or allocation of resources. A go-it-alone approach can backfire, as the following situation illustrates.

An association we studied was engaged in a facilitated strategic planning exercise in which 42 volunteer leaders participated. As part of the effort, the chief staff executive gave a state-of-the-association-and-the-industry report, raising certain questions and challenges that frequently came up in board meetings about the association's need to become more international. Following the speech, the chief staff executive put up a mock logo that simply dropped the word "national" from the association's name. No one said anything at the time. When the planning process was complete, however, the board went into executive session, where it discussed the chief staff executive's continued employment because she had raised this idea, though only to the board as a thought provoker and not as a unilateral action by staff. She was accused of kowtowing to the majority of the membership because she allowed the strategic planning process to raise the specter of "governance" changes. This was hardly a fair criticism given that this issue had been raised at every meeting since 1985. But it pointed up a valuable lesson, namely, that organizational leadership needs to be kept informed and its support ensured before staff makes unanticipated suggestions for change.

Influences of Technology on Trust in Governance

Technology facilitates communication, and its effective use can contribute to perceptions of authenticity and respect. Technology can facilitate regular communication between the organization and members, and the way the organization uses it can contribute considerably to the trust factor. Does governance use technology to solicit input and feedback? Does governance use it to convey information consistently? Does governance use it to communicate with members but then ignore the information received? Does governance take into consideration the need of some members for face-to-face experiences? All these questions affect perceptions of organizational credibility and trust.

Technology is also a vehicle to reach broader constituencies. Organizations need to consider both generational differences that exist today (e.g., in the way different generations may want their information conveyed) and what is known as the "digital divide" (an economically based disparity in both access and availability). An organization not attuned to these issues cannot build trust.

A critical relationship exists between evolving technologies and governance, with an up side and a down side. The up side of a potential technology-enabled governance mechanism can be the following:

- Increasing access and broadening knowledge distribution (ease of access to knowledge that promotes understanding of issues through Web site postings and customized e-mail messages).
- Speeding up decision cycles (with dialogue, knowledge sharing, and preliminary thinking about alternatives executed in Web-based chat rooms or discussion boards).
- Involving a wider population of people in work and decision making without sacrificing time or efficiency (targeting access and distribution virtually to groups who could not otherwise afford to be a part of the conversations).
- Keeping a larger body of people equally informed more easily (through the simultaneous use of both Web- and paper-based technologies such as fax to ensure that all stakeholders, whether technologically literate or not, have access to the same information and insights).
- Reducing the amount of paper people have to carry to meetings (by creating CD-ROM-based board books and sending those ahead of time, or by e-mailing board information or creating downloadable locations on the association's Web site).
- Illuminating issues before groups come together to make decisions (such as facilitating virtual discussion boards or chat rooms addressing the relative advantages and disadvantages of a particular action).
- Enabling work groups to keep governance informed of progress and problems without requiring board members to spend huge amounts of their time together reviewing the work of others (consent agendas or regular committee reports distributed by e-mail or Web site, so that the board does not have to spend its time together reviewing work that has already been done and in which no immediate governance action is required).

The down side to the use of evolving technologies in governance concerns a problem relating to trust. In dealing with the most complex and controversial issues, particularly where judgments are being made without full knowledge of what is occurring or being able to anticipate the future with any certainty, confidence in a decision is often premised on a group's comfort that it has exercised sufficient due diligence. Up to 80 percent of what an individual uses to understand what is really intended has to do with nonverbal cues. But the ability to access the cues that support the exchange of trust is significantly diminished in a virtual environment.

Technology also has implications for developing a culture of transparency that builds greater trust. With the continued evolution of technology, broader access to more information—either consciously or accidentally—needs to be an expectation. It was always difficult to keep a secret in a community as small as an association, and now, with governance operating in a virtual world, keeping a secret is "virtually" impossible.

Technology, Community, and Trust

Trust is most important in places where people care. When people are part of a community, they tend to care the most. By definition, successful associations are a community—this is why they view community as a strategy—and the presence of strong community has implications for trust in effective governance.

The ASAE Foundation's study, "Community as Strategy—People Make it Work: The Social Fabric of Community on the Web" explores the need to pay attention to the "people" side of Web communications in order to create effective community. The work notes that although associations have been the front-runners in building networks that unite their members and serve a broad range of needs, emerging online technologies can also be a dislocating force. "The real key is to pay attention to how people actually use technology. . . . Associations will need to deploy 21st-century technologies to serve social needs that have been with us since the beginning of time." And our work suggests that many of those social needs have to do with the elements of connection, enfranchisement, and trust.

How an organization uses technology relates also to its role as an enabler of community. If it is able to effectively connect all stakeholders to the processes of work and decision making in the organization, members will feel enfranchised and will have trust in the organization and its processes. But technology is only a part of this. As suggested in the "Community as Strategy" abstract, "Web technologies offer wonderful tools for strengthening member engagement. But as powerful as these tools are, the greatest value is found when associations weave together online and face-to-face connections, consciously and strategically integrating them in the service of the whole."

The "Community as Strategy" study further suggests that in order to take advantage of these opportunities, associations will need new kinds of facilitation. We believe they will also need new kinds of leadership and governance. Successful associations know that online interaction will not just take care of itself, and in order to make effective use of online community in an association, leadership must ensure that the dialogue process is seen as credible—open and accessible to all stakeholders in the organization—and that the processes are focused on issues that will deliver value to members and help move the organization forward. Elsewhere in this text, we refer to governance's obligation to the "management of attention"—making sure the organization is focused on the right things. As the "Community as Strategy" study notes, "successful initiatives require someone to nurture energies, connect people, and seed efforts and ideas. . . . The two big jobs are keeping things connected, and getting people to do things." Our work suggests that this is a critical element of success in governance that is viewed by itself and others as having the will to govern well—a focus on both what is done and how it is done.

In many of the associations we studied, the result of the successful establishment and nurturing of community is an increased level of trust. As the "Community as Strategy" study notes, "in an online community, trust is the result of things like shared experience, the opportunity for authentic interaction, persistent identity, reciprocal disclosure, testable expectations, and experience to suggest that the 'Test' will be passed." We observe that if the association and its leadership are able to use technology in support of an effective sense of community among the organization's stakeholders, a community in which dialogue on issues important to the membership is open and participative, and in which the context of decision making is understood and credible, it will have moved forward toward developing a culture of trust and sustaining the will to govern well.

Trust at the Board Level

Profound changes will need to occur at the board level to engender trust in governance and the organization. For years, many boards have been "talking the talk" and "walking the walk" when it comes to change in governance behavior. However, the truth is that some still want to maintain the same level of control they have always had. Collectively they want to succeed, but change is difficult, so the focus needs to be not on how much control they have but on what tools they employ to execute that control. A knowledge-based governance strategy allows governance to build trust and yet maintain an adequate level of control by assessing the extent to which the association is satisfactorily achieving declared outcomes and by causing intervention where it is unsatisfied with results. This allows for the exercise of control through oversight rather than through meddling or "snoopervision."

The Role of Staff Leadership in Trust

Staff leadership is also critical. Perhaps the greatest influence in the creation of a culture of trust is leadership. An inspiring, knowledgeable staff leader who acts as mentor and guide, who is visible to both members and leaders, and who presents a credible face to the community engenders trust. While the quality of volunteer leadership is also an important element in trust, the turnover in volunteer leaders is high, emphasizing the importance of effective, consistent staff leadership.

Question 4

What are the ethical implications relative to trust in governance models and practices emerging as choices for the 21st century?
Creating a culture of trust requires associations to expand their idea of what constitutes ethical behavior. While illegal and immoral behavior will continue to be the traditional realms for ethical consideration, issues involving disenfranchisement and trustworthiness will also require ethical scrutiny.

The Trust Commitment

In today's association environment, more than ever before, trust will require an ongoing commitment to good faith and righteous intention. The increasingly less organized environment of associations will require comfort with ambiguity in both internal and external transactions. The traditional sources of comfort provided by definition and clarity about who does what and how are not as readily available. Environments that seek to respond nimbly to rapid, discontinuous, and unpredictable change can achieve and sustain trust more easily when they clearly define and communicate expectations. Increasingly, governance finds itself wrestling with issues where reasonable expectations may not become clear until after movement in a particular direction has already begun, suggesting that governance will have to trust that others will be trustworthy.

The larger and more contentious an issue is, the more likely it is that stakeholders involved with it will want to be trusting and trustworthy to provide a source of common comfort. It is equally important for member and staff leaders involved in governance to identify for any given situation the specific behaviors likely to erode or dissolve trust among key stakeholders. A common attribute of successful governance is that partners examine their behavior for the purpose of consciously determining what will earn trust and what will diminish it.

Chapter 11
What Change Strategies Will Promote Trust in Governance?

A Culture of Trust

A culture of trust allows associations to abandon politically motivated permissions to proceed that add little or no value to the quality of a decision. Practicing a culture of trust requires the association to define what constitutes this type of culture and implement strategy to support it. Trust is a critical part of culture, but culture is full of intangible elements, so it may at first be difficult to identify essential characteristics of a culture of trust. A culture of trust cannot exist in the following situations:

- Volunteer leaders vote one way in a board meeting and another way around the coffee urn.
- Staff managers must have three sets of signatures before creating new products.
- Committees go to the board for validation only to have the board invalidate their work.
- The chief staff executive withholds important information from volunteer leaders for the sake of shortening the board meeting.
- National organizations and state component groups do not communicate or recognize each other's value to the members.
- Members constantly question the board's actions because they do not understand the rationale behind those actions.

An association culture of trust exhibits the following characteristics:

- Board members have knowledge and expertise and engage in the dialogue necessary to make informed decisions with confidence.
- Staff and volunteers have well-defined roles and interrelationships, within a particular context, so that leaders can make efficient decisions without "command and control" approvals.
- The board has responsibility for strategy and direction setting; member and staff workgroups have accountability for the detail and implementation of strategy.
- The chief staff executive is considered an integral part of the association's leadership team, understands the members' marketplace, and maintains an open flow of communication to volunteer leaders.
- National organizations actively solicit the opinions of leaders of state and local component groups in creating the future for the industry, profession, or cause they represent.
- Leadership constantly informs members and, where appropriate, asks for their opinions so that they feel part of the decision-making process and are adding value to the overall community.

Trusting Oneself

Literature that examines the nature of trust in organizations recognizes that trusting oneself is a prerequisite for creating a culture of trust. If association governance, staff, and volunteers do not trust themselves to make the right decisions and create a trusting environment, such a culture cannot emerge. Associations that are viewed by themselves and others as having the will to govern well make an effort and a commitment to seeing that the individuals involved build and sustain a culture of trust.

Governance must trust its ability to make the right decisions; this trust is basic to leadership success. Before trusting others, individuals must be able to trust themselves, and before they can expect others to trust them, they must earn a reputation as trustworthy. Though it is not meant to be exhaustive, the following is a list of behaviors common among governance and staff leaders who have the ability to create and maintain a culture of trust.

- Listen well.
- Have respect for diversity of opinion.
- Are willing to share common and appropriate information.
- Are committed to open communication and facilitated dialogue.
- Have complete confidence in the abilities of others.
- Are committed to honesty and integrity.
- Delegate responsibilities effectively.

- Practice transparency.
- Are committed to "open book" financial accountability.
- Are open to criticism and willing to admit mistakes.
- Are aware of what they do not know.

Trusting Each Other

For a group of individuals who associate together to define their interactions as trustworthy, the relationships among them need to be built on trust. To establish and maintain a trusting environment among volunteer leaders and staff, governance must recognize the unique leadership partnership among all parties. This is critical to achieving and sustaining the will to govern well.

Trust is transferred from one person to the next. When one person trusts another, the trustee usually reciprocates in some way. This reciprocation continues to spread trust and goodwill among groups of people passing it along. Mistrust spreads the same way. Communities, including associations, will begin to fragment if trust is repaid with dishonesty and disloyalty. If associations are committed to building a governance structure founded on trust, members of the leadership team must be willing to trust each other and risk vulnerabilities through open and honest communication.

In a knowledge-based governance strategy, the use of dialogue as a tool for illuminating issues and choices of strategy before deliberation engenders a culture of trust. Sustaining trust in governance requires individual and group commitment to keep the following two key promises

1. to inquire about thoughts, beliefs, and feelings until one understands sufficiently the basis of views and opinions, and
2. to be honest and open about thoughts, beliefs, and feelings when one is asked questions.

In successful governance, the commitment of the group to keep these promises manifests in the way the group itself behaves. In other words, the governance culture of the group becomes the aggregate of the commitment of all the individuals. When governance designs a process to solicit and reward effective behaviors, the trusting culture becomes institutionalized. Commitment to the process provides coherency in the culture over time, regardless of the particular combination of individuals at any given point.

Association leaders of the future will need to be free to delegate authority and responsibility and then get out of the way. If they cannot trust volunteers and/or staff, the organization and its members will demand that they be watched, thereby creating an environment unfit for nimbleness and change. Leadership must examine the relationships of staff to staff, staff to volunteers, volunteers to members, and members to the organization before they can create a culture of trust.

Trust in Organizations

When an association makes a commitment to trust, the individuals involved are free to create, experiment, and lead the organization to greater heights of success and opportunity—and governance has an obligation to enable this commitment. Trust links to nimbleness in at least two ways. First, absent trust, the need for bureaucratic permissions to proceed will encumber the organization, slowing decision making and implementation. This diminishes nimbleness. Second, absent trust, the creative talent of the organization is less likely to take risks and innovate. This also diminishes nimbleness. Nimbleness is not just about doing things quickly; it is about doing the right things quickly.

Articulations of Core Ideology

Governance's need to articulate core ideology and core values is not just a theoretical or academic exercise. The communication of core values has a strategic utility to organizations. Governance must undertake a serious commitment to and enforcement of core value if it is to be successful. When an association's leadership establishes a set of core values, it creates energy, motivation, and commitment to creating a trusting environment. It also provides the parameters needed for creative thinkers to feel sufficiently comfortable to take the risk to innovate. Examples of core values that assist in communicating a culture of trust include:

- Visionary leadership forever open to new ideas.
- Service to society.
- Belief in the value of collaboration. *Synergy* is the belief that the group can accomplish things that cannot be achieved individually. Synergy requires respecting others in the industry, valuing individuals' time and contributions, sharing information and opinions, and embracing a spirit of unity, both as an industry or profession and as an organization.
- Being grassroots driven, with those served by the organization defining policy and direction.
- Demonstrating respect and acknowledgement for the contribution to values of gender differences, as well as of ethnic and cultural diversity.

Associations that are viewed by themselves and others as having the will to govern well demonstrate core values as critical principles upon which they base their behavior, make decisions, and build trust. Understanding and using core values as parameters for action enables nimbleness in staff and workgroups as well as in governance. Governance does not make decisions that conflict with core values; its behavior is consistent with them.

Earned Trust

Commitment to continuous reflection and practice defines and sustains a culture of trust, not just through values recorded on paper, but also through the continuous practice of those values. For trust in governance to be fully realized within the association, those on the outside looking in must perceive it. The culture of the association will become the combined perceptions of those actively involved and of those observing from the outside.

If an organization is unwilling to practice its core values, then it is better not to create them in the first place. Most people can relate to the hotel experience where one has a confirmed room reservation, guaranteed with a credit card, and finds upon arrival that no room is available. Worse yet, the inexperienced hotel staff member relaying the message to the weary traveler may be standing in front of a gold-plated sign stating in bold letters the hotel's "commitment to exceeding the customer's expectations." At that point, the traveler concludes that since she does not have a room, she must not be a customer, and she walks out vowing never to return.

For these reasons, it is an essential requirement that leaders define both what will constitute value and what values it will reflect in behavior, and effective governance uses these definitions to measure success. Member and staff leaders who exhibit the will to govern well appreciate that the articulation of value assists their ability to guide the organization without micromanaging activity that can best be done by others.

Successful associations recognize the necessity for creating a culture of trust and living out that culture through daily actions that, over time, will establish the organization as a trustworthy entity. In this environment, while controls are present, controlling tactics are nonexistent. Staff and volunteer leaders are free to perform their defined functions within understood parameters, without hierarchical constraints; work is done quickly and efficiently, and those involved receive personal gratification from what they are doing—and perhaps even have a little fun.

Three Prerequisites for Creating and Sustaining a Culture of Trust

There are three prerequisites for creating a culture of trust in associations. They include clarity and consensus on what will constitute success, open access to common information, and confidence in the competence of leadership partners.

Clarity and Consensus on What Constitutes Success

When an association lacks sufficient understanding of the future and its implications, it frequently remains neutral on a variety of critical issues. This can be worse than doing the wrong thing, because members—seeking value, benefit, and an association that will help them navigate the relevant environment successfully—will migrate elsewhere. By the time governance has determined what it is comfortable doing, the association has lost the critical mass needed to do anything well. Hence, clarity and consensus on what will constitute success is critical.

If governance is able to define its vision and goals in ways that describe what it would like its world to become, it can make judgments about what it will or will not do within that changing context. When associations make assumptions about the future, they may not always know the specific solutions required should those assumptions come to pass. By thinking about the future in this manner, however, associations are better able to illuminate issues, identify choices of strategy, and select rational paths of action.

When governance has taken the time to reach clarity and consensus on what will constitute success, the outcomes—issue-by-issue and assignment-by-assignment—are clear. In this case, the board does not merely give a committee a charge; it ensures that the committee also has a series of tangible objectives to achieve—specific products consistent with the behavior ascribed to good governance, resulting in a recommendation, a study, or a new program.

Good governance understands and employs the distinction between oversight and supervision. Board process should enable oversight while diminishing the opportunity for mischievous "snoopervision." If both parties are clear on what they are trying to accomplish, the leaders are then able to provide oversight, leaving the committee to do its work. Together they find places where both assess progress toward desired outcomes. They do not conduct assessment to document a problem, but to see whether progress toward the goal is satisfactory. If it is unsatisfactory, they can make adjustments to increase the probability of success.

Organizations can apply this difference between oversight and supervision together with the need to be clear on outcomes. These are the ingredients critical to achieving a knowledge-based environment characterized by trust and the elimination of unnecessary controls.

At all levels of the governance structure and in all relationships where there is a need for oversight, accountability, and fiduciary responsibility over another party, trust is key to successfully completing work. Whether the relationship is between the board members and staff, board members and committee chairpersons, committee chairpersons and their committees, or committees and their staff liaisons, there need to be clearly defined and articulated outcomes in addition to defined roles and responsibilities. Then those responsible for doing the work can operate freely, using their own judgment. Not only must the organization define the outcomes, but it must establish an environment that encourages the freedom to create and follow through on a chosen path. Once they have established outcomes and parameters that people on the association's staff and volunteer workforce know and agree to, overseers need to step aside at let others execute.

Regarding the overseer's fiduciary responsibility, at given points in the execution path, both parties should review progress to make sure it is moving toward the defined outcome. Overseers must set these reviews in advance, and both parties must agree to them. This helps eliminate the tendency to supervise rather than oversee. If overseers continue to supervise, they will lose trust, and their organizations will forfeit their ability to attract good people and create significant movement forward.

Associations define success in many ways, such as member retention. Members define value in products and services delivered. If an association has designed its strategic plan well, *it* will be the best answer to the question members may ask, "What have you done for me lately?" Clarity and consensus on what will constitute success is a critical obligation of governance in defining the future. If there is agreement at the highest levels in the association on vision and direction, there will be higher levels of trust. The organization will be able to respond more quickly, more nimbly, and with a higher degree of success.

Open Access to Common Information

Open access to common information does not mean that everyone should know everything. But we have observed that in a trusting culture, individuals working together will have open and common access to information about stakeholders' opinions on an issue; beliefs, values, or interests as the reasons for each opinion; alternatives as possible paths to solutions; and respective advantages and disadvantages of each of those alternatives and paths. Common understanding of context and options is essential for establishing and sustaining trust. In an association, perception is reality, and if there is a perception that that the organization is withholding knowledge and information on any issue critical to membership, trust is eroded.

Trust can occur in associations only where there is reasonably open access to the dialogue about what association leaders are doing, why they are doing it, and how well they are doing it. What enables this in a knowledge-based organization is systems for exchanging information and use of "informed intuition" and "dialogue before deliberation" in decision making.

Association leaders exhibiting the will to govern well understand and appreciate the radical change in the paradigm of knowledge and power driven by the rapid and dramatic evolution of the Internet. The Web has significantly altered the world's views and expectations regarding information. The world now expects information to be free or at the very least accessible. Hoarding information no longer creates power. Instead, sharing and using information with like-minded partners now creates power—the competitive advantage lies with alliances and partnerships providing increased information and knowledge rather than keeping secrets and building walls around information.

A culture of trust requires open access to common information. This does not mean that an association makes all information available to everyone. What it does mean is that when the association is considering who should know what, it errs on the side of access rather than inaccessibility.

Suppose, for example, that governance tasks a group to work on a particular policy or program initiative. The group needs open access to common information about all relevant stakeholder views on this issue. It needs to know who all the voices are and what they are saying, particularly those that might not be at the table on any given day. The group needs to understand not only what their opinions, interests, experience, expertise, and values are, but also why they hold these ideas—not just what they think, but why they think it. The group also needs to understand alternatives, along with the advantages and disadvantages of each.

Technology allows an association to increase or decrease the size of governance or decision-making groups at all levels without sacrificing participation. By using a variety of technologies, associations can allow broader groups of members to engage in deliberations that create information bases for making decisions. The effort is to place higher levels of authority in smaller groups that can meet more frequently and, therefore, can assimilate more information to make decisions about targeted sets of problems. This is a shortcut, but the direction is clear and enhances trust.

Confidence in the Competence of the Leadership Partners

The third prerequisite for a culture of trust is confidence in the competence of the leadership partners. If members do not have confidence in the competence of the board, they will not trust the board. If the board does not have confidence in the competence of its officers, it will not trust the officers. If member leaders do not have confidence in the competence of senior staff, they will not trust the senior staff and, conversely, if the staff does not have confidence in the competence of member leaders, they will find it difficult to trust the member leaders.

In an effective leadership partnership, staff recognizes volunteers as subject-matter experts in their particular area or profession and incorporates their input and value in a meaningful way. Volunteers view staff as professionals in terms of the mechanics of running an association, accomplishing meaningful work, and getting things done.

In work undertaken for the ASAE Foundation that led to the 1993 publication of *Successful Association Leadership—Dimensions of 21st Century Competency for the CEO*, and in a related article in ASSOCIATION MANAGEMENT magazine by Glenn Tecker and Catherine Bower, "Why Good Executives Get Fired" (December 1992, pp. 32-40), we identified three interrelated dimensions of staff competency especially germane to a voluntary environment.

1. **Functional competencies**—knowledge about effective operation of core business lines of associations (e.g., government relations, member marketing, nonprofit law, publications, and chapter relations).

2. **Personal and professional competencies**—44 competencies organized into six clusters: interpersonal skills, value and use of technology, acquisition and use of information, understanding of complex relationships, deployment of resources, and personal characteristics common to all clusters.

3. **Process competencies**—knowledge about methods employed to make certain critical decisions within an association (e.g., strategic planning, budgeting, project management, and performance appraisal).

Board members are increasingly better informed about what is possible, so they have higher expectations about the professional expertise and competencies for which they are paying. In 1993, we observed that it was not merely knowledge of the competency that predicted success but also the ability to apply it successfully in context. Because the relevant contexts (mission, political dynamics, functions, program of work, etc.) differ markedly among trade, professional, and philanthropic/cause-related organizations, even where the competencies expected may be similar, the understanding necessary to demonstrate them effectively within context are fundamentally dissimilar. Governance holds senior staff accountable not just for what they do but also for how they do it. Because the peculiarities of organizational culture drive the expectations about how senior staff perform, the mechanisms used to sustain trust between member and staff leaders will need to be sensitive to differences in role and behavioral expectations.

This dynamic is particularly complicated in philanthropic, charitable, and cause-related organizations. In trade and professional associations, member leaders tend to share a larger book of common experience than do volunteers in these other groups. In trade associations, because members tend to be companies, volunteer leaders may share a common view of organizational operations based on their business expertise. In professional associations, volunteer leaders tend to share educational or training experiences and often a common set of personal preferences that led them to their field. In charitable and cause-related organizations, members share little other than common interest in the cause. Widely divergent and deeply held views exist of how an organization should operate, what the role of staff should be, and what constitutes effective process. This divergence of opinion, when coupled with the natural messianic zeal that most likely led them to donate their discretionary time to the cause, creates a different set of necessities around the issue of trust than those that exist in trade and professional organizations.

Trust between members and staff leaders in charitable and cause-related organizations is at special risk, and in some instances, is seriously eroding. In many such organizations, the conversation about trust focuses on issues of accountability. Some organizations are pursuing a misconstrued version of what constitutes successful accountability at the expense of partnership, resulting in the inhibition of the culture of trust rather than its enhancement.

Successful accountability is shared and formative rather than imposed and summative. Summative evaluation, in its simplest form, is about catching someone doing something wrong, documenting it, and imposing a penalty. Systems for summative evaluation, while necessary, are in and of themselves insufficient to sustain a culture of trust. It is necessary to bring to justice a staff executive who misallocates funds or spends organizational funds on personal items, but successful accountability goes beyond such measures.

Formative evaluation is about assessing progress toward a declared end to allow course adjustments to improve the probability of success. How governance chooses to approach accountability will have much to do with achieving and sustaining the necessary trust culture. A summative philosophy inhibits trust. A formative philosophy promotes it. Absent a culture of trust, the enterprise is unlikely either to achieve the nimbleness required in the 21st century or provide an enjoyable participation experience to attract talented volunteers and staff.

Because there tend to be fewer common organizational experiences and values within the governing body of organizations focused on a cause, sustaining trust may depend more on the process used for governance than in any other kind of organization. Where these organizations sustain trust, governance process ensures that considerations of core ideology (core purpose and core values), envisioned future (mission and audacious goals), and ethical dimensions inform every conversation about an important issue. It is the institutionalized expectation of such conversations between volunteer and staff leaders that establishes a shared and formative philosophy of accountability. The organization examines the appropriateness and efficacy of each important decision collaboratively on an ongoing basis, preserving partnership. Both partners find themselves better positioned to ensure that each of them is in fact holding itself accountable for appropriate performance.

In one association we studied, governance identified the lack of trust as the primary reason why the organization was experiencing a significant downturn. Over several years, the association had experienced an annual decline in membership, meeting attendance, and exhibitors. The waiting list of potential exhibitors dwindled to zero. Governance was not overly concerned with the annual incremental declines the association was experiencing because it had built up significant reserves from previous successful years. But behind the declining numbers was a larger issue and the core of the problem.

Research showed that members no longer trusted the volunteer leadership to make good decisions, volunteer leaders no longer trusted staff to execute, and staff no longer trusted the industry to support the value of the association. The organization needed to perform a major overhaul of its volunteer leaders and staff. It also needed to establish a firm foundation of trust before rebuilding and creating the kind of nimble organization that could respond quickly to marketplace changes, create more value to the membership, and create a community to which members would feel proud to belong.

Creating a culture of trust must be deliberate. It will not happen overnight, and the association's stakeholder groups will interpret it over a period of time through their own combined experiences, impressions, decisions, and actions. This chapter provides strategies from other associations that have successfully created and sustained a culture of trust.

Organizational Behaviors Supporting a Culture of Trust

Associations that view themselves or are viewed by others as having the will to govern well have employed the following strategies (among others):

1. Hire, Elect, Choose, and/or Appoint Trustworthy People

Whether hiring staff or electing volunteer leaders, these associations believe that trust begins with the individuals involved and the basic beliefs, values, and experience they bring to the table. An organization can create a trusting environment only by choosing the right people with integrity of the highest order who understand and support the importance of doing what is right "for the good of the whole."

A core competency of governance is the management of trust. Associations and their members rely on their leaders to set direction, consistently follow through on promises, focus the association's stretched resources, and maintain authenticity throughout the process. Some associations we studied, which elect or appoint volunteer leaders, employ mechanisms that provide some method of screening for trustworthiness among governance candidates. Some of the mechanisms include the following:

- Conducting a thorough reference check and asking specific questions about the candidate's integrity and honesty.
- Creating scenarios for candidate responses that assess characteristics such as openness to the opinions of others, willingness to put the organization's agenda above personal aspirations, listening and communication skills, and personal commitment to the organization's mission. Scenarios can begin with questions such as, "What would you do if . . . ?" "How would you respond to . . . ?" "What role would you play as a member of the team responsible for . . . ?" "In the past, how have you handled . . . ?"

- Testing commitment to the association's core values. If the association has stated core values, it can ask the candidate to respond to them with such questions as, "What does this statement mean to you?" "How do you see the association implementing this statement?" "What would the association not do because of this statement?"

2. Articulate Core Values in the Association's Strategic Plan

The associations we studied determined that articulating commitments to create and sustain a trusting environment in the form of core values is paramount. Core values provide the foundation for building a trusting culture, recruiting trustworthy people, and creating a nimble infrastructure that can respond quickly to changing marketplace dynamics. Many associations we studied ensured that the organization's strategic plan articulates vision and strategy that supports the implementation of those core values.

3. Create a Decision-Making Process Founded on Knowledge Collection and Analysis

As associations become increasingly positioned as sources of information and knowledge for the industry, profession, or cause that they serve, their ability to make the right decisions becomes more and more important. Dialogue promotes trust through an understanding of why people think as they do rather than just what they think. When an association has successfully downsized its governance groups, it has done so by adjusting size, structure, and process. Many of the associations we studied make every level of decision making smaller, not larger, and have been able to do it without sacrificing participation. By using a variety of technologies, they have allowed broader groups of members to engage in deliberations that create information bases on which they make decisions.

4. Increase Enfranchisement

Associations experience an exchange of trust when members feel fully enfranchised. The associations we studied linked enfranchisement to the opportunity members had to participate in the dialogue from which the organization made decisions. The associations implemented regular and consistent communication to members. Opening up channels of communication between staff, volunteer leaders, members, component organizations, and other important stakeholder groups was pivotal in transforming cultures of mistrust. They focused deliberately and specifically on groups of members that might feel most disenfranchised—those who are most distanced through gender or cultural experiences from the membership majority.

Some associations feared that disenfranchised groups would be most apt to form splinter organizations or take their business elsewhere. In some associations, such groups could include suppliers, vendors, and business partners;

members from minority ethnic backgrounds; and members from younger generations. In other organizations, groups believed to be in danger of becoming disenfranchised could include the house of delegates; state, local, and regional component leaders; at-large or nonvoting board members; and mid- and lower-level association staff members. The associations we studied identified key stakeholder groups that might feel disenfranchised and created mechanisms to communicate with and obtain feedback from those groups. Examples of communication formats associations employed include the following:

- **Town hall meetings, forums, and knowledge cafés.** Face-to-face gatherings where volunteer leaders can listen, with very little "official response." Not only is it important to listen at these meetings, it is also important to provide feedback when acting upon a response.
- **E-mails from the "desk of the chief staff executive."** Technology has created opportunities for inexpensive and efficient communication to stakeholder groups. In most organizations, members appreciate personal e-mails from association leaders as long as they are not direct advertising venues for products and services.
- **Ongoing Web-based feedback tools.** Research shows that, generally, Web users are no longer primarily technology-savvy young people. The demographics of Web users are growing closer and closer to the average demographics of the U.S. population; therefore, Web users have become a legitimate and statistically significant population to survey. Associations should be using their Web site as an inexpensive, quick, and reliable source of member feedback and responses from other constituencies on issues important to the organization. Doing so helps create an environment in which otherwise disenfranchised members can feel connected to the organization and provide legitimate feedback leadership can use in forming decisions and creating new products and services.

5. Create Gatherings to Celebrate the Community's Accomplishments

As noted earlier, trust builds over time through constant interaction and continuous commitment. Missed communication opportunities and lack of commitment destroy trust quickly. The associations we studied viewed the communities within their organizations as gathering places, whether face-to-face or in virtual space, and as important outlets for celebrating accomplishments and building a culture of trust. Trust tends to build in more intimate settings where relationships can develop, but opportunities for the full community to gather sustain a culture of trust. These gatherings validate and strengthen trust as members of the association have the opportunity to interact and contribute to the future direction of the association. In future virtual work, meeting face-to-face early on will speed the development of trust.

Virtual space can deepen trust and relationships over time, but face-to-face encounters contribute to the desire to work together.

Case Study—One Association's Experience

The following case study documents the mechanisms an organization employed to transform itself from an association with a culture of mistrust on all levels to an association with a culture of trust.

This association had a rich history of service and support to a well-known and vital profession. The oldest association in the industry, it had a reputation for being the premier leader. At one time, it set the example for professionalism within the association community representing this profession.

Before a massive undertaking to rebuild a culture of trust, the organization was fraught with fiscal irregularities, dysfunctional governance structures, staff incompetence, and archaic processes and systems. The board was arrogant and ignored the wants, needs, and preferences of the membership. Without sufficient board oversight and management, the staff was directionless and incapacitated, unable to move the organization forward. In summary, the volunteer leadership and staff disagreed on what constituted organizational success, thereby creating a chaotic and untrustworthy environment for staff and volunteer leaders.

The board represented special interest groups that over the years had formed into a hierarchy based on industry prestige. Those at the top of the hierarchy usually got their way, and those at the bottom did not have a voice. The governance structure was subject to a silo mentality. The board did not believe in strategic planning. The organization had never developed a strategic plan. Consequently, the board made bad decisions and continually changed the organization's direction. The board also had a reputation for not keeping promises. The staff became confused and disillusioned with the board's attempts to provide leadership to the organization. Membership declined annually at a time when membership in other industry organizations was growing. Splinter associations were forming to accommodate the needs of disenfranchised members. Staff worked behind locked doors, and staff turnover was extremely high, resulting in frustrated volunteer leaders, poor customer service, and lack of continuity of services. With the exception of the chief staff executive, staff was not involved in association decision making or the governance structure.

The situation was desperate. The board eventually terminated the chief staff executive and began a two-year search for a replacement. During this time, the board managed the association and experienced close to 100 percent staff attrition. The new executive the board finally hired had significant work to do to stop the bleeding. The organization recognized that lack of trust was at the core of its problems and decided to develop a culture of trust. What emerged incorporated the following principles:

- The association has a clearly articulated definition of what constitutes success.
- The association engages in continuous monitoring of member needs, wants, and preferences.
- The organization disperses power rather than allowing a few to hold it.
- Volunteer leaders and staff participate as equal partners with distinct and well-defined roles.
- The association shares information rather than hoarding it.
- Association activities and finances are transparent to members; the organization has discarded "closed book" accounting practices.

Over several years, the organization also employed the following strategies to effect its transformation to an organization with a culture of trust:

Creation of a strategic plan. When the association created its first strategic plan, all volunteer leaders and staff understood what constituted success for the organization. Volunteer leaders and senior staff were equal partners in creating the plan. At present, the organization structures all reports and board agenda items around the goals and objectives of the plan. Even the chief staff executive organizes the annual report to the members and the staff with the strategic plan as the outline.

Adoption of a knowledge-based governance structure. The association committed to making informed decisions using the knowledge-based governance approach discussed further in Part 5 of this book. The board backs all significant decisions with available market and marketing research along with insights and intuitions developed through group dialogue before deliberation.

Redesign of staff workspaces. The organization removed the locks from staff's doors. An open-space design helped break down department silos and encouraged communication. The association organized products and services along with staff in business units rather than functional areas. The chief staff executive established an open-door policy for staff, and the organization outsourced all staff functions that did not align with the core competencies. The association became customer-centric—servicing the customer became a top priority. Staff generated weekly reports to assess customer service levels. The organization makes constant modifications in staff service support as a result of the weekly reports.

Clear lines between staff and volunteer roles. Staff has complete autonomy from the board for the association's operations; the board does not interfere with staff operations. In turn, staff operations are completely transparent to the board. The association's volunteer treasurer receives monthly financial updates, and the board receives quarterly updates. The association has adopted an open-book policy with regard to financial information. The association's finances are also completely open to members. Corporate subsidiaries create clear lines between the association's nonprofit and for-profit functions.

Complete change in governance structure. The organization created three-year staggered terms to maintain a level of leadership continuity that was nonexistent before. All board members are elected at large rather than from special interest groups of the association, thereby eliminating board silos. The organization increased power to the full board and removed it from the executive committee. The senior staff management team sits with board members during board meetings; they are nonvoting members of the board but have equal say during board dialogue. The organization eliminated all special interest group councils and shifted work to temporary task forces and workgroups that meet electronically for efficiency.

All members solicited to become involved in the association. Through the task forces, all members have the opportunity to become engaged in the association in a meaningful way—providing expertise and intellectual capital rather than perfunctory busywork.

New product delivery process instituted. Volunteer leaders conduct and analyze regular member surveys to assess new product opportunities. Currently, no products and services are more than three years old. The association has developed a formal process to review products and services annually to identify those that need to be eliminated and to recognize gaps in the association's product-and-service portfolio.

Increased communication. Every other Monday, the chief staff executive sends all members a personalized e-mail update on association happenings. This communication provides regular contact with the members and allows them to give feedback to the association. It creates an open channel of communication between members and association leaders. In addition, the organization holds several regular, face-to-face meetings to obtain member feedback, including an open-forum session at the association's annual meeting. At this session, members can share thoughts, ideas, and concerns in a facilitated dialogue session led by volunteer leaders. The chief staff executive also established weekly meetings with senior staff and monthly meetings with the full staff.

Redesign of membership categories. The organization eliminated special membership categories to create equality among the members and to break down silos and volunteer fiefdoms.

Part 4
The Role of Nimbleness in Governance Systems

Chapter 12
Nimbleness: A Definition

At the highest level of vision, nimbleness is the presence of clarity and consensus on what will constitute success at a more discrete level of outcome-oriented goals. Nimbleness exists in organizations with strong core values that guide decision making at all levels of an organization. When values are understood, parameters for action become clearer. Nimble organizations allow thoughtful groups, guided by strategic principles, to determine whether the work they propose to do in support of the organizations' agreed-upon outcomes fits within the parameters of strategic direction and governance's intent, without having to seek permission from management or governance before they act.

Nimble associations are able to achieve universally understood clarity and consensus on what will constitute success, are able to define strategic principles and boundaries that act as guidelines for the associations' staff and volunteer workforces, and then empower those groups to innovate within those boundaries. A nimble organization is like a gymnast performing a floor exercise—within the boundaries defined by the mat, the gymnast is free to do whatever she thinks is necessary to succeed. In doing so, she exhibits extraordinary flexibility and can instantly change direction or move in totally new ways, with grace and purposeful movement, leaving the audience breathless and amazed.

In terms of effective association governance and sustaining the will to govern well, it is important to define what nimbleness is and is not. Nimbleness is not just about doing things quickly. Rather, it represents the ability of the organization to seize opportunities. It is work done in an appropriate amount of time and in an appropriate way. The amount of time it takes may not necessarily be the shortest.

Nimbleness is about being responsive. This definition may seem paradoxical, implying that nimbleness is about reacting to something rather than moving proactively toward decisions and actions. But one should not confuse nimbleness with being "reactive"—rather, it is reacting, but with purpose.

Nimbleness is the ability of an organization's leadership—volunteers in partnership with staff—to identify and act on the right things and to make decisions in a timely manner. Often, it's about trying new things.

Nimbleness is also about determining what *not* to do, because in order to be nimble, an association must be able to juggle existing resources and redeploy them from one project to another as appropriate. Therefore, it may imply the need to stop doing something in order to do something else. It is leadership's ability to shift from one thing to another, to change directions quickly in order to continue to deliver value to members and be relevant to their world. In unpredictable environments, the ability to be nimble is essential.

Nimble organizations can tolerate risk and mistakes. They carry a cultural implication that it is permissible to take informed risks and to make honest mistakes, as long as work and decision-making groups are able to find appropriate solutions and move onto the right path in a timely fashion.

Another paradox is that while nimbleness needs boundaries, parameters must be wide enough for the organization to seize opportunities. Appropriate boundaries, articulated in agreed-upon strategic principles, allow staff and volunteer workgroups to respond quickly and effectively to opportunities without having to "ask permission."

New, technology-enabled methods of work (i.e., ways of accomplishing things other than through meetings) tend to enhance nimbleness. Technology has created an expectation for nimbleness—because obtaining answers more quickly and reaching outcomes faster have contributed to higher, more complex expectations for customized member services.

Chapter 13

Nimbleness in Current Governance Practices: What We Know, Believe, and Predict

This chapter will use a knowledge-based approach to examine the following mega-issue question: "How can governance (systems, structures, role, process, and culture), in its decision making and behaviors, ensure and sustain a nimble organization?"

Question 1

What do we know, believe, or predict about association members' needs, wants, and preferences relative to nimbleness in governance?

The number of members who do not care will decrease. With more choices of where they can belong, people who continue as active participants will be invested in the work of the organization, and there will be a smaller number of inactive or "checkbook" members. Further, members who remain active will have increased expectations about their involvement in association governance and decision-making processes. The implications of this situation for nimbleness are that these involved members will most likely be committed to their ideas and priorities, and ideas will need to move to outcomes more quickly. If the organization lacks nimbleness, members will go elsewhere, and nonmembers will not seek out the organization.

An increased level of trust will be necessary between the association's volunteers and staff leaders. Members will expect associations and their decision-making processes to move faster, but they are not always comfortable giving up approval authority, even at an operational level, for decisions that involve risk and change. What we see currently in the associations we studied is that although volunteers are impatient with decision-making processes, they are not always willing to commit to behaviors or philosophies that will delegate decision making at a strategy level to staff. Hence, timeliness of decisions in association governance will rest not just on nimbleness, but also on trust, and the elements of knowledge-based governance strategy are imperative to generating trust.

There will continue to be diverse expectations among members. How any given membership at large connects to the governance of its association is often unclear. Older generations may be invested in the cultures and processes that have facilitated their involvement in the organization's decision-making processes. Younger generations, in many cases, do not know or care how governance works and may have less tolerance for its mechanisms, but they certainly care about outcomes. Hence, associations often do not know whether members expect to be more involved in the governing process, or how this may affect nimbleness. Increased involvement runs the risk of inhibiting nimbleness, but insufficient involvement may result in a lack of buy-in to the association's work program.

As deliberative bodies begin to improve work and decision-making processes, members often do not feel a sense of connection to the governance process. But if a board develops a reputation for addressing substantive issues in a way that creates learning opportunities for those involved, it will attract and retain the best, brightest, most talented, and most influential participants.

Because of their comfort with, capacity to absorb, and competence in utilizing technology, emerging generations of members will expect nimbleness and responsiveness from their associations' use of technology. They will also expect the association to use technology in meeting their needs and managing their involvement. Four assumptions emerging in this area suggest that members will want their association to use technology in the following ways:

1. To identify and anticipate their needs, making valuable offers to them before they even know to ask for them.
2. To give them instant, easy access to useful knowledge, programs, and services—when they want these things and in a format they want.
3. To enable them to participate actively in the work and decision making of the association without having to travel to or be in a particular place at a particular time.
4. To create a sense of community that fosters emotional attachment and connection.

Associations seeking to be nimble must address these assumptions and use technology as a delivery system for instantaneous access to knowledge and involvement.

Members may want to be proactive and involved in both the organization's work and in governance processes, but in many cases they do not know how to connect. There is a real difference between volunteers and members. Sometimes, governance is only for the "plugged-in" volunteers of the organization, whose degree of comfort with dialogue and decision making often depends on their participation in the organization's work. Lack of information about how members can become volunteers will significantly hinder an association's ability to mobilize a nimble and knowledgeable workforce when governance identifies a particular need. If members are not sufficiently connected to the organization's work, the association may miss opportunities to meet needs or provide value in areas that only the volunteer workforce can identify.

Members will expect associations to respond quickly, provide outcomes, and create value. Driven by an increased sense of accountability, associations will need a greater focus on tangible outcomes and benefits to members, thus moving the most successful associations away from internal politics and agendas. Associations will need to understand the strategic value of information and knowledge in their industry or profession and will need to play a role as knowledge creators. Achievement of these goals will affect their ability to shape the future of their members' world.

Associations will need to focus on things that members believe are important and will need to report on progress in a timely manner. As members increasingly have more resources for meeting their needs, those who commit their time, effort, and interest to the work of an association will want it to focus on things of particular interest and value to them. They will also want instant information on progress toward meeting their needs. This will have implications for nimbleness, as associations will need to achieve a balance between executing work and striving for outcomes while constantly having to communicate progress to an increasingly impatient membership. People will not feel enfranchised in a system that moves too slowly or too rapidly, and associations will need to make decisions based on what is appropriate for the given situation.

Question 2

What do we know, believe, or predict about current realities and evolving dynamics of associations relative to nimbleness in governance?

Members will still expect stability from their association, even in the face of rapid change. Paradoxically, members will want their association to keep pace with change in their profession or industry, but they will still perceive it as a place of stability in a changing environment. If an association becomes too nimble, it may alarm members who have come to view it as a sort of safe haven, far from the chaos of their workplace or marketplace. The challenge for governance is to keep a balance between what needs to change and what needs to stay the same. Further, governance will need to communicate fully to membership the reasons for any change that members might perceive as radical.

External demands will force associations into nimbleness or loss of relevance and critical mass (resources, enfranchisement, assets, etc.). If associations cannot be nimble, they may not be able to sustain critical mass or the resources necessary to provide value to members and their industries. An association loses relevance when it is either performing poorly on an issue important to members or doing an outstanding job on something of no consequence to members. If the association loses relevance, it loses engagement and commitment. And if it loses engagement and commitment, then it loses the critical mass of support it needs to be successful.

Though no association has ever intentionally selected obscurity as its desired future, many have achieved it. To maintain relevance, associations must begin to anticipate rather than react. But anticipation requires risk, and most associations are notoriously risk averse. Even those that can anticipate future needs and that are philosophically and emotionally committed to nimbleness may have difficulty compressing the timeframe between deciding to do something new and actually accomplishing it. This is particularly true where deciding to do something new and getting it done will require multiple loops of permission to proceed. Implementation comes easiest to those organizations that have committed to a consistent process for new product development with predetermined criteria for determining success at defined times. A common attribute of successful governance is the presence of rational, businesslike, and defensible tools in the processes that enable the making of intelligent decisions. Without such tools, governance risks lack of nimbleness and loss of relevance and does not have the knowledge it needs to make good decisions.

Fun is back. In the recent past, associations have gone from being social to focusing on business. But with the involvement of emerging generations, the pendulum may swing back to the social element. After decades of the baby boomer demand that says, *"Get me in, give me what I need, and get me out,"* joy is once again in demand. Baby boomers are aging and realizing that not everyone will achieve the resplendent material wealth promised them in the 1980s and 1990s. As a result, they are embracing an earlier value of being part of something bigger and more important than themselves. Having spent a large part of their lives trying to win a "rat race," many boomers are realizing that pursuit makes them just rats. Now, they want more. However, in their current search for meaning, the maturing members face some challenges. First, the sources of community that supported previous generations are no longer available: neighborhoods are too mobile, church and cultural groups are not sophisticated enough, and people do not even keep the same career—never mind employer—for a lifetime. Second, a large part of self-image for baby boomers has often been based on what they do for a living. They were the generation that defined the difference between a "job" and a "career" through "certification" of one sort or another. While the value of acquiring material goods has diminished for many, few have abandoned their affection for their profession, industry, or issue arena. So where can this largest cohort of the adult population look to satisfy its recommitment to gregarious but meaningful affiliation with others? Obviously, in appropriate association communities.

The opportunity for associations to become that source of community is enormous—if leadership understands the dynamics at work. Historically, the decision to become involved in associations was made based on the match between the perceptions of (a) one's needs, and (b) the benefits offered by a particular association product or service. If the programs and services satisfied those needs—meaning that the value matched the price of membership—then the individual joined. With this as an assumption, an organization would use certain techniques to strengthen its membership. For example, if an organization wanted to attract new members from a nontraditional population, it would add programs targeted at that group. If an organization wanted to encourage existing members to become more involved, it would upgrade its programming to better match those members' needs. If the match was already sound, it would simply reinvigorate promotion of its offerings to keep people interested.

Though these dynamics are still important, our research has identified a third variable driving the decision to belong—namely, the extent to which people perceive the organization earns a perception of being the "kind" of organization in which they can proudly claim membership. In other words, the key traits of the organization need to be congruent with a set of values and an identity that people desire. For baby boomers, the organizational image generally shares equal weight with the factors of a match between one's needs and the benefits offered. However, for younger members who are gradually replacing boomers in the prospective member marketplace, organizational image is often *the* deciding factor.

Most not-for-profit organizations are just beginning to wrestle with the issue of attractiveness to the generation that is following the baby boomers. Like the baby boomers, this demographic group will be big enough to demand commercial and community attention.

To this generation, raised with the interactivity of the Internet, the primary reflection of an organization's "age" is its integrated use of computer and communication technology. Generation "Next" does not look at a computer and anticipate the passive experience of a television screen. It sees an electronically enhanced, three-dimensional board game that allows for the instantaneous exchange of information and opinion. With the right focus and format, the computer will also be part of the entertaining experience expected in a modern association community. "Edutainment" is not merely a concept to tomorrow's members and customers; it is a prerequisite for participation. They do not expect just to sign up—they expect to sign on.

Collaborative organizations have the opportunity to do even better in the future what they have always done well in the past. Their only limitations are the imagination and experience of current decision makers.

The era of broad, expansive vision is over; it is being replaced by an equally powerful desire for an instantaneous and easily communicated bottom line. Newer, younger leaders are not interested in long-term, long-payback expansive visions that espouse a "make the world better" mentality. Members will increasingly need to face huge, immediate dilemmas, and hence will not see the need for a distant and possibly irrelevant vision. Instead, they will value nimble, responsive, relevant outcomes from their organizations.

Question 3

What do we know, believe, or predict about the capacity and strategic position of associations regarding nimbleness in governance?

Effective knowledge systems will inform governance and eliminate the necessity for volunteer and staff work groups to seek permission to reassess the appropriateness of what they are doing. Work groups with the necessary understanding of the board's strategic intent for their assigned tasks do not have to go to the board for constant feedback. Having a board that requires work groups to ask for permission to proceed with work will diminish nimbleness. Furthermore, if the board invalidates work that has been accomplished, it destroys trust. The key to building an effective partnership between governance and work groups is an efficient system of knowledge that gives everyone access to the related content and context within which governance makes decisions and work groups execute work.

Many association staff are overwhelmed and underpaid when compared to the corporate world, and this condition may contribute to a "brain drain" and a lack of nimbleness because of staff turnover. The recent economic climate notwithstanding, there have been increasing pressures on association staffs to do more with less, and associations have notoriously not been comfortable investing in their future through the development of staff. Higher-paying corporate positions have lured some of the best staff away from the not-for-profit world, and as member expectations have risen, staffs have been overwhelmed and less equipped to meet demands.

Almost all associations wonder if they can afford to be nimble. Most express a commitment to managing their program portfolios and business models in ways that enhance nimbleness. Yet few associations actually execute strategy in this fashion, not through a lack of willingness as much as a lack of understanding. However, in associations we studied there was often a lack of willingness to *develop* understanding. There is also a lack of commitment by associations to become financially secure, to identify multiple sources of revenue, and to understand how to manage the risk of spending more to make more. Perhaps many wonder whether they will ever be in a financial position to be "nimble" (i.e., have sufficient assets in dollars, staff, volunteers, culture, members, etc.).

Associations continue to face increasing competition for programs and services through electronic providers. The dot-com boom has gone bust. Gone are the for-profit organizations that sprang up overnight, seeking to compete with associations to be the one-stop source of knowledge and insight for a particular profession or industry. Those who predicted the demise of associations and the critical role they play in being a source of unbiased information and insight on the industry, profession, or cause-related area they serve were wrong. Although the decision-making processes of not-for-profit organizations may not be as nimble as those in the entrepreneurial world of the dot-com boom, associations were able to survive as sources of information and insight, largely on the strength of internal community and their ability to deliver relevant, insightful information. But despite surviving this challenge, there are still many other sources for the information, education, advocacy, and networking services that associations have traditionally embraced as their primary business lines, and they will need to become even more nimble in product development and service delivery.

Technology is evolving faster than most associations can adapt. Pressures not only from the corporate world but also from technologically savvy members have pushed many associations to adapt the wrong technology at the wrong time. Most associations are typically several years behind the for-profit world in terms of the use of technology, both in external product and internal support applications. In many cases, well-meaning but misguided boards pressure their associations to adapt new technologies in a haphazard way. In order to make the best use of technology, an association must have an integrated strategy that allows it to build base capabilities and then use them in multiple product, service, and support areas. It must also ensure that technology is being deployed in support of activities that deliver value to members rather than for technology's own sake. In an attempt to be nimble and member responsive, many associations end up with multiple systems, multiple platforms of incompatible technology. Add to this mix the fact that many associations create technology committees whose perceived charters in many cases overlap those of staff (i.e. making decisions about technology in support of the organization's operations rather than in terms of how technology is used in the profession or industry), and associations are left with islands of incompatible technology. Technology will continue to evolve faster in the for-profit world, but associations that exhibit the will to govern well will invest in technology in a nimble manner—with appropriate timing, focus on supporting the delivery of outcomes to members, and integration with the association's overall strategy.

Question 4

What are the ethical implications of nimbleness in governance models and practices emerging as choices for the 21st century?
Values will be more important. If there is disagreement on facts but agreement on values, an association can still be nimble. Core values are essential to attracting diverse people. If members feel they are accepted on the basis of their values and not just on their diversity, they will feel more integrated. Hence, associations need to share their values more explicitly.

Decision-making bodies will need to be groups of smart people, committed to making good decisions on behalf of the organization as a whole, but comprising a variety of perspectives and perceived by the membership as highly ethical individuals. Unfortunately, even if an association is able to achieve a truly representative body, there is no assurance it will act in the best interest of the greater whole. There are tradeoffs to being nimble, since not everyone can be involved in everything. Associations will need to ensure adequate representation in decision making—broad enough to encompass the majority of member views. But they will also need to be nimble in decision making so they can deliver value to the greatest possible percentage of the membership and maintain relevance among that population. Everyone may want to be involved, but not everyone can contribute to final decisions. A knowledge-based governance strategy will be imperative to ensure that dialogue occurs among the widest possible population of the membership. A process of thoughtful, knowledge-based deliberation yields confidence in decision-making processes, even for those who will not be directly involved.

If ethical decisions equate with fair decisions, then the definition of what is "ethical" will evolve. As associations become more nimble, broad definitions of "ethical" will change. It may become more acceptable for certain groups of people to be left out of decisions but not be excluded from accessing their benefits or disenfranchised in other ways. In many associations, it may even be possible for those in charge to make fair decisions without the direct involvement of the group most affected.

Chapter 14

What Change Strategies Will Promote Nimbleness in Governance?

Change Strategies Regarding Direction, Values, Focus, and Boundaries

Direction

A common and universally agreed-upon understanding of an association's direction is critical for nimbleness. The long-range goals of an organization must be highly attractive, open, and inviting of enfranchisement, as opposed to goals an organization defines as specific and discrete activities in a particular area. When a goal directly articulates member value, it describes a condition or attribute that members prefer. Associations who exhibit the will to govern well ensure that the strategic plans of their organizations are focused on delivering external value and benefit to members, with a compelling vision and a clear path to achieving the vision. Strategic direction is communicated in many ways at many levels so that all who are part of the organization know where it is going and, when there is agreement on direction, have the ability to act more nimbly to get there.

Values

Core values will become essential to achieving nimbleness. If there is disagreement about the content or specifics of a particular decision or situation without an agreement on core values, there will often be more frequent conflict. A conflict over what to do can result either from (a) disagreement over facts or (b) absence of congruence of values. If the conflict over what to do results from disagreement over facts, leadership can require the collection of information that is sufficiently objective and defensible to members. If, however, the conflict comes from the absence of congruence of values, then the intervention available to leadership is to reference the declared core values of the group and ascertain which of the proposed choices is most consistent with those values. If an association does not have explicit core values, leadership cannot use them as a tiebreaker in controversial and complex issues, nor can the thought and work units of the organization use them as an *a priori* guidance system for avoiding recommendations that may cause conflict.

Focus

To be nimble in the 21st century, associations must have clear focus. The issue of focus is still a huge challenge for most associations. Focus is a critical and difficult element in managing risk. Indeed, the greatest risk an association takes is in its decisions about what it will do and not do, whom it will serve and not serve, and how it will serve or not serve. If those fundamental judgments of strategy are wrong, little else will matter.

A knowledge-based governance strategy allows the selection of strategy on key issues in a knowledge-based manner and with a reasonable degree of confidence. It also has a built-in mechanism that constantly assesses the efficacy of a decision so the organization can alter or abandon it if the risk or action taken on it appears to have been improper. The most risk-averse form of governance includes boards whose decision processes are so lacking in knowledge that they have no confidence in their ability to identify and manage risk. The absence of a process to assess and navigate risk is the source of risk aversion. The antidote for risk aversion is the presence of process and tools to assess and navigate risk. There is a critical relationship between nimbleness and relevance. The riskier the environment, the more nimble the association will have to be. The more nimble the association is, the more frequent will be its need to consider risks. If an association is serving an industry, profession, or cause whose stakeholders are operating in an environment characterized by rapid and dramatic change, or if the world of the association's constituents is changing rapidly and the association wishes to remain indispensably relevant to them in that world, the association must have mechanisms in place to change at a pace at least consistent with the pace of change in their world.

One future critical competency for associations may lie in this issue of focus. Having and sustaining focus will require that associations develop the discipline of strategy. Strategy is an organized response to a particular set of conditions. It is not the act of doing everything on a particular issue or even doing some things quickly. Nimble associations whose leaders develop the discipline of strategy choose the path that creates the greatest value for the member; understanding that the association can only go as far as its resources and focus permit. Associations cannot be everything to everybody, but they must often be different things to different people and different groups of people. Associations will need to assess new opportunities in light of the parameters of a selected strategy or path in order to remain focused.

Boundaries of Service Niche and Strategic Principles

Nimbleness will require governance to articulate a unique service niche and then direct the organization to take advantage only of opportunities that fit that niche. Associations must identify what it is that they are better positioned to provide to members than any other enterprise—what essential needs they meet. This will require a core competency for associations in market and marketing research. They may obtain this competency through internal or outsourced resources, but it must be continuous and deep to provide the information governance needs to govern well.

Strategic principles will help an association assess whether an opportunity fits within a defined service niche and whether the association has the tools to fulfill that opportunity effectively. In many associations, as governance becomes more and more comfortable delegating responsibility for the development and execution of strategy to staff, there is an increasing need for a set of boundary rules, which articulate the board's strategic intent without proscribing, and which provide focus for staff and volunteer work groups by defining the types of opportunities governance would like to see the association pursue or avoid.

In nimble associations, staff can make decisions at an operational level without direct volunteer involvement. Nimble associations need a set of boundaries, based on values. Strategic principles can provide these as they allow for nimbleness and free staff from having constantly to ask for permission. Nimble governance requires constant flexibility to readjust boundaries as conditions change for an association, its members, their marketplace, and the work it must do to deliver value and benefit.

Part of an association's knowledge base includes capacity and strategic position. Capacity refers to what the association has the resources, knowledge, time, and expertise to do. Strategic position refers to the external view of the marketplace in which members have their needs met, as well as the extent to which an association is well positioned to meet those needs.

An association whose governance exhibits the will to govern well builds on its knowledge of which opportunities to capitalize on and which to ignore. Guidance in these decisions comes from strategic principles that help an association determine whether an opportunity fits with its defined service niche. Strategic principles help achieve clarity of focus and nimbleness in actions, in congruence with an association's core values and envisioned future. A strategic principle is a concrete statement, often grounded in the association's core values, that gives guidance about direction and provides parameters for action. It is a template that helps an organization make tradeoffs—decide which opportunities to pursue and which to reject. A strategic principle helps an organization achieve simplicity and focus.

Associations that exhibit the will to govern well will establish strategic principles *before* an opportunity arises. They are an integral part of both the long-term process for planning strategically and of an annual review of the strategic plan and a setting of priorities. They are not a set of dictums or decrees handed down from governance to the workforce. The establishment of strategic principles takes place in a conversation entered into in a collaborative manner within the leadership partnership, with staff and governance as equal partners. Staff is often able to provide a critical knowledge base of the association's capacity and strategic position, and governance is able to balance that with its knowledge of member needs, dynamics of the industry or profession, and/or other knowledge bases to articulate strategic intent and to provide guidance through the declaration of these principles.

The associations we observed construct strategic principles through consideration of five perspectives or sets of rules:

- *Boundary rules:* These provide focus by defining boundaries for opportunities to pursue. They ask governance to consider, "What kinds of programs or services should we pursue or not pursue?"
- *Priority rules:* These help rank opportunities. They ask governance to consider, "What kinds of programs or activities should we pursue before others?"
- *Timing rules:* These relate to pacing and timing. They ask governance to consider, "How long should projects and activities take?"
- *Exit rules:* These provide guidance on when to pull out or abandon. They ask governance to consider, "Under what circumstances should we stop doing something?"
- *How-to rules:* These spell out how to execute a key process. They ask governance to consider, "What should we make sure we do or do not do when developing, executing, or delivering a program?"

Strategic principles sometimes focus on resource allocation, fiscal strategy, or rules applied to new opportunities, such as the following:

- Pursue opportunities that serve at least 75 percent of the membership.
- Pursue opportunities of interest only to all the key segments of membership.
- Pursue only those opportunities that can demonstrate a reasonable breakeven point within two to three years.
- Pursue opportunities where we already have staff competence.
- Do nothing that competes with member businesses.

Strategic principles define parameters and allow for nimbleness. When an organization clearly articulates and agrees to them, staff has no need to ask for permission. The challenge is to create principles that will not fit every opportunity. The current reality in many associations is that everything fits the strategy, so the organization can justify almost anything. Strategic principles should instead frame the development of priorities and the determination of what associations should do and not do. Other examples include the following:

- Ensure that the association is able to continue to meet the needs of members' core businesses.
- Execute strategies required to sustain critical mass needed to be a unified voice for the industry.
- Develop programs of interest to existing members that may also interest other stakeholders, and that are likely to generate revenue or demonstrate a reasonable benefit.
- Pursue opportunities that leverage staff capabilities and/or strategic partnerships wherever possible, but be ready to increase financial and human resources of the organization if necessary to get work done.
- See that the board, in partnership with staff, prioritizes new and existing opportunities and shares with the membership a rational basis for prioritization.

In associations that exhibit the will to govern well, the articulation of strategic principles that provide focus, direction, values, and boundaries ensures a significant degree of nimbleness.

Change Strategies Regarding Structure and Processes
Acting Nimbly on New Product Ideas
Associations will need to start thinking like businesses in identifying new sources of revenue and will need an organized process to take advantage of and develop new ideas. How should governance prepare an association to respond to emerging opportunities? What are the processes and what role does the governance body play in developing new products and identifying new sources of revenue? In the future, all associations will need to customize products and services to customer/member needs much more rapidly and specifically. Associations will require critical organizational processes to manage new product development (NPD) efficiently, including managing risk and measuring progress, while at the same time increasing speed to market and member/customer satisfaction. As associations struggle to adopt more businesslike practices while at the same time retaining a mission-driven focus, it is significant to note that many leading

corporations have been using NPD processes for years. An NPD process institutionalizes a market-driven philosophy in the development, design, and delivery of an organization's products and services. The process is engineered for responsiveness to what members need and value, sensitivity to the organization's strategic plan, innovation, and speed.

All too often, planning for a new product or service moves through the phases of investigation, development, and production with insufficient thought given to whether the project is ready to move ahead to each subsequent phase. An NPD process involves satisfying sets of criteria before moving into or through any phase to ensure that sufficient thought has been given to any needs, resources, or obstacles that could affect the upcoming phase. Each phase takes inputs (prescribed deliverables), considers criteria (hurdles or questions for judging the project), and yields outputs (the decision to proceed, delay, or recycle an action path). These decision points between phases serve as a check-and-balance system to ensure that the organization can correct problems before moving on to the next phase. Associations will require a structured but efficient approach to creating new products or becoming attuned to increasingly customized member needs in the future. The typical outcome of most associations' needs assessment process, until now, has been to package existing products differently. The next wave of success will belong to associations that can nimbly develop new products to meet the needs of members effectively.

The following case study describes one organization's experience in implementing an NPD. This association, a mid-sized professional society in a health care–related field, was facing competition from other associations seeking to serve its membership. The organization needed to ensure that its program portfolio remained relevant to its members' needs.

Prior to instituting an NPD, the association had no systematic process for developing new programs. It did not regularly budget for emerging program ideas and, consequently, focused too much time and attention on trying to salvage existing programs—some of which were no longer serving member needs effectively.

There was no shortage of good ideas for new programs and services, but there was also no systematic process for idea generation and screening. Some ideas came through the board, some from the association's member listservers, some from committees, and others from staff. When the association initiated development of a new program, resources were often an issue. Because there was no process for screening, the association tended to embrace the first good idea that came along, or one presented by a board member with the greatest clout. Consequently, staff resources were immediately dedicated to ideas that were not sufficiently fleshed out.

When new programs did progress through development, there was an over-reliance on volunteers, limited staff, and a culture that did not support the risk taking required to be successful in new ventures. As a result, the association experienced a hit-or-miss success rate with new products, was not able to adjust its program portfolio, and was in danger of becoming irrelevant to its members.

A staff and member task force examined generic NPDs and decided to customize one for the association's use. Four types of program development efforts now use this process: new business or product lines, new products in existing business lines, enhancements to existing products, and regular revisions for existing products. Each type of initiative has a slightly different set of milestones within a common framework.

For new programs, idea generation comes systematically from the following:

- the strategic plan and annual plan review,
- an annual strategic program assessment and review, and
- ad hoc ideas from members (e.g., via phone calls, from information on membership forms).

Criteria for idea screening includes the following:

- a brief definition of the product concept,
- an explanation of why the association should consider the program idea,
- target audience,
- needs served,
- potential life cycle, and
- potential competition.

The process progresses from idea generation to preliminary market assessment, concept analysis, design and development, testing, launch, and review and evaluation. Throughout the process, developers define, gather, and evaluate the metrics of cost, time, resources, and quality, so that at any point in the process, there is ample information about the true progress of the project. Mid-course corrections, changes in direction, or even abandonment of the program are all possible and justifiable actions. Before it implemented its NPD process, the association committed resources over a multiyear period to accomplishing a specific project. There was no way to change course if, over the development time, the need for the program changed or disappeared. The nimbleness achieved through the association's NPD process has contributed greatly to its success, allowing it to bring new products to fruition that meet member needs and ensure its relevance in the eyes of its members.

The association gained the following key insights in its development and implementation of this process:

- There is a need to forecast staff requirements accurately, including number of staff, staff time and capabilities/skills, and time for evaluating all new ideas.
- Only staff will be able to execute many parts of the program development process. While it is important to view volunteers as content experts in their industry, profession, or cause, they do not always possess the knowledge or expertise required to design and implement program ideas. In any project, there is a need to determine what staff and volunteers will be responsible for, to identify realistic expectations of volunteers' time commitment, and to have back-up plans if the original content suppliers (usually volunteers) are not able to deliver in a timely or acceptable fashion. (The association found that with a formal process in place, volunteers had a greater understanding of how their contributions fit into the overall program scheme. The member who had taken two years to write one chapter for the association's new publication now understood that he was responsible for the association's failure to meet a window of opportunity for launching the product and serving a market need.)
- When members share their input and ideas, they expect to see action resulting from their contributions. Having a clear process for evaluating new ideas helps to communicate the rationale behind decisions about members' suggestions for product ideas. Such a process is especially helpful if the association decides to revise or cancel a product that is nearing completion. Ideally, if the association cancels a product that is being developed, it should come as no surprise because of the constant flow of information.
- If it is not completely understood and implemented well, an NPD process carries a danger of making the association even less nimble, as those using the process may see it as an inflexible set of tasks to accomplish rather than as a dynamic method of managing resources, assessing risk, and measuring progress.

Managing the Program Portfolio—Strategic Program Assessment

Once governance has defined focus, values, direction, and boundaries through the articulation of strategic principles, key questions arise regarding how it should adjust its current portfolio of programs and services to reflect the identified boundaries and service niche.

Many of the associations we studied analyze their portfolio of programs and services at least every three to five years to ensure that it reflects work in support of the new strategic plan. In some associations, this analysis is part of the annual cycle of operational planning. Issues commonly explored include the following questions:

- Is this program a fit with our core business?
- How would it improve or detract from our image?
- Will the time spent on this program generate at least the same revenue and result in the same or greater member value as the association is generating now?

Associations that are viewed by themselves and others as having the will to govern well *have a rational process for deciding what to do and what not to do.* They have ceased to do "stuff" that is unimportant to the majority of members or that does not add value.

Not-for-profit organizations have not traditionally been concerned with competitive orientation. Many have been the "sole source" of products or benefits. There have been few incentives to limit programming as long as funding has been available. Therefore, associations have lacked incentive to question the status quo, to determine whether they are meeting stakeholder needs, or to examine cost-effectiveness of services.

Competitive realities are now forcing associations to change their thinking on all of these issues, to develop effective systems for analyzing their program mix, and to make rational decisions about what to do and what not to do. Questions they now ask include the following:

- Why is this service needed?
- Is this the most effective way to meet the needs of stakeholders?
- Are we the best organization to provide this service?
- Are we meeting a need that is not being met elsewhere?
- Are we spreading ourselves too thin?
- Does this program fit within our "service niche"?
- Does it build on our distinct competencies?
- Are we trying to be all things to all people?
- Can we be all things to all people?
- Should we try to work cooperatively with other organizations to provide some of our services?

(Adapted from Michael Allison's and Jude Kaye's 1997 *Strategic Planning for Nonprofit Organizations: A Practical Guide and Workbook.*)

In 1983, professor Ian MacMillan of Columbia Business School published one of the first works on this topic. His article, "Competitive Strategies for Not-for-Profit Agencies," is cited in *Strategic Planning for Nonprofit Organizations.* The article included a matrix to help organizations assess their programs within the context of decreasing funds to support the needs of clients. Tecker Consultants LLC has worked with MacMillan and has further evolved this matrix into a methodology called Strategic Program Analysis, which involves an assessment of both current and potential programs in the following three dimensions:

Program Attractiveness: Factors contributing to judgments about whether the program is attractive to the organization as a basis for current and future resource deployment.

Competitive Position: Factors contributing to judgments about whether the organization is in a strong position to support the program.

Alternative Coverage: The extent to which other organizations can or may be positioned to serve the same clients through similar programs.

Strategic Program Analysis uses the following three assumptions:

1. There are more opportunities to respond to member needs, wants, and expectations than there are resources to meet those expectations.
2. Given the need for resources, the organization generally should not directly duplicate the services of other organizations.
3. Focus is important; providing mediocre or low-quality programs in many areas is inferior to providing higher-quality programs in response to a set of focused interests.

The analysis defines a program as a product, service, or set of products and services that the association provides or delivers to a specific group of customers/clients/users/members. In using Strategic Program Analysis, associations may need to view program structure differently than they have traditionally perceived it. The organization must determine the level of specificity at which it is appropriate to assess programs. For example, education could be viewed as one program or as a group of related programs, such as management education, technical education, etc.

The decision as to how the organization will define its programs should be based on their relationship to major resource allocation decisions. How an organization will fund and staff a program and how it will be of value should figure in any decision to expand, maintain, partner, or eliminate that program. Further, there are a number of essential operational activities of the organization that are not programs—for example, membership development, financial planning.

As defined for Strategic Program Analysis, programs involve the delivery of products or services to a specific group of members or customers. It is important to distinguish programs from the mechanisms used to deliver them and to avoid defining these delivery mechanisms as the programs themselves. For example, professional continuing education is a program; its delivery mechanisms may include one-day seminars, three-day workshops, sessions at the organization's annual conference, and so forth.

In employing this tool, background material for each program to be discussed is prepared for the facilitated dialogue that follows, during which each program is assessed against a set of criteria related to the dimensions of program attractiveness, competitive position, and alternate coverage. The composite group determination suggests the appropriateness of one of a number of generic strategies, suggesting what kinds of adjustments to make to approach and delivery, what kinds of resources could and should be devoted to it in the future and what priority to assign to it in the overall program portfolio. Examples of generic strategy include the following:

- **Aggressive competition**—This strategy encourages the association to compete to maintain a powerful position in areas where the association is currently strong. These programs can play a vital role in an organization's future in that they may function as a growth base, as well as generate surplus resources for other programs.

- **Build strength or sell out**—Generally, this is a transitional strategy. Programs that fit this strategy are often, but not always, new programs or services that attempt to meet recently developed, rapidly growing needs that the association does not yet have the necessary skills in place to fulfill effectively. If the programs are truly attractive, if the association has the resources, and if it does not anticipate exit barriers, then it should rapidly deploy the necessary resources to develop needed skills. If the resources are not available, the association should identify other organizations with appropriate skills and advocate their offering the program, even aiding them in skill building if necessary. Once again, it will take strong leadership to recognize that in the long run, the stakeholders served will be better off if the association does not take the easy short-term option of continuing a program with inadequate capabilities.

- **Aggressive divestment**—Programs fitting this strategy have substantial competition. If these competitors are able to provide superior services, there is no justification for the association to offer them, no matter how attractive they may be. The decision to concede such programs is often difficult, requiring strategic vision and leadership. If there is any clear competition in the marketplace, continuation of such programs will be detrimental to the organization; these programs are consuming resources the organization could use better elsewhere.

When the association has analyzed its current portfolio, it then should align it with future strategy. In order to transition the current portfolio to one that supports the strategic plan, the organization needs to ask the following questions:

- What existing programs can support goals, objectives, and/or strategies in the strategic plan?
- In what areas will the organization need to reposition or enhance existing programs?
- Are there new programs the organization will need to develop?
- Are there entirely new business needs that will emerge and/or new business lines that the organization will need to create?
- Are there any implications for which programs the organization could eliminate?

Traditionally, in many associations, programs have become artificially attached to either a particular constituency or facet of organizational culture. Even in those cases where it is clear that (a) the program is no longer meeting the original need, (b) another source is providing a better solution to the need, or (c) the need no longer exists, associations find it difficult if not impossible to stop providing a particular program and to utilize resources in other ways that will deliver a greater member return on value. However, associations with the will to govern well make knowledge-based, rational decisions about what to do and what not to do. There will always be more ideas than resources, and there will be a critical need in the future to prioritize investments in time and capital effectively and rationally. Knowledge-based organizations use defensible tools based on rational premises in order to make real decisions about what will grow and what will go.

Balancing Market Opportunities and Member Perspectives

Members are usually an association's primary market, but they may be only one of a number of markets the association serves. A key issue that governance must guide the association in considering is how to recognize and reconcile competition, opportunities, and threats among and between various markets served (e.g., members' components, the business sector, government, academia, the media, and society).

Although associations serve a unique group of members, the sources of revenue of most organizations have diversified well beyond member dues. Even in trade associations, where the primary business line is usually a focus such as advocacy that is not revenue producing, only 32 to 45 percent of the revenues come from dues, according to ASAE. Many associations have decided to serve marketplaces beyond members with products and services that are not necessarily mission related.

Given the limited amount of time and resources available to most associations, they need to focus on those things that are most appropriate for fulfilling their purposes. If governance and the organization move too far in the direction of trying to serve other customers, they will draw their focus away from serving member needs. An example of this in one association we studied was the implementation of an insurance program that serves both members and nonmembers. Because of the enormous fiduciary responsibility needed to ensure a successful program of this type, governance in this association focuses a huge amount of time and effort on this program, which is tangential to core member needs and does not serve the organization's mission well.

Some of the associations we studied fear they may be "getting ahead of their members." Many have allowed a corporate mentality to slip into the boardroom, which has not helped. Association structures are still very traditional and risk averse, but the drive to a more "businesslike model" is causing governance in some organizations to shoulder inordinate pressure in trying to make their association into something it may never become—nor ever should.

Associations that seek to be nimble must sustain an understanding of their market and serve its needs. Governance must guide decisions about these factors. There is currently considerable focus in associations on adopting corporate strategies for enhancing market share, revenue, and customer bases. But if this focus goes too far and becomes the core of how an association views itself, the association may not only begin to treat its members as customers but to view itself as a vendor rather than a community, thereby losing its unique competitive edge. As it becomes less committed to creating opportunities for members to do things together that create value for the community, it assumes a vendor-like dependence on staff to provide something the community wants.

This dynamic has the potential to unravel the delicate DNA of associations. The point where an association is more concerned with markets than members is dangerously close to the point where there is no longer any difference between a 501(c)(3) and a for-profit vendor, especially if the not-for-profit engages with its members in the same way the vendor engages with its customers. Associations that do not recognize this dynamic are doomed to failure. When they become "just like a vendor," they will struggle unevenly in a marketplace where competitors will overwhelm them with superior capital, nimbleness in governance and decision making, and flexibility.

Another current dynamic is increased attention to accountability. Many associations have begun to use corporate-like measurement tools such as the balanced scorecard, which was introduced in the corporate world by authors Robert Kaplan and David Norton in the early 1990s. (For more information on the use of this tool, see Jim Dalton, CAE, "Strategic Score-Keeping." ASSOCIATION MANAGEMENT, June 2002 pp. 53–57.) While these are extremely valuable tools, if they are not used well, they, too, can contribute to the association viewing itself as a vendor rather than as a community. Such approaches to accountability have been constructed for businesses. They are designed to ensure that a business does what is necessary to make a profit. But tools that are legitimate for for-profit businesses require adaptation to the triple helix dynamic when associations use them; otherwise, they may do more harm than good.

As stated earlier, a key set of issues governance must help associations consider is how to recognize and reconcile competition, opportunities, and threats among and between various markets served (e.g., members' components, the business sector, government, academia, the media, and society). By using a knowledge-based governance strategy, which considers the four basic perspectives of knowledge and insight (sensitivity to member needs, dynamics of the marketplace, capacity and strategic position, and ethical implications of choices), governance can facilitate dialogue and decision making on any critical issue. To ensure nimbleness, those who will engage in the dialogue must be sufficiently educated in how the association does business to ensure that the opportunity for discussion of these issues happens on a timely basis (i.e., the association does not have to miss a market opportunity because the board only meets once a year). The process of decision making must be sufficiently transparent to members that they understand how the organization makes decisions on serving various markets and customers. And a culture of trust must support systems for measuring success and outcomes of various market endeavors to provide clarity on what will constitute success, open access to common information, and confidence in the competence of governance and its leadership partners.

Employing Knowledge-Based Decision Making
Nimble associations must have in place a knowledge-based approach. This must include a defensible decision-making process, which allows the association to move faster or slower, depending on what a situation calls for. Nimbleness allows an association to change direction quickly and to do so with universal buy-in, because the association's leaders have confidence in the process of decision making and do not need to second-guess everything.

Removing Intermediaries to Achieve More Nimble Communication
Governance will need to create mechanisms that allow direct communication with members, customers, and other stakeholders. Some associations we studied are dismantling the use of intermediaries as sources of information or insight about members' needs, wants, and preferences. An increasing number are seeking knowledge directly from those whose behavior they are trying to influence, rather than depending on committees, task forces, or advisory groups as sources of filtered information from the "customer."

Reinventing Planning Cycles
Associations will need to free themselves from traditional planning and budget cycles because they require prescience much further into the

future. The practices that many associations are now finding too convoluted and tied to the past are goal setting and budgeting. Some suggest that the board should not even approve a budget—it should merely set financial parameters for the organization. Nimbleness will require more flexible systems for assessing conditions, determining action, allocating resources, assessing progress and value delivered, and then changing course as required.

Making Sufficient Resources Available
In some cases, nimbleness does require significant resources. Some organizations dedicate a portion of the annual operating budget to work in support of emerging opportunities. A common action of successful governance in associations we studied was the establishment of a pool of unencumbered resources they could dedicate to experiment and innovation, thus allowing for nimbleness in a changing environment. Mechanisms employed included such strategies as establishing reserves sufficient to manage risk but deep enough to encourage creativity, and developing "creativity funds" to support projects that arise midyear without having to get board approval. The presence of this kind of "opportunity fund" has enabled a number of organizations to take advantage of previously unforeseen prospects for partnerships and new products. Other organizations we studied, however, believed an association did not necessarily need a special fund to be "nimble" as long as there are sufficient assets of dollars, staff, volunteers, knowledge, and insight, along with a culture of trust. These associations, which are viewed by themselves and others as having the will to govern well and which use a knowledge-based governance strategy, are able to evaluate emerging opportunities, shift resources wherever necessary, and assume a reasonable level of risk to take advantage of new opportunities.

Internalizing Core Competencies and Outsourcing
Keeping core competencies internal while outsourcing other functions can enhance nimbleness. This approach ensures that the intellectual capital and skills necessary to execute the core competencies of the organization are resident within the organization but allocates some funds for contracting with outside sources in order to access special skills and competencies as needed. Dedicating resources to this contingency enhances nimbleness, as the association is able to take advantage of emerging opportunities quickly.

Change Strategies Regarding Culture
Institutionalizing Nimbleness
Associations that exhibit the will to govern well establish a process for building nimbleness into leadership succession. This process encompasses leadership development, orientation, core values, and a commitment to training board and staff. Associations that create nimbleness will be able

to pass the baton to future leadership successfully, making good governance self-perpetuating. Associations that do not put systems in place for good leadership succession may lose nimbleness because of the nature of revolving-door leadership. In some associations, the succession of officers is not known from year to year, and when a newly appointed leader has no knowledge, context or enfranchisement in the direction set by a previous leader, the organization will be set back while a new leadership agenda takes hold. Associations that exhibit the will to govern well have effective systems for leadership succession and effective ways of gaining the broadest possible involvement and enfranchisement in the organization's direction, so that those who ascend to leadership will be invested in a long-term vision, enabling the association to transition leadership more nimbly.

Rewarding Risk Taking
Risk taking is a key component for building nimbleness within associations, and organizational culture must tolerate it within reason. Risk is the link between trust and nimbleness. In the future, governance will need to become even more tolerant of risk. However, there is still a need to ensure sufficient safety nets for staff and volunteers, so that "living at the edge" feels less risky. Associations we studied that are successful in this area have created cultures in which board and management are partners in exploring new opportunities so that no one feels "out on a limb." A culture of risk taking is critical, but to be nimble, the association must be right more often than it is wrong.

Change Strategies that Clarify Accountability and Establish Performance Standards
Systems for Measuring Performance
In any association that aspires to achieve the will to govern well, appropriate systems for measuring success are critical. An effective performance system yields improved knowledge, giving governance and staff sufficient information and insight into the progress the association is making toward its goals. Measures of success, coupled with open access to common information and clear accountability lines, build increased levels of trust within governance. When there is clarity and consensus on what will constitute success, and a consistent, credible stream of information reflecting the association's progress toward goals, there will be increased confidence in the competence of the partners—governance, staff, and the volunteer workforce.

To be nimble, an association needs measures of progress and clear lines of accountability. We have already discussed the systems and processes many associations have begun to put in place to manage and measure the quality, delivery, and effectiveness of their portfolios of new programs and services. These metrics help governance ensure that the outcomes it has committed the organization to are in fact being achieved, and that when it is necessary to change course, the association will move in appropriate directions and timeframes to achieve success.

Measures of performance are also critical to achieving nimbleness, and clear lines of accountability are essential to acting nimbly. In an effort to achieve higher levels of responsiveness, many associations have restructured staff organizations toward becoming more customer-centered. These associations have implemented teams, clusters, and circles in an attempt to replace traditional hierarchical structures. On the surface, this is positive, but in many organizations, there is no longer a clear line for decision making. In associations that reorganize into staff structures that focus on program or business areas, the lines of authority, responsibility, and accountability may blur to such an extent that accurate measures of success are almost impossible to ascertain. The following case study describes one association's experience in adjusting organizational structure to maximize resources and clarify lines of accountability.

Case Study—One Association's Experience

This health care–related organization operated in an environment that was undergoing significant change. Key external shifts that were to have significant implications for the organization's future included the following:

- The specialty served by the society was fighting to keep its niche; there was significant challenge and potential encroachment for scope of practice both from higher- and lower-level practitioners.
- Emerging sources of power in the industry (namely, health care decision makers and health care providers) did not play a significant role in the work of the society.
- The society was not well positioned to meet the needs and expectations of the next generation of members.
- The society's governance did not represent the future of the profession.

The society had historically been well positioned to address opportunities and challenges where advocacy was the path to the solution. But as the industry environment began to change significantly, it became apparent that for its continued success, the society would need to attract the best minds and the most influential players in the profession to lead and participate in its work. If it was unable to do so, the society would lose its ability to execute its core business of advocacy.

To move toward an organizational strategy supportive of its core purpose, vision, mission, and goals, the society needed to do the following:

- increase the speed with which it made important decisions;
- implement systems, structures, processes, and a culture that would

ensure that people with appropriate expertise and experience were making decisions and executing work; and
- establish clear lines of accountability for measuring progress.

Achieving these objectives required the society to do the following:

- Uncouple thinking about the role the national organization fills versus the role the state associations fill with respect to meeting individual member needs.
- Abandon the traditional political model of decision making in favor of a more knowledge-based culture of decision making.
- Uncouple the volunteer structure from the program and staff structure. Structure staffing around core businesses, and structure member committees around strategic objectives; use team-based workgroups with a mix of knowledge and experience to reduce time and dollars spent in initiatives with little or no payback for members.
- Refocus the volunteer structure on the strategic objectives of the plan, rather than on functions or program areas of the organization.
- Focus the organization's valuable volunteer resources on essentials, and decrease volunteer time in areas where staff or outside experts can better serve the members' interests.
- Uncouple the membership structure from the governance structure and the staff structure from the volunteer structure, and eliminate member committees that parallel each of the major staff functions.

The previous organizational structure consisted of six individual centers established to create coordination among various parts of the society. Unfortunately, the original implementation of this concept included minimal changes in work processes, resulting in fragmentation of the society's organizational structure. As a result, each center was operating almost as a mini-association, with a shadow board of directors, committee structure, and staff liaisons. Some of the centers had similar, if not overlapping, functions, thus creating duplication of effort and poor use of resources. The structure also did not provide for a clear link of the society's strategic priorities to committee and workforce objectives, systems, or accountabilities.

To remedy this situation, the society implemented a new organizational structure that uncoupled the staff structure from the volunteer structure so that one no longer paralleled the other. It consolidated the six centers into three, more focused entities:

- Advocacy Center—This included government relations, public relations, professional relations, and industry relations (including managed care initiatives).

- Standards and Research Center—This included clinical practice standards, clinical guidelines, quality assessment, industry demographics, and trends.
- Delivery Systems Center—This included coordination of services to the society's state organizations and special-interest sections, conferences and meetings, publications and communication, and other member services.

Each group, led by an accountable group leader, is now able to draw upon the expertise of staff, members, and external experts. This framework enables the society to execute the work set forth in its strategic plan more effectively and to focus lines of accountability and performance. Strategies defined in the strategic plan are now assigned to the right work group and executed through the appropriate functions and processes of the society. The society monitors progress through a comprehensive management accountability process.

A Management Accountability Process

One change strategy adopted by associations with the will to govern well is the establishment of a comprehensive performance management process, with metrics clearly linked to the strategic plan and its outcomes.

In many associations, traditional performance appraisal has become almost counterproductive. The process is difficult to execute effectively, and even when an association does so, it is often counterproductive in terms of motivating people. The average staff person never seems to have sufficient feedback to know how he or she contributes to the organization's achieving its mission and vision. With the decentralized, nonhierarchical team structures many associations adopt, this connection is even more difficult to make.

A management accountability process enables associations to establish sound and practical performance appraisal, link compensation to decisions about performance effectiveness, and connect evaluation and recognition of performance to achievement of organizational objectives. A successful management accountability system merges the association's planning process with its appraisal of professional performance. If designed properly and implemented seriously, it provides a structure for purposeful and continuous attention to effectiveness. The organization can evaluate performance in a framework that promotes successful management and balanced attention to achievement of mission, efficient operations, and successful personnel. In associations that exhibit the will to govern well, it serves as a critical link between knowledge, trust, and nimbleness—providing *knowledge* of performance against the strategic plan as well as against day-to-day responsibilities, promoting *trust* because it provides clear measures of accountability, and facilitating *nimbleness* because it gives governance the tools it needs to assess progress and determine whether and when a change in direction is necessary.

A management accountability process can be an especially valuable tool in associations that have instituted nontraditional, nonhierarchical staff structures. Establishing clear lines of accountability in terms of outcomes minimizes confusion and accomplishes work toward those outcomes more nimbly. In itself, a management accountability process provides clarity and consensus on how the organization will measure success.

An effective management accountability process demonstrates a number of important characteristics, including the following:

Collaborative Decision Making—A management accountability process involves collaborative decision making that results in shared accountability between governance and management. It allows for identification of critical objectives through data collection, analysis, and discussion. Everyone owns and understands decisions about what needs to be accomplished. The person responsible systematically develops plans for achieving identified objectives. The process builds collaboration into decision-making procedures.

Merging Planning and Evaluation—Management accountability processes merge planning and evaluation activities. Part of the planning process is to determine the standards to be used for measuring accomplishment of objectives. Developing standards helps to clarify the objectives and test the feasibility of plans proposed to achieve the objectives. The organization can use the standards, suggested by the staff responsible, to judge whether it has implemented plans successfully *and* whether the implemented plans have achieved their purpose.

An Early Warning System—Because planning and evaluation activities are integrated, a management accountability process has a built-in "early warning system." Formative evaluation lets planners, doers, and evaluators monitor whether plans are leading toward achieving stated objectives; it allows decision makers to correct a plan during its use rather than waiting for it to fail. A management accountability process has an inherent bias toward success because it promotes continual adjustment of activities to improve the probability of achieving desired outcomes.

Coordinated Activities across Organizational Units—A management accountability process promotes coordination of activities among different units, which is especially critical in a team-based staff structure. Because planning and decision making are collaborative in nature, and because participants produce written statements of objectives, measures, and plans, each organizational unit understands what the other units are doing and why.

A Clear and Common Understanding—By coordinating activities among the association's units, a management accountability process results in a clear and common understanding of "where we're going," and "how we'll get there." This promotes understanding of individual roles and commitment to the association's central objectives and contributes to greater levels of trust and nimbleness.

Preventing Surprises with Formative Evaluation—Because the management accountability process is formative in nature, adjustments to action plans increase the probability that objectives will be achieved. If an objective is achieved partially or not at all, those involved in the planning, implementation, and formative monitoring of progress will know it far ahead of the final evaluation. This allows associations to be nimble and make "mid-course adjustments" in especially complicated or risk-intensive program initiatives. In formative evaluation, the responsible staff member and superior know when an objective isn't being achieved, and actions are probably underway already to respond.

An Evaluation Record—A management accountability approach to integrated planning and evaluation produces a clear and defensible record of association and individual performance that is a critical tool for governance to use in evaluating progress. By linking management accountability to performance compensation, associations can establish both monetary and nonmonetary reward systems for effective performance. A management accountability process also contributes to sound personnel decisions about selection, assignment, promotion, and retention.

Effective management accountability processes require commitment, clarity, and competence. Governance must be accountable for ensuring that the management accountability process fulfills its purpose. That requires money, energy, and time. In associations with the will to govern well, governance supports this effort visibly and encourages the chief staff executive to ensure that all staff are involved and supportive.

Boards have a special role in management accountability processes. The board should participate actively in the association-wide planning and appraisal components. The nature of board interaction with the chief staff executive in developing and implementing a management accountability process at the organizational level serves as a model of the values and behaviors other staff members should emulate. The board interacts with the chief staff executive in developing objectives, indicators of achievement, and action plans. The chief staff executive and the staff management team replicate this interaction, as do the staff-management team members and their staffs. The board must support the effort and demonstrate its commitment to sharing accountability with staff. Staff often judges the real importance of efforts based on how much time and money the "boss" and the "board" spend on them.

A management accountability program also enables the board to merge organizational planning with its performance appraisal of the chief staff executive. It accomplishes this through performance evaluation policies and procedures that evaluate the chief staff executive's performance on the basis of the following criteria:

- progress toward predetermined objectives as measured by predetermined indicators of achievement;
- demonstration of position skills, responsibilities, and/or competencies as measured by criteria and competency descriptors; and
- the board's evaluation of its own effectiveness and the extent to which its performance affected the ability of the chief staff executive to accomplish designated objectives and responsibilities.

Performance appraisals tend to be a reflection of assumptions about the chief staff executive's role. If the process, instrument, and content are those one would use with an administrator, the organization tends to treat the chief staff executive as an administrator. If they are those one would use with a manager, the organization tends to treat the chief staff executive as a manager. If they are those one would use with a senior-level executive, the organization tends to treat the chief staff executive as a senior-level executive.

Appraisal systems can either reinforce stereotypes about the chief staff executive as hired hand or can promote understanding about the contemporary role of the chief staff executive as a valued partner. In successful associations, board officers and the chief staff executive will discuss role expectations and design a performance appraisal process, instrument, and content accordingly.

A considered discussion of role is often far more valuable to the chief staff executive and the organization than merely marking a checklist of responsibilities, functions, or traits. Executive evaluation systems are not easily transferable from one context to another. The subtleties of cultural expectations that distinguish the worlds of trade, professional, and philanthropic organizations from one another are not always transparent in prepackaged systems built on an unannounced set of assumptions about the context in which they will be used.

In associations that exhibit the will to govern well, there is no substitute for ongoing, honest, and informed conversation about progress toward strategic objectives, fulfillment of job responsibilities, and demonstration of professional competencies. Reducing assessment of a modern association executive's contribution to a traditional performance appraisal checklist may be a step in the wrong direction.

One final component of performance management in associations that exhibit the will to govern well is that board self-evaluation demonstrates both symbolically and tangibly governance's commitment to performance appraisal as a constructive mechanism for promoting continuous improvement. The board's willingness and demeanor in evaluating itself will say more to association staff about the integrity of evaluation and compensation policies than any spoken or written declarations.

Some associations employ a strategy wherein board self-evaluation is the final event in the association's annual summative evaluation. Because planning and evaluation are cyclical, board self-evaluation can serve simultaneously as the first and last event in the planning/evaluation cycle. This activity provides an opportunity for the board and chief staff executive to begin discussions about problems, issues, and needs that will serve as the basis for recommended critical objectives for the next year. Planning and evaluation activities merge in fact, not just in theory.

The process of defining and measuring accountability is a critical change strategy that promotes knowledge, trust, and nimbleness in associations that exhibit the will to govern well.

Part 5
Evolving Governance:
Strategies for Change

Chapter 15
The Relationship of Process, Behavior, and Culture

Thus far, this book has established an imperative for associations that want to evolve in terms of how they think about, organize, and execute governance systems, structures, and processes. It has highlighted the roles of knowledge, trust, and nimbleness in creating more effective governance systems.

The most effective overall change strategy an organization can use to improve governance is to change the process; when the process changes, behavior changes, and when behavior changes, the culture changes. Years of working with associations in many different industries, professions, and cause areas are the basis for the observations we offer here.

The following case study illustrates the relationships between culture, process, and behavior, and provides compelling evidence for the critical linkages and relationships among these three areas. Looking at a relevant situation and "reverse engineering" it will help illustrate the efficacy of this change strategy.

This case study involves two organizations that served the same human services–related profession and that had virtually identical membership demography, size, and assets. The two organizations sought to unify, merge, or consolidate. Members and staff leadership of both organizations unanimously agreed on assumptions about the future of their profession as well as on the core purposes of any organization that would serve the profession. Members and staff leadership of both organizations also unanimously agreed on the core values guiding the behavior of any organization that would successfully serve that profession, as well as on what conditions or attributes, once achieved, would improve their world.

Finally, members and staff leadership of both organizations unanimously agreed that they would serve their profession better by pooling available resources and speaking for it with one voice. The primary obstruction to unification was a significant and definable difference in the cultures of the two organizations, which we will refer to as Group A and Group B.

Group A's primary mission was advocacy, which requires the ability to respond rapidly to a diverse set of needs. Group B's primary mission was to provide practitioners with education and the practical application of relevant and meaningful information. Both groups were engaged in each of these areas.

The value discipline for Group A was eminent influence, while for B it was customer intimacy. In the culture of B, community was important; decisions evolved from openness and the constant exchange of information. Group A desired tangible results, which meant its culture valued the achievement of definable outcomes. Group A was willing to sacrifice some elements of community to get results quickly, while group B was willing to sacrifice efficiencies to sustain a deeper sense of community. To provide customer intimacy, Group B had to maintain community. To sustain a reputation for eminent influence, Group A had to achieve results rapidly.

Group A's culture prided itself on the shortness of its decision cycles and the degree to which it empowered its staff to make decisions consistent with desirable outcomes for members without having to ask permission. Group B's culture prided itself on ongoing conversation among members and staff leadership, from which emerged judgments about who should do what.

Group A's culture took pride in staff getting work done successfully. Group B's culture took pride in sustaining an appropriate and sufficient emotional attachment with members.

The process. Group A employed Policy Governance, John Carver's system of board process. It articulated desired outcomes in the "ends" policies but placed significant limitations on the "means" by which work would be accomplished. Group A had recently implemented a strategic planning process to create opportunities for board and staff to discuss outcomes and strategy, regardless of how they would then distribute responsibility.

Group B used a knowledge-based governance strategy. It did not have a formal process but was committed to creating the opportunity for all interested persons in the organization to engage in formal and informal conversation—face-to-face and virtual. It used those conversations as a source of possible and preferred alternatives on any given issue.

Group A designed its process to make decisions quickly and sustain pre-event clarity on who had what authority. Group B designed its system to ensure comfort with and commitment to all the decisions that resulted and paid attention to the degree of common agreement about what the organization should do.

Distinguishing cultural characteristics of the two groups manifested themselves in governance's expectations about the behavior of the chief staff executive as well as about how he or she should execute the role. Group A congratulated its executive for being an aggressive bulldog, an assertive leader, and an activist. Group B congratulated its executive for being a source of stability, a convener, and a facilitator. In other words, the processes each organization had in place both caused and commended certain behavior from the chief staff executive. Policy governance caused and commended the activist behavior of Group A's executive; collaborative decision making caused and commended the facilitative behavior of Group B's executive.

What each group has done in the past and how it has done it—in terms of culture, behavior, and process—has matched its primary mission. However, these two groups now understand that if they are going to create a new organization, they will need to develop new processes, behaviors, and cultures, because neither of the existing frameworks is appropriate for a newly combined mission or comfortable for the membership of the existing organizations. Through unification, the two groups hope to build a stronger organization by combining resources to support both missions. But neither of them has a culture that will be as well matched to an organization executing both missions as each of them currently has with their respective missions.

Chapter 16
What It Will Look Like: A Vision for the Future

Our study indicates that there is no "one right model" or best answer for governance that will serve all organizations. Instead, there are multiple approaches and lessons to be learned from studying the experiences of others. Different organizations have arrived at their own solutions, but the composite picture suggests that a new knowledge-based approach—one that will reflect, nurture, encourage, and demonstrate the will to govern well—can help virtually any organization in developing its own unique governance strategy. This philosophy suggests the will to

- build a nimble infrastructure that enables an association to seize opportunities for creating value more quickly, while becoming more rational and open and less political in structures and procedures;
- direct the board to focus its time on direction and policy setting, operational oversight, and strategic thinking;
- attract those with the skills and expertise needed for organizational leadership;
- create a collaborative partnership between leadership and staff; and
- employ a knowledge-based form of strategic governance—a mechanism for consultative leadership that recognizes strategy as the necessary and appropriate link between the board's role in governance and the staff's role in management and implementation.

Case Study—One Association's Experience
The following case study is a compendium of our findings from associations that have successfully embraced the elements of knowledge, trust, and nimbleness in order to promote a culture supporting the will to govern well. This

study does not represent a profile to be copied. Rather, it demonstrates key elements emerging from a wide span of associations that are documenting their conversations about their future and what they want their governance systems to be. It includes the processes used to build support, describing what one organization's governance did to transform a culture of politics and organizational inefficiency to one focused on knowledge, trust, and nimbleness.

This professional association was among the oldest in its industry. It had once had a reputation as the top industry group, but in recent years, ineffectiveness, inefficiency, and infighting had eroded its influence and, some maintained, its integrity. Its organizational structure had been deemed "dysfunctional," and its governance process was described as "isolated, bureaucratic, and nonresponsive" to the challenges facing the organization.

Before the organization made a decision to transform itself, its burdens included divisive member segments competing for time, resources, and power; weak staff leadership; aging programs and processes; and the need to balance the preservation of 100-year-old-plus traditions with a new vision for the future.

New leadership on the association's board took on the challenge of remaking the association. At the beginning of the new president's two-year term, the board adopted an education process about best practices in association management and leadership that allowed governance and senior staff to learn together. The board embraced new practices in its own process and championed an organization-wide change effort. It established a task force to define the association's future, with broad representation from all constituencies both within the organization and from external organizations serving other segments of the profession. This task force, supported by the board and senior staff, engaged in a year of intensive work designing a new strategic plan and organizational model for the association. At the same time, the board became actively engaged in the work of the task force and accepted the challenge of evolving its own processes with a knowledge-based governance strategy. The board's actions modeled the culture, processes, and behaviors the task force hoped to engender in the rest of the organization.

In its organizational design work, the task force articulated the following design criteria for the new organization:

Represents a model for the future.

- Builds trust.
- Builds what is needed, rather than relying on what is.
- Is visionary.
- Is action-oriented, especially in terms of how to accomplish things.
- Builds what unifies rather than what separates.

- Is fluid and flexible.
- Fosters open communication.
- Is alert to all opportunities for collaboration, being inclusive, not exclusive.
- Assesses and responds to competitors, anticipating and making adjustments based on environmental factors.
- Is simple, elegant, and easily communicated.

Enjoys support from all segments and major elements of the industry and profession.

- Integrates efforts toward a common agenda.
- Fosters interdependence while preserving autonomy.
- Shares resources.
- Encourages collaboration and economy of effort across the profession.
- Reflects both the synergy and the differences within the profession.

Employs an inclusive stakeholder structure.

- Connects to both the individual and the organizational member, supporting multiple membership options/entry points based on how and where people want to connect with the association, and encouraging individual members to choose the access point—at the state, national, or local level—most relevant to their needs.
- Embraces the profession's entire workforce, and represents the continuum of a member's career.
- Seeks to minimize structural barriers between and among stakeholders and affiliated organizations.
- Enhances the voice and autonomy of special interests/related entities and identifies their respective accountability.
- Attracts new populations to active involvement, including international members, consumers/industries, communities, and other industry players.
- Facilitates collaborative relationships between and among state and national members and national and individual members.

Invests in the leadership development of its membership (i.e., mentors future leaders).

- Attracts new faces in leadership positions.
- Provides a variety of leadership opportunities across the organization, wherein action teams and ad hoc task forces provide members with opportunities to demonstrate leadership skills and encourage involvement.

- Identifies leadership development, education, and mentoring as business lines at the national level.

Provides a structure aligned with the association's strategic long-range plan. Is efficient, seeking to maximize use of resources.

- Ensures that all members will see value and benefit in participation and return on their investment.
- Sets priorities and goals, focusing on critical issues and key opportunities and allocating resources to achieve goals.
- Ensures financial viability, responsibility, and accountability.
- Creates opportunity for new revenue streams.

Includes a new governance structure.

- Delineates roles and responsibilities for all governing bodies, as well as for organizational members.
- Supports autonomy, accountability, and responsibility in terms of decision making and governance.
- Encourages decision making that is nimble, flexible, inclusive, and timely.
- Facilitates participation, access, and input of all stakeholders.
- Employs knowledge-based decision making, ensuring availability of relevant information, experience, and expertise needed to make quality decisions.
- Embraces a knowledge-based governance strategy—a process that includes collaborative dialogue on important issues affecting the profession.
- Acknowledges differences of opinion and explores underlying assumptions in order to build understanding and increase the likelihood of consensus.
- Provides an opportunity for all members to feel a sense of direct involvement.
- Supports the process of addressing key issues, reaching consensus, and establishing policy.
- Sets priorities and goals by focusing on critical issues and key opportunities.

Supports the association's role as convener of a knowledge community.

- Serves as a clearinghouse for information, including collection, interpretation, and dissemination of information for members and others.
- Ensures easy access to information once a source has developed it.
- Supports real-time, two-way communication and rapid dissemination of information.

- Supports members' sense of connection to the organization by recognizing that the organization serves as a national information coordinator.
- Promotes enhanced communication and facilitates advocacy at the national level.
- Allows for broad input.

Respects the association's workforce.

- Empowers all participants.
- Uses staff and volunteers' time and talents effectively.
- Shows appreciation and recognition of volunteer efforts.
- Recognizes, respects, and accesses the expertise and autonomy of members, and turns over work relating to specialties to the appropriate industry group.

Develops an organizational culture characterized by trust.

- Supports open and honest communication and information sharing.
- Is more responsive to environmental changes, increasing potential sources of information and expertise from a broader member base.
- Uses easily articulated values as guides.
- Supports dialogue among members as equals, viewing conflict as healthy, agreeing to disagree, and respecting differences and diversity.
- Has a commitment to outcomes, following through to implementation.
- Builds trust and respects differences.
- Brings organizational members together to work on larger issues, even though they may not always agree on more specific areas.
- Focuses on outcomes because of the nature of member connections.
- Has a small governance body, whose size contributes to enhanced responsiveness.

During the year, the board engaged in a knowledge-based governance dialogue about the change process itself, considering the question, "How can we conduct association business differently during the transition to a more futuristic organization?" The motion crafted as a result of this dialogue was as follows:

Motion: Doing Our Business Differently
Background

- WHEREAS, this is a transition year for implementation of the work of redesigning the organization; and
- WHEREAS, there is a need to communicate where we are going in the next few years and what is driving change; and
- WHEREAS, historically, the association has adopted organizational changes but has not fully implemented them; and

- WHEREAS, we need an implementation process that we define and commit ourselves to; and
- WHEREAS, we perceive timelines for organizational changes to be unacceptably long; and
- WHEREAS, we need more information about different organizational and business models (e.g., alliance relationships and/or nonmember-directed models); and

Action
THEREFORE, BE IT RESOLVED THAT
The board of directors will facilitate ongoing dialogue about

- Communication of how we are conducting business differently (toward a knowledge-based approach).
- Communication of the desired outcome, process, and timeline needed to get there.
- Open dialogue will be promoted throughout this transition year relative to this work.

The house of delegates will allocate a portion of its meeting time this year for strategic dialogue; meetings of other related entities throughout this transition year will model knowledge-based strategic governance; and we will find means of sharing the strategy with other stakeholders.

Guiding Principles
This work must take into consideration the following concerns/issues:

- Commit to the implementation plan. (No stop/start; no modification.)
- Make sure that we base our choices of organizational models on as broad an information database of potential choices as possible; this approach may include benchmarking other organizations.
- Develop tools to help the states prepare their delegates in advance for how to participate better when they get to the house of delegates.

Throughout the process, governance demonstrated the will to govern well in its support for the process of change, as well as in its willingness to adjust its own processes and to model new behavior publicly. It exercised influential leadership in championing the process, and it used an approach to leading this change effort that relied on influence rather than on power. It focused both on what governance needed to do to exercise leadership in this effort and on how it needed to execute that leadership.

Chapter 17
Knowledge-Based Governance: A Strategy for Change

Among the strategies employed by associations that exhibit the will to govern well is one that is paradoxically both simple and complex: refocus the attention of the board on those things that matter to the members or the greater community served—making time at the board table to talk about strategic issues critical to the future of the organization. The problem is that it requires refocusing not only on how the board functions, but also on what it pays attention to, who participates in the conversations, and how it handles other things that previously dominated the time of board meetings. It means, essentially, rethinking roles, an approach that also means rethinking the kinds of people the association wants to attract to leadership, the types of skills and competencies they must possess, and their ability to deal in a far more ambiguous environment than the traditional world of parliamentary procedure.

Having examined the elements of knowledge, trust, and nimbleness and how they contribute to creating a culture supporting the will to govern well, our discussion will now explore the application of these three elements in the implementation of a knowledge-based governance strategy—a mechanism for focusing governance on appropriate things, in the appropriate way for a given organization.

When an association moves toward a knowledge-based governance strategy, when it creates opportunities for members or stakeholders to participate in conversations relating to various issues before the board, members' views of the organization's efficacy undergo a significant change—because they sense that the organization is directing attention to things that matter to them.

In a knowledge-based governance strategy, the board executes an organizational role for which it is well positioned. There are certain decisions that only governance is legitimately capable of addressing. In some organizations, especially trade associations, the board may view staff as so effective that on many issues, governance almost questions whether its input is necessary. But because there are some judgments that only boards can make, chief staff executives need to encourage governance to provide meaningful input on critical issues. One way to do this is for the board to engage in strategic dialogue on a particular issue. Situations where the board is so satisfied with the competency of staff and with what the organization is doing can almost create a ticking time bomb— without a sense that they are playing a meaningful role, board members will withdraw from participation. Hence, chief staff executives need to bring issues and problems to the board to keep it active and to sustain trust. If they fail to keep the board actively engaged, trust decreases. If the association is executing well in current-day programming, the board should move out of its operational oversight role and start focusing on how to sustain the organization into the future. It must constantly seek to answer the question, "What's next?"

What Is a Knowledge-Based Governance Strategy Like?

The traditional governance process has had the following six steps:

Step 1—Someone who has credibility with others identifies an issue he/she says is important.

Step 2—A committee, task force, or members of the staff think and talk about the issue and make a recommendation.

Step 3—The issue appears on the board's agenda.

Step 4—Board members make and second a motion to approve the recommendation.

Step 5—The board debates the issue.

Step 6—The board votes yes or no on the recommendation.

A different perspective on what is possible would involve members of a constituency group. Suppose a board member comes around to explain an important board decision that is going to create some disadvantages for a particular constituency. The board member's problem is that he or she has two competing values of equal importance. One is the value of authenticity. The second is that when a member of the board signs on, it is his or her responsibility to support decisions the board has rendered as a body politic.

The board member addresses the group: "Ladies and gentlemen, this is a very complicated decision. There were several schools of thought. One was A, which said that these were the things that would matter, and that we should worry about. Here are the advantages and disadvantages of school A. Another school of thought was B, whose idea was that such-and-such would occur; the advantages and disadvantages of B were these. Personally,

I thought B looked like a reasonable course of action to take at the time. A third school of thought was C. The advantages and disadvantages of C were these; the risks and consequences were these. The board chose C because it believed C was a superior decision for the following three reasons. Yes, I liked B, but I didn't make a big deal out of it."

What the board member did was to defend the efficacy, rationality, and credibility of the board's process in reaching the decision—expressing support for the final decision, while articulating appreciation of the fact that there were different sets of advantages and disadvantages for each decision choice and the impact of the possible choices on different groups. The board member used truth in defending the credibility of the board's decision process.

For a board member to be able to behave in this manner, two things are necessary: first, knowledge that it is permissible to explain the situation this way; and second, a board meeting that actually proceeded in the way the board member described it. How could the board member go before a constituency group and say, "The board considered these three alternatives; here were the advantages and disadvantages of each; the reason this alternative was selected was because it appeared superior for these four reasons," if that is not the way the board meeting really happened? The board members could not give that logical explanation if what actually occurred was that a committee politically composed of one stakeholder group presented the idea to the board, made and seconded a motion on it, and the board passed the motion.

This description of a board member's report of a meeting to a constituency group represents the kind of approach a board would use on a significant issue when following a knowledge-based governance strategy. Its purpose is to create an approach to decision making that produces better decisions: decisions governance can have more confidence in, that are better understood by participants and are likely to be more supported by groups not necessarily participating. This process for making decisions is an eminently more enjoyable leadership experience than the traditional, political, opinion-rich-and-information-poor approaches that some, but not all, associations have found themselves engaged in for many years.

Some boards find the idea of not using Robert's Rules of Order distasteful. They want an issue framed at the outset, and they need a motion as a focus of discussion. They want the intended action expressed right away, with a background paper to follow describing the intended action and the pros and cons of the issue. Some governance bodies find this type of structure of great value in focusing them on the discussion. Without it, they might spend hours on discussion before someone would decide on a direction to take and would make a motion.

In a knowledge-based governance strategy there is still a motion, the difference being that it is not constructed prior to the board's conversation about the issue. Rather, the motion *emerges from the dialogue* about the issue, and the board is fully invested in both the process and content. In a knowledge-based governance strategy, the dialogue about the issue is enabled by the presence of a background paper. The background paper, prepared by a group, examines what is known about the four knowledge bases, identifies possible solutions, and frames the relative advantages and disadvantage of each; it can facilitate a board's examination of a complex issue.

Another difference is that in a knowledge-based governance strategy the question to be examined, rather than a motion, becomes the source of focus. So in effective dialogue, there is still a focal point—it is the question on which the board is working. The motion that emerges from the conversation becomes a subsequent focal point.

There are a variety of ways to get to this point, but governance must be sure the judgments it makes are knowledgeable, that it has considered alternatives, that all the participants understand and broadly support the judgments, and that they represent decisions about important issues confronting the association. If those elements are in place, then whether the board dialogue results in a motion is less important than the quality of the judgments reached and the experience governance is having.

Some leaders believe they should come away from a board deliberation with full consensus, and that is the only thing they should report to the membership. But in a knowledge-based governance strategy, there is a shift in values and norms. The old paradigm valued the appearance of unanimity, so it limited disagreement to the greatest extent possible; the new paradigm recognizes that in today's world, complex issues will invite a variety of views. While one view might appear to be most propitious at the moment, governance in this new organizational approach recognizes the legitimacy of other views as well. This represents a shift in values within the culture.

In a knowledge-based governance strategy, as practiced by leading-edge associations, the person or group who placed the item on the agenda develops background information addressing each of the four knowledge-based questions for each decision point on the agenda. The board begins discussion of an agenda item not under Robert's Rules, but as a committee of the whole. During this period of dialogue, no one proposes resolutions or motions; rather, the group has discussion between board and staff in equal partnership.

When the dialogue is complete, the board reconvenes, someone introduces resolutions that have been created as a product of the dialogue, the board undertakes formal deliberation and debate on motions or resolutions, and it then takes a vote. In a two-day meeting, the board may devote the first day to dialogue on a series of items, author resolutions overnight, and on the second day, engage in deliberation and voting. An alternative approach is to alternate, conducting dialogue and deliberation on an item-by-item basis.

While there is a need to customize this approach to an association's culture and process, best practices in many associations have led us to document a series of steps, presented in the next chapter, that represent a critical path for executing knowledge-based governance strategy.

Chapter 18
A Nine-Step Process for Change

Following is a methodology for institutionalizing a knowledge-based governance strategy. It is based on our work with many associations seeking to sustain the will to govern well. Those desiring to use it should consider it as a framework, not a cookbook. Every association we know of that has begun to employ these methodologies has done so in a manner suited to its particular culture and membership. Associations choosing this path should recognize that it involves hard work over time and does not fulfill its potential overnight.

Although boards of directors are in practice the most frequent users of this approach, a number of associations have begun to apply it to encourage informed dialogue in broader governance venues, such as houses of delegates, councils of representatives, annual membership meetings, and other deliberative bodies. Bringing this philosophy to agendas that have traditionally been less than intellectually stimulating has energized more than a few houses of delegates and has helped them find a meaningful role in governance and decision making (i.e., the role of the board is to govern the association, while the role of the house is to govern the profession).

As we detail these steps, we will refer to the experiences of one particular association as a case study to illustrate each step's products. This trade association served a transportation-related industry. Advocacy was a major business line, and governance and the membership were very appreciative of the staff's efforts to advance issues related to the industry's growth. In this association, the governing body of more than 50 members met twice a year for half a day. A smaller executive committee of 20 met quarterly to exercise operational oversight.

Because the staff did such a good job and were so knowledgeable about the industry, and because they had forged a strong and effective partnership with the volunteer workforce, the board felt all it needed to do as a governance body was to approve positions and recommendations staff and volunteers would bring to it. However, some board members questioned their role and process and believed they could spend their time in a more meaningful way. Others believed the board should not meet at all or perhaps just once a year. At one meeting, the board engaged in a spirited discussion of how it conducted its work and how governance might restructure its meetings and processes to (1) make the board a more effective leadership body for the association and (2) make membership on the board a more meaningful experience for individual directors. The board agreed that it would be valuable to consider further changes to meeting format and processes that would

- focus the board's time and attention on providing *strategic leadership* for the association,
- make the board a *more proactive* and *less reactive* body,
- *decrease* the amount of time the board spent receiving reports on activities and objectives the organization had already accomplished, and
- promote the *active participation* of all directors in board meetings and discussions.

The board determined that one way to do this might be to reformat the board agenda to include time for focused discussion of one or more significant strategic questions facing the association. As a result of a thoughtful and thorough analysis of its governance process, the board began to adopt a knowledge-based governance strategy.

At a recent board meeting, board and staff collaboratively addressed the following mega-issue question: *"How can our association more effectively utilize members in advocacy work?"* The following discussion of the nine steps for instituting a knowledge-based governance strategy will detail the group's process of dialogue on this issue.

Step 1. Identify the Mega-Issue Question.

In an effective process of planning and thinking strategically, there is a constant dialogue about what will need to happen next, whether it involves the next day or the next five years. In the latter case, the strategic plan and progress against three- to five-year goals reflect what the organization has already committed itself to, and there should be constant monitoring of progress against objectives and strategies. But the organization should also annually review the plan, including assumptions about the future, to determine the issues the association and its membership will need to face in the coming year, and whether those issues reflect a change in direction or the intensifying of a long-term issue.

Such discussions should yield mega-issue questions, and in any good annual strategic planning process, the board or executive committee should review, prioritize, and select those questions the board should deal with in the coming year. These questions cannot be answered with a "yes" or "no." They require illumination and begin with phrases like

- *"How can we . . . ?"*
- *"How could we . . . ?"*
- *"What should our role be in . . . ?"*
- *"What would most effectively address . . . ?"*

Additional subquestions, again adhering to the same rules, may help inform them. Some examples might be the following:

- *How can our association contribute to a long-term solution to the increasing labor shortage in our industry?*
- *How can our association more effectively utilize members in advocacy work?*
- *How can our association best support the "XYZ" segment of our industry?*
- *How can we neutralize barriers to increased client participation in our programs and services?*

Such subquestions can address the bigger question of what should happen next—this week or this month or this year. The board can use a knowledge-based governance process to develop strategy and illuminate choices regarding existing program or policy issues. An example would be staff taking a question about the association's publishing program to the board, looking for guidance in how to deal with new competition from for-profit sources.

Step 2. Prepare Background Information.

In either case, the preparation of background information is the next step. Staff, a committee, a staff/taskforce team, or some other group that represents broad perspectives about the issues can prepare this information, framing it around the four knowledge-based questions. Many associations prepare this information prior to board meetings using Web-based technology, with conference calls, e-mails, listservers, chat rooms, and so forth.

However the organization gathers the information, the associations we studied commonly executed the following tasks in preparing it:

- Test the questions with key stakeholders/constituencies (*Are these the right questions to ask?*).
- Inventory where there is information related to this question that might illuminate understanding. (*Who knows about this? What has been written? Who has this information?*)

- Draft preliminary insights using the four knowledge-based questions as a template.
  - Question 1. *What do we know about the needs, wants, and preferences of our members/prospective members/customers that is relevant to this decision?*
  - Question 2. *What do we know about the current realties and evolving dynamics of our members' marketplace, industry, profession, or issue arena that is relevant to this decision?*
  - Question 3. *What do we know about the "capacity" and "strategic position" of our organization that is relevant to this decision?*
  - Question 4. *What are the ethical implications of our choices? (Does this "smell" right? Who may be advantaged or disadvantaged?)*
- Prepare a preliminary background information document in a relatively simple, declarative format that uses bulleted insights to help inform the dialogue.
- Test again with key constituencies and/or staff (*What do you think about these insights? Do you have anything to add or challenge?*)
- Revise/redraft background insights.
- Submit package for board meeting.

Although it is preferable to prepare background information prior to a meeting, knowledge-based governance allows for brainstorming without a background paper, leading into the other phases of dialogue and deliberation. This flexibility is extremely valuable in situations where the board must consider an urgent issue that has just popped onto its radar screen. In such a case, the four knowledge-based questions serve almost as a checklist for managing risk in determining how to respond to an issue. (*"This is known, but that is not; therefore, these are the risk factors of acting at this time."*)

Case Study Example of Background Materials Prepared for the Question, "How Can Our Association More Effectively Utilize Members in Advocacy Work?"

Question 1

What do we know about members' and stakeholders' wants, needs, and preferences relative to this issue?

- Advocacy is the reason for our existence and the principal motivation for membership in our association.
- At the most basic level, members want and expect us to minimize the negative impact of government policies on their business.

- Increasingly, members also want us to implement policies that will have a positive impact on their business.
- While all members want and expect advocacy success from our association, their advocacy priorities vary, depending on such factors as industry sector, company size, and company philosophy.
- Many members belong to multiple associations and expect coordination among these organizations to achieve desired policy outcomes without duplicative effort or unnecessary expense.
- Some members are heavily involved in the association's advocacy work (with Congress, the administration, and/or the states), but many more are not. We don't know why this is so. (*Do the majority of members not want to get involved? Do they not know how? Do they not feel they've been asked?*)
- Most members have limited time to participate in association work and need to see a direct correlation between their involvement in the association's work and their companies' interests.
- Members who are not involved in our association's advocacy work today may need education and training in the advocacy process and/or more communication about our organization's priorities to feel comfortable getting involved.

Question 2

What do we know about the current realties and evolving dynamics of our members' marketplace, industry, profession, or issue arena that is relevant to this decision?

- Constituents, contributors, and supporters most effectively influence external "customers" of our association (e.g., Congress, administration officials, and state legislatures).
- Other organizations in our industry employ tools to involve members in advocacy work (e.g., legislative fly-ins, e-mail alerts, editorial board visits, local media outreach) that we do not.
- The high rates of congressional member and staff turnover require an ongoing effort to educate Congress on our association, our industry, and its policy priorities.
- We cannot approach every decision maker in the same way. The executive branch differs from the legislative branch, and congressional office styles vary considerably from member to member.
- As information and communication technology evolves, decision makers are increasingly inundated with communication from interest groups seeking their attention.

- Political campaigns are becoming increasingly expensive, requiring members of Congress to raise funds continuously. This creates an increasing demand for political action committee contributions.

Question 3

What do we know about the "capacity" and "strategic position" of our organization that is relevant to this decision?

- People perceive us as the leading voice for our industry in Washington, D.C.
- We are more visible with decision makers and have more effect and credibility than at any time in the past. Successful regulatory programs, our image campaign, and past advocacy successes have contributed to this improved perception.
- We are an association of modest size and financial resources compared with potential competitors in the public policy arena (e.g., other associations, environmental organizations, and labor unions).
- Our industry is a low-profile one of modest size and economic impact compared with many other industries competing for the attention of policy makers.
- Given the current level of member participation in the association's advocacy work, there appears to be much untapped potential and greater capacity for member involvement.
- Our members are geographically diverse; they reside in and do business in many states, congressional districts, and media markets.
- We have limited information on the extent to which our members currently have contacts with members of Congress or participate in the advocacy process independently of involvement in our association.

Question 4

What are the ethical implications of our choices? (Does this "smell" right? Who may be advantaged and disadvantaged?)

- Becoming involved in our association's advocacy work can potentially increase the value an individual member company derives from membership.
- At the same time, members speaking or acting on behalf of our association must remember that they are not simply representing their company's interest but the interest of the association/industry as a whole.
- Clear and honest communication is essential. If a member company does not support our association's position on an issue, that company

should not represent itself as speaking for our organization or its members in the public policy arena.

- Not finding ways to increase the involvement of members in the association's advocacy work decreases the effectiveness and value of our association to its members and gives them less return on their investment in our organization than they could or should get.

Step 3. Conduct Dialogue for Informing the Issue.

The next step moves from the pre-meeting into the actual meeting process, and represents the first part of a two-part dialogue process. The first phase addresses the question, *"What do we know?"* and the second addresses, *"What could we do?"* There are two conditions under which dialogue on a mega-issue can begin.

1. **If a background paper has been prepared**, the dialogue might be facilitated in the following manner.

   Let us use the information provided in the background paper as a starting point for dialogue. As you consider this information,

   - *Which points are particularly significant?*
   - *On which points are there questions or disagreement?*
   - *What else do we know? What is missing?*
   - *What do we wish we knew but do not?*

2. **If a background paper has not been prepared,** the dialogue becomes a brainstorm, which should include the board, staff, and any volunteer work groups and/or leaders present. The discussion uses as its basis the following questions:

   - *What do we think we know about this issue in each of the knowledge bases?*
   - *How do we know? What can we observe? What is the basis of our thinking?*

In a knowledge-based governance strategy, committee work sometimes occurs after board conversation about an issue, not before. Perhaps the board has an agenda item in the form of a question. There is dialogue and deliberation on the item. The board illuminates the issue using the four knowledge bases, but it discovers it does not have sufficient information to identify its choices. At that point, it might ask a committee or an ad hoc group to explore possible choices and return to the board with alternatives and an assessment of the advantages and disadvantages of each. At that subsequent meeting, the board might invite the committee chair or the entire committee to participate in the dialogue, thereby using the committee's thinking as a running start.

Another possibility would be for the board to define the choices as well as the advantages and disadvantages of each and to author a motion that says, "Here are things we want to do and how we want to do them." At that point, the board would charge a committee or build a task group to assume accountability for designing and executing whatever strategy or work might be required to achieve those desired outcomes. There is still a relationship between the workforce and the board, but in this approach, the board will almost always have a conversation about the important issues before it assigns work.

Case Study Example—*How Can Our Association More Effectively Utilize Members in Advocacy Work? What Information Do We Still Need?*

After engaging in initial dialogue, the group identified the following information gaps concerning why members didn't get involved in advocacy efforts: A major realization for the board was that the association does not have sufficient data as to why members don't get involved in advocacy efforts. Questions centered on the following:

- *Are they waiting to be invited?*
- *Do they not have the training?*
- *Are they not aware of options for involvement?*
- *Are they afraid of conflicts of interest in association positions with their own businesses or employers?*
- *Do they prefer to be involved at the local rather than at the national level?*

Step 4. Conduct Dialogue on Identifying Choices

This step involves looking at the information base as a whole and determining possible choices of action, response, or strategy. It uses discussion questions such as the following:

- *What could we do with regard to this issue?*
- *What strategies could we employ?*
- *Are there alternatives or choices among the strategies we have identified in formulating our response to this issue?*

Case Study Example—*How Can Our Association More Effectively Utilize Members in Advocacy Work? What Choices Do We Have?*

In its dialogue, the group identified the following as possible choices of action:

1. Maintain status quo—continue as we are and hope for greater involvement in the future.
2. Conduct additional member research to better understand members' needs and preferences in this area.

3. Conduct training programs this year for all members to ensure that they have the knowledge and skills to participate.
4. Extend formal invitations for involvement.
5. Build a database of members' knowledge and interests in industry issues and topics.

Step 5. Conduct Dialogue on Evaluation of Choices

This step involves discussing the relative advantages and disadvantages of each possible choice. In many associations, boards have found this step to be somewhat difficult in the beginning, as it is the place where advocacy and deliberation usually take over. When there is a choice to act or not, members in most deliberative bodies eloquently state their positions for or against an issue, and the most convincing opinions put forth in the deliberations often sway the group's ultimate decision. But this does not mean the group has necessarily considered all information and implications. By thoughtfully separating dialogue from deliberation and limiting this part of the conversation to the relative advantages and disadvantages of each of the choices, governance obtains a more balanced view of the implications of actions. Also, by focusing this part of the dialogue on information sharing and not on connecting any of the positions to one individual, much of the conflict and contentiousness that usually surrounds deliberation dissipates before it begins. The approach depersonalizes debate and focuses the group's attention on the full implications of the products of its dialogue.

Case Study Example—How Can Our Association More Effectively Utilize Members in Advocacy Work? What Are the Advantages and Disadvantages of Our Choices?

An excerpt from the group's dialogue yields the following thinking on two of the identified choices:

Choice 1—Status Quo
Advantages

- It will give us the chance to study the problem more closely and not take any premature actions based on lack of information.
- We will be able to save our resources until we make a decision, so it will be more cost-effective.
- We would avoid alienating the majority of our members—possibly losing members and revenue.

Disadvantages

- Key issues may arise that, without the support and active involvement of our full membership, will not go our way.

- We may lose strategic position and influence in the industry.
- Member apathy may spread to other areas of the association and its activities.

Choice 3—Conduct Training Programs This Year for All Members
Advantages

- We would be able to provide tools for members to get involved in advocacy in preferred ways and in a consistent fashion.
- We would be able to achieve results fairly quickly, and on issues we know our industry faces this year.
- We would avoid alienating the majority of our members—possibly losing members and revenue.

Disadvantages

- We still wouldn't know if training alone would encourage members to be actively involved.
- It would require deployment of staff and financial resources in a year where we have already made many commitments.
- We might alienate members who do not want to participate if we were to make a strong push for their involvement.

Step 6. Determine Areas of Consensus or Information Needed to Reach a Decision in the Future

If consensus on the choice emerges, what actions does this suggest for the board, the staff, or other work groups? If the need is to declare the ends that the board would like to see accomplished, the motion that articulates it says, "Here's what we want to accomplish." If the need is to detail the strategy by which the work is to be done, then the motion should be to construct or identify the work group and make it accountable for the development, implementation, and execution of that strategy. Sometimes, governance discovers it does not know enough to make a final decision. Then the motion should be to acquire the additional information governance needs in order to make a confident decision. Sometimes the most important question in this phase is, *"What is it that we wish we knew, but do not?"* There is still a motion, action still happens, and the group still moves ahead.

By this point in the dialogue, it is rare for all of the choices to still be standing. Overlaps, combinations, or outright rejections of a particular course of action usually become apparent to the deliberative group, and in many cases, consensus begins to build. At this point, the dialogue refines the list of choices, asking the following questions: *"Are there any choices that we can eliminate? Are there any choices that we can combine with others? Is there any choice on which the group can agree?"*

If consensus does not emerge, a critical question to address is, *"What additional information would we need to make a confident decision?"* This is the point where many good board dialogues break down. The group eagerly discusses an issue, but when clear consensus does not emerge, the board tables it either for another day or for the great beyond. (Should this occur, it would be at least useful to document the points of the discussion; years from now, the question may come up again, and it will be helpful to the board of the future to know how thoughtful dialogue tried to address the question.) Another negative scenario along these lines would the one where the board engages in impassioned and stimulating dialogue, but when it fails to reach closure, board members (and staff) feel frustrated—they believe the effort was wasted and that the organization is not moving forward on the issue. This situation can cause an association to risk inertia, disenfranchisement, and even irrelevance.

If there is consensus that the group can eliminate some choices, combine others, and find more information on still others, this step is important in identifying those areas.

If a declaration of what outcomes or ends the organization needs to achieve emerges from the dialogue, the board is accountable for providing that information. If what emerges from the dialogue is the need to develop strategy or an action plan or program, then the workforce—either staff, a member committee, or some action team composed of both—will become responsible for developing it.

It should be clear how different this process is from the way decision making used to be. Board and staff are in dialogue together about the outcomes they need to accomplish and the means to achieve them. But the board retains the authority to declare its strategic intent—what it wants to see happen. When it is time to detail the means by which the association will achieve those ends, the workforce becomes accountable. The board exercises oversight by constantly assessing whether the workforce is accomplishing those ends. When it is not, the board intervenes in the strategy, action plan, program, or initiative.

The traditional political model of governance differentiated roles and authorities between board and staff. In the old days, a brick wall existed between the board and the member leaders. The board set policy and established direction on one side of the wall, and the staff implemented policy and administered programs on the other side. In today's world, the nature of work required for success necessitates the perspectives and expertise of both members and staff leaders. Even in situations where member leaders may understand more than the staff, most of the work done today requires full-time attention. Since most member leaders have other jobs as well, associations need able staff leaders, because nimbleness significantly diminishes when an association is entirely dependent on volunteers to make decisions and get work done. If no one within the association can devote the time and day-to-day attention to the work itself, regardless of the association's intent, the effect on nimbleness is significant.

Case Study Example—*How Can Our Association More Effectively Utilize Members in Advocacy Work? Are There Areas of Agreement?*

An excerpt from the group's dialogue yields agreement on the following general ideas:

- We must do something, thereby eliminating the status quo choice of "continuing as is."
- We have a significant information gap as to why members do not get involved today, and acting without information may carry a greater risk than not acting.
- The board must play some role in encouraging active involvement among the membership.

Step 7. Identify Actions, Intent, and Accountability

By asking what actions this choice (or need for additional information) suggests about who should do what, the board begins to articulate its intent on an issue, even if that intent does not suggest final closure. Key questions are the following:

- *What are the implications for the board, staff, and/or other work groups?*
- *Who will task whom for what?*
- *Who will be accountable?*

These are all important questions; when the board asks them, it is articulating its intent as an active outcome of its own dialogue, not rubberstamping thinking that has been done elsewhere.

Step 8. Craft a Motion

The next step, crafting a motion, empowers the board to articulate its intent as a product of its own dialogue on an issue. What usually occurs is that during the dialogue the attractive content of the motion emerges. Sometimes in such cases a small group, perhaps a committee person and/or a staff member, will assume responsibility for keeping track of the dialogue. It is not uncommon for this tracking to be done on a laptop connected to an LCD projector. As the board moves through its conversation and consensus begins to emerge, the trackers will project the elements of the dialogue onto the screen, and the participants will discern what the motion ought to be. "Whereas" and "resolved" clauses go up on the screen before the dialogue ends. If the board agrees on the substantive points of the motion, it can either wait for its formal business meeting to consider it, or it can move directly from dialogue to deliberation and entertain a formal motion to approve.

One board's strategy, when dealing with extremely controversial issues, is to report on details of the advantages and disadvantages of possible choices in the association's newsletter. This gives members the opportunity to understand the basis of the board's decision and to know that governance gave adequate consideration to all aspects of an issue. Although they might not agree with the final decision, members understand that their views received adequate consideration.

Other associations employing a knowledge-based governance philosophy follow the standard rules of order, where there is a motion and a vote on the motion, and hence use a very parliamentary-style format. A motion under this approach creates a record not merely of the decision but also of the rationale for it. Such a motion becomes a powerful communication tool. This is not the only way to handle tracking motions, but it is a tool that helps move groups forward.

As indicated above, the three parts of the motion are background (key discussion points), action (policy reflecting the will of the board), and guiding principles (parameters, boundaries, or other statements reflecting the board's intent on the issue). The crafting of a motion with these three parts represents a rich articulation of the board's intent as well as an effective recap and documentation of the manner in which it has thoughtfully considered an issue. This approach can be useful not only as a historical record of the board's consideration of an issue, but also as a vehicle for communicating to the broader membership both the decision reached and the process the board used to consider the issue.

This kind of motion is usually crafted on a break from the meeting, over lunch, or on the evening of the first day of two days of meetings. Many boards devote the first day to dialogue, craft their motions overnight, and return to deliberation and board business on the second day of the meeting.

Case Study Example—*How Can Our Association More Effectively Utilize Members in Advocacy Work?*
A Motion Reflecting Dialogue
Background

- WHEREAS, members expect the association to be an effective advocate for the industry and work to maintain our success and position; and
- WHEREAS, our association, despite its strong industry position, is an association of relatively modest size and must use all available resources effectively; and

- WHEREAS, member involvement in the association's advocacy efforts is critical to our success; and
- WHEREAS, there is no current consensus on why members do not participate in advocacy efforts;

Action

- Be it resolved that the board assigns a task force of volunteers and staff to conduct additional member research and gather relevant information about member needs and preferences for being involved in the association's advocacy efforts. This group should have a report prepared for the next board meeting, which should include analysis of the data and recommendations for next steps.
- Be it further resolved that the board of directors will immediately take an active role in promoting, encouraging, and mentoring membership involvement in advocacy efforts at the local, regional, and national levels.

Guiding Principles

- All efforts and recommendations should be respectful of the possibility that members may have conflicts of interest with their employers or businesses on particular positions the association may take.
- The organization should structure advocacy activities in a way that both contributes to the success of the association and allows members to perceive greater value in participating in the association that represents their industry.

Step 9. Deliberate on the Motion

However the meeting agenda has been organized, when the board concludes its dialogue and creates a motion, it also makes a motion to leave the committee of the whole and adjourn back to parliamentary procedure and board process. The board then returns to normal deliberation and acts on the motion it has created as a product of its own dialogue.

When the process comes to this point the chair might say, "Ladies and gentlemen, I'd like to entertain a motion to adjourn from committee of the whole." This is a nondebatable, majority vote. The board moves back into regular board process, and the chair asks to entertain a motion on the issue. At this point, it is not uncommon for someone to point to the screen and say, "So moved." Then there is a second to the motion. The board may then use Robert's Rules for debate, advocacy, and argument. When the board believes it has heard all the views, someone calls the question. Then a minimum of 51 percent of those present and voting may move the question; the vote is either "yes" or "no." In many associations, if the board has an opportunity to dialogue about the issue and build the elements of a motion that articulate its intent, those voting will rarely challenge or vote down the motion. Further, in the associations we studied, there is greater understanding of decisions that result from conversation than a board can achieve when simply debating a motion that came from somewhere else; under these circumstances, there is also more support for the decision once it is made. And, not least of all, the board is better able to communicate both the context and content of its decisions to a constituency group that otherwise might oppose it.

Changes as a Result of a Knowledge-Based Approach

A knowledge-based approach affects the following elements of a governance system most:

- The nature of what kinds of items should go on the agenda and what kinds should not is reconsidered. The proportion of operational versus strategic issues on the agenda changes in favor of strategic issues.
- The board will spend its time using information, not collecting it; it will move from focusing on reviewing what was done to determining what should be done next.
- Background materials will be organized differently.
- The board will adopt a meeting process that facilitates the movement from dialogue to deliberation.
- The board will not require a motion or resolution to initiate dialogue on an issue.
- The board will spend up to 80 percent of its meeting time in dialogue, deliberation, and decision making about issues of strategic direction and/or policy.
- The board will routinely consider issues of capacity, core capability, and strategic position in deciding what to do.
- Volunteer leaders and staff will jointly facilitate, catalyze, and encourage dialogue on key strategic issues.
- The planning process will become a basis for shared accountability. The board and senior staff will operate as partners, using a clearly defined management accountability process to identify things they see together as most important to address.

Knowledge-based governance also commonly includes member leaders and staff members as co-chairs of committees; this is an excellent shortcut for improving committees' accountability. The staff member, naturally, has a somewhat different incentive for accomplishing work. But this practice positions the staff member as a co-leader rather than as a servant or source of information and truly cements this collaborative relationship. Staff and volunteer work groups report only when an obstacle arises with which the board must deal. The practice of rewarding committee chairs by having them give dog-and-pony shows to the board is passé. Instead, their reward is meaningful participation that provides important work and the chance to dialogue on issues where they have expertise.

The power of this process is multifold. It energizes boards to spend time talking about issues that matter and allows them to contribute their intellectual capital by considering and doing real work on issues that affect their industry, profession, or cause. This is especially beneficial in an association where board views staff as very effective and almost questions the need for its own role of oversight.

In associations employing a knowledge-based governance strategy, staff is also more invested in the decisions it has an opportunity to implement. By being a part of the dialogue leading to the decision on an issue, staff can feel comfortable that the board has considered capacity concerns, that is, areas where staff members have unique expertise but usually do not have a chance to inject that knowledge into board deliberation.

Many associations have begun to put technological mechanisms in place to extend the dialogues occurring in their annual house of delegates (HOD) meeting to a broader timeframe throughout the year. This not only makes better use of the intellectual capital resident in the broader membership, but it serves to enfranchise members in the governance process for longer periods of time in a more meaningful way and also extends knowledge throughout the organization. Using technological mechanisms to extend dialogues requires trust. If members believe the process the association's deliberative bodies use to consider an issue has taken into account all critical information, including that which represents their views, and if their support allows an organization to make appropriate decisions in an appropriate amount of time, it will promote the nimbleness associations will need to sustain success well into the 21st century.

Transitioning to a Knowledge-Based Governance Strategy

Getting to this point may not be easy. Some boards or board members may not be willing to release control of the opinion-rich-and-information-poor processes that permit the most persuasive individuals to control a group's thinking. But just as the new strategy will threaten some, it will invigorate others. As one elected leader put it, "This allows us to talk about what matters—which makes the commitment of time and energy worthwhile."

What is involved in beginning to adopt such a process? How can governance learn to rely more on knowledge and less on opinion? Good board training/orientation is essential, as board members bring to the table a wide range of experience, knowledge, and expectations. Absent a good definition of roles and expectations, they will do what they think is appropriate based on past experience—they will act with good intentions, but they may likely be wrong, and focusing at the wrong level takes valuable time away from strategic discussion and critical thinking.

Given the publicly documented board missteps at both the corporate and volunteer levels in recent years, some board members may believe that by focusing strategically, they are failing to pay attention to the important operational details of running the organization—what they view as due diligence. It is imperative that the board understand what constitutes appropriate board due diligence in this era of rapid change.

The use of a knowledge-based governance strategy shifts the role of the board in several other ways as well; manifestations of the new dynamic include transitioning board members from personal problem solvers for constituents to direction setters for the organization. In its behavior, the board becomes more nurturing and open and less political. Work becomes more transparent and less closed. Staff become partners, not "executive secretaries and indentured servants" who carry out pronouncements. There is increased accountability for the group as a whole. What constitutes appropriate behavior at the board table is different for both board and staff. Focus of responsibility shifts from having the right answers to asking the right questions and ensuring time to discuss them.

What indicators determine that the time is right for such a shift? Increased competition has enhanced awareness that there is no exclusive association franchise on enfranchisement, knowledge, education and community. Associations must position themselves effectively to anticipate future challenges, to move beyond today's successes, and to take risks. That cannot happen without greater knowledge of the environment, their marketplace, and their capacity as an organization; it can happen only if an organization articulates a clear vision and spends time in strategic dialogue more often than once every three years.

In addition, increasing use of technology creates more and more data—making the job of filtering out the chaff more complex but even more essential. Good analytical skills will be critical for both staff and volunteers and will be an essential internal staff core competency, whether the organization gathers its data internally or externally.

Another key contributor to readiness for a knowledge-based governance strategy is that good people stop being willing to waste time on unimportant "stuff." There are more options and more competitors for their time and dollars, and fewer are willing to sign on just because "It's the right thing to do." The mantra now is, "Make better use of my time and my travel, and make it meaningful, or I'm not interested." The need for value and meaning is equally important in trade, professional, philanthropic, or cause-related organizations. The roles of boards have become more differentiated among these different types of organizations. There may also be an impact as each new generation of association members arrives at a unique definition of community and desires something different from their leadership experience.

The use of a knowledge-based governance strategy will also increase organizational willingness to be more risk tolerant. This is because governance will discuss both risks and the dangers of not acting as a routine part of dialogue. Such a discussion is important to success and to ensuring the association a corner in the marketplace. But change in the level of risk tolerance requires a shift in culture that must begin with a shift in governance processes.

In the 21st century, governance will be less concerned with distribution of power and more concerned with whether the organization is delivering value; distribution of power will be important only when the perception exists that the organization is not providing value.

The leaders of associations choosing the path of knowledge-based governance understand that it involves hard work over time and does not realize its full potential overnight. They are also learning that each association employing these mechanisms must construct them carefully to be sensitive to its own particular character. An association must design and implement its knowledge-based governance strategy according to its own unique structure, process, and culture.

In the associations we studied, although no two organizations approached this transition in exactly the same way, they did experience common phases in institutionalizing the process.

First, governance receives an orientation to the concepts, including an opportunity to understand the philosophy, the values, and the mechanisms for dialogue. If, in that orientation, which may include a mini-case study, the board is comfortable with the approach, it examines one or two issues as a prototype at the next board meeting. Perhaps one might have a prewritten background paper, and one might not. At the subsequent board meeting, the nature of the agenda changes. Many of the associations we studied employ a consent agenda, where they approve all committee reports in one motion, but any member of the board can pull out an issue for separate discussion. The agenda at this point includes a higher proportion of meeting time focused on issues of strategic direction and high-level policy, with sufficient time reserved for the traditional business meeting. Many boards will schedule the strategic dialogue portion of the meeting at the beginning of the agenda, when minds are freshest, and schedule the business portion at the latter part of the meeting (sometimes resulting in faster movement through that portion of the agenda). This meeting design also facilitates having the motions crafted as a result of strategic dialogue on the board's business-meeting agenda so the board can formally vote on them.

Our study of a wide variety of organizations showed that for an association to execute this kind of change strategy successfully, the following set of conditions had to exist:

- An experiential opportunity—the organization gave people who had to be the users of the governance system active opportunities to experience a new methodology and to participate in its customization for the organization.
- A group of champions within the association constantly exhibited a belief in and articulation of how the new way was significant, meaningful, and exciting.
- Real issues of importance formed the basis of training and orientation efforts.
- The organization would bring in outside expertise and energy at critical points in the process. The first experience people had with the new way, because experts guided it, created a good mental model of success.

Together, these change strategies were always *recursive*—meaning that what results is an example of the strategy, and the strategy bears within it the elements that will bring about the result. For example, the way board change was achieved was itself an example or reflection of how work would get done in a knowledge-based governance culture.

Over time, associations refine and adjust their processes, never attaining perfection but always evolving and changing. The nature of the experience of wrestling with each new issue, while consistent, is novel. It never gets boring. Our belief is that governance in associations that exhibit the will to govern well in the 21st century will need to operate with knowledge-based strategy.

Chapter 19

The Will to Govern Well

When Governance Leads—It's Not Just What You Do but How You Do It

Knowledge-based governance is a process that institutionalizes strategy and policy in directing the resources of the organization over time, ensuring that the body politic rather than a political someone makes decisions about strategic directions and positions.

In many associations, the will to govern well is about establishing a set of righteous and meaningful principles and then behaving consistently within those principles. Elected leaders in associations that exhibit the will to govern well commit to "rules" about what they will do and how they will do it. These rules represent evolving governance philosophies that characterize the will to govern well.

The following list, while it is not meant to be exclusive or totally comprehensive, provides a sense of what leaders in associations that demonstrate the will to govern well focus on in executing their governance roles.

What They Choose to Focus On

- Desired outcomes rather than the activity.
- Strategic intent and core values rather than how to achieve an outcome or reexamine already completed work.
- What needs to happen next rather than what has already been done.
- Using information rather than collecting it.
- Honestly considering issues of capacity, core capability, and strategic position in deciding what to do.

How They Choose to Do It

- Making the investment in individual and group behavior that earns and sustains trust and consciously avoiding overt or inadvertent behavior that diminishes or demolishes trust.
- Sustaining a process that gives governance the tools it needs to lead intelligently.
- Encouraging policy making as opposed to political behavior.
- Focusing on value of what the organization produces for its stakeholders rather than on the distribution of power.
- Understanding that governance's fiduciary responsibility in the 21st century is to define what will constitute value and ensure its delivery, making the choice to drive important decisions at all levels from clarity and consensus on what will constitute value. Members and staff leadership collaboratively assume accountability for paying constant attention to value in an honest, open, and well-informed partnership.
- Choosing to view mistakes as a natural correlate to risk taking and innovation and as a rich opportunity to be diagnosed and learned from, rather than covered up or repositioned by organizational spin-doctors as successes on the basis of reasons unrelated to the original objectives.
- Redefining measurements of success on the basis of indicators of quality rather than quantity.
- Deciding to neither enable nor accept dishonesty or manipulation, even when such a decision is the path of least consequence.
- Being willing to change individual opinion or perspective based on changing context or experience but not on the personal whim or political influences of the moment. Avoiding dependency on any particular leader, because really important things are likely to take more than a single leader's term to accomplish, and an organization that constantly redirects its energy will lose essential momentum.

Good governance finds a way to remain a student of its own organization, thinking strategically about it as an enterprise. At a macro level, this is the essence of strategic thinking in an association, while at a micro level, it is the path to designing governance well matched to the unique needs and dynamics of an enterprise. Many organizations have employed the following common strategies in improving governance in their organizations and achieving the will to govern well:

- Define the governance philosophy they wish to employ—what they will pay attention to and how they will do it.

- Design work processes that enable them to accomplish their work intelligently. Part of the work process will involve deciding how such structures as an executive committee, committee infrastructure, or outsourced contracting can support the board's selected approach to governance.
- Decide the outcomes the association seeks to achieve.
- Determine what work they need to accomplish to achieve those outcomes.
- Decide how best to organize to accomplish work.

Planning a Leadership Strategy

Leadership groups sustain the will to govern well when they consciously make choices about how they can be most successful in leading. They must make those choices continually and on a case-by-case basis. This act tends to promote (a) the knowledge necessary for strategic thoughtfulness, (b) a commitment to behavior that earns the trust necessary to get others to follow, and (c) a disciplined flexibility consistent with nimbleness.

Bennis' Four Competencies of Leadership

Amid changes to governance processes, structure, or culture, the actions of leadership remain a critical key to improvement. Leadership in governance focuses both on what the organization does and how it does it. It focuses on behaviors leadership exhibits to achieve success.

In Chapter 5, "The Four Competencies of Leadership," of the 1994 book, *An Invented Life: Reflections on Leadership and Change*, Warren Bennis defined the following four competencies of leadership that we believe have implications for developing the will to govern well in general and for governance's development of leadership strategy on any particular issue:

1. Management of attention
2. Management of meaning
3. Management of trust
4. Management of self

Management of Attention

One trait Bennis says is most apparent in successful leaders is their ability to draw others to them because they have a vision. They communicate an extraordinary focus of commitment that attracts people, managing attention through a compelling vision that brings others to a place they have not been before. The idea of vision is not used here in a mystical or religious sense, but in the sense of outcome, goal, or direction.

Management of Meaning

Bennis suggests that to make dreams apparent to others and to align people with them, leaders must communicate their vision. Communication and alignment work together. Leaders make ideas tangible and real to others to gain support for them. For no matter how marvelous the vision, the effective leader must use metaphors, words, or models to make that vision clear to others. The leader's goal is not mere explanation or clarification but the creation of meaning. The more far-flung and complex the organization, the more critical this ability is. Effective leaders can communicate ideas through several organizational layers, across great distances, even through the jamming signals of special-interest groups and opponents. Those in leadership positions hear so much about the importance of information that they may overlook the significance of meaning. Actually, the more bombarded a society or organization, the more deluged with facts and images, the greater will be its thirst for meaning. Hence, effective leaders integrate facts, concepts, and anecdotes into meaning for the public, getting people to understand and support their goals in a variety of ways. It is not enough to use the right buzzword or a cute technique, or to hire a public relations person to write speeches. The ability to manage attention and meaning comes from the whole person.

Management of Trust

Bennis suggests that trust is essential to all organizations. The main determinants of trust are reliability and constancy. When talking to board or staff members in associations exhibiting the will to govern well, we hear certain phrases again and again, such as, "She is all of a piece," "Whether you like it or not, you always know where he is coming from, what he stands for." Studies show that people would much rather follow individuals they can count on, even when they disagree with their viewpoint, than people they agree with but who shift positions frequently.

Management of Self

The fourth leadership competency Bennis describes is management of self, knowing one's skills and deploying them effectively. Management of self is critical; without it, leaders and managers can do more harm than good. Effective leaders know themselves; they know their strengths and nurture them.

Bennis' leadership competencies have to do both with what governance chooses to focus on and what behaviors leaders exhibit in executing work to achieve those priorities. In associations that exhibit the will to govern well, governance consciously uses competencies like these in deciding how it will lead the association through any particular issue.

Case Study—One Association's Experience

The following case study demonstrates how one association built a leadership strategy on a given initiative. This association, a professional society in a technically related profession, was involved in a broad visioning process and related organizational change initiative. It had tasked a work group with identifying organizational specifications necessary for recommending a new set of bylaws. The new bylaws would clarify the definitions of organizational oversight between the association's board and HOD, as well as the board's primary role as governing the association and the house's role as governing the profession. The new bylaws would eliminate a cumbersome set of checks and balances hindering the society's nimbleness in positioning itself as the advocate for its membership. Also involved in this change effort was the board's implantation of a knowledge-based governance strategy and its desire to have the HOD and other work and decision-making groups adopt it as well.

The board accepted the work group's report and proposed a set of bylaws to be placed before the HOD during the coming year. The board viewed itself as a champion of the effort but recognized significant barriers to universal acceptance of this new set of governance parameters, both within the HOD and among other groups, such as the state organizations and the general membership. The board was operating with another hindrance—attachment to the old paradigm was causing discomfort with the new way of doing things. The organizational culture continued to cause a sense of distrust related to the board: The board distrusted itself, it distrusted other elements of the organization, and other factions in the organization distrusted the board. There was also a lack of understanding of the national organization's role and perceived value. The board decided it needed to develop and execute a leadership strategy in order to win member acceptance of the new bylaws through use of a Tecker Consultants' tool based on Bennis' four leadership competencies (see figures A.12 through A.20 in the appendix for a full template of the tool). Excerpts of the strategy follow:

Management of Attention
(Leaders manage attention through a compelling vision that brings others to a place they have not been before.)

- *What is the goal?*
  - To gain the HOD's approval of the new bylaws and to achieve broad member support of the change effort.
- *Who are the stakeholders?*
  - HOD
  - Members at large

- *For each stakeholder, what are the formal and informal communication opportunities?*
    - HOD—formal methods are virtual HOD listserve and paper mailings; informal communication opportunities are meetings at section and state events and personal contact at other society functions.

Members at large—formal methods include the annual report to the members directly; all other formal methods are indirect, such as newsletters, reports about board activity from regional liaisons, and; personal contact is ad hoc.

- *What are the primary messages, the most important things they need to understand?*
    - HOD—that the new bylaws will allow greater clarity of role and increased nimbleness; that the organization will have a better chance of achieving and sustaining its envisioned future; and that although the new bylaws will require the HOD to give up oversight of society operations, it will gain a powerful role in policy development for the profession and a new tool for its work through implementing a knowledge-based governance strategy.
    - Members at large—that although there is a concern about the ability of the national board to look out for the interests of its members, clarifying the role of the national board and passing the new bylaws will better allow the Society to meet member needs and remain relevant into the future.

Management of Meaning
(Leaders make ideas tangible and real to others in order to encourage support.)

- *What is the goal, and who are the stakeholders?*
    - To gain the HOD's approval of the new bylaws and to achieve broad member support of the change effort.
    - HOD
    - Members at large
- *What are the self-interests for each?*
    - HOD—would like to retain power and influence.
    - Members at large—would like to ensure a continued voice in the running of the society.

- *What would be the values/benefits to them?*
    - HOD—would play a broader role in defining the future of the profession and would spend their meeting time engaged in meaningful dialogue instead of reviewing operational information and "rubberstamping it" (sometimes after the fact).

- ○ Members at large—would be part of a vibrant, successful professional society; the new governance paradigm would ensure that should they become involved in the organization's work and decision making, their experiences would be that much more meaningful and enjoyable under the new bylaws.

- *How will they be affected by the goal positively and negatively?*
  - ○ HOD—positively by taking on a new policy role, and negatively by giving up authority for operational oversight of the society.
  - ○ Members at large—little direct impact.

- *How can we ask them to support the goal?*
  - ○ HOD—by embracing a new broader policy role for themselves as a body.
  - ○ Members at large—by voicing their approval to their regional delegates.

Management of Trust
(The main determinants of trust are reliability and constancy.)

- *For this goal, what are the leader/governance behaviors that can earn and enhance trust for us as a board?*
  - ○ Painting a vivid picture of what achieving the envisioned future will be like for the society and how the world of members will be different and better as a result.
  - ○ Creating an understanding that to achieve the envisioned future, the society must undergo structural change to take advantage of new opportunities and operate efficiently and effectively.
  - ○ Communicating both the positive and negative elements to all stakeholders.
  - ○ Being balanced and fair rather than self-serving in attempting to gain greater oversight of society operations.

- *For this goal, what are the leader/governance behaviors that can inhibit or diminish trust?*
  - ○ Doing all of the above in public while privately focusing on the balance of power issues and how the board (or any individual member) will benefit.

Management of Self

- *For this goal, what are the primary strengths that individual board members need to bring in pursuit of this goal?*
  - ○ Good communication skills.

- ○ Honesty and integrity.
- ○ Ability to see the big picture.

- *For this goal, what other strengths/competencies/skills/abilities will the board need to pursue this goal, and what are the sources for obtaining them?*
  - ○ Access to individuals both in governance and the general membership who can provide a realistic picture of the wants and concerns of all stakeholder groups.
  - ○ Assistance in and support from staff and other resources that can help us get our message out and communicate with stakeholders.

Using this framework, this group's board created a leadership strategy for executing its role in guiding the bylaws through to successful acceptance. It allowed board members to think not only about what they wanted to do (i.e., help the bylaws pass) but how they wanted to do it (i.e., demonstrate consistency and authenticity in their behavior, thus earning trust of the membership). After much spirited dialogue and many twists and turns along the way, the organization passed the bylaws. As a result of the behaviors the board exhibited during this time, it built new levels of trust between the general membership and the national governance bodies and began to chip away at decades of mistrust.

Four Portraits of Influential Leadership

Good governance makes conscious choices both about what the organization will accomplish and how it will lead. Associations are by nature collaborative enterprises, with dual lines of authority and accountability shared between members and staff leaders. Leadership in associations is therefore unique in many important respects. For example, in an association, unlike for-profit enterprises, seldom if ever is any one individual permitted to make an important decision alone.

In voluntary organizations, leadership does not enjoy the usual perquisites of power that enable it to direct or order certain behavior from others. This difference suggests that traditional approaches to leadership founded on distribution of power and authority will not succeed in an association environment. Governance must lead through influence rather than power.

In "influential leadership," the primary vehicle is communication, and the essential currency is information. Individuals, groups, or enterprises execute successful leadership most often by using information to affect the beliefs, perceptions, and understandings upon which people base their choices.

We have found that influential leadership strategy manifests in organizations that demonstrate the will to govern well in one of four portraits catalytic leadership, servant leadership, visionary leadership, and expert leadership. These are not styles or personality traits but are coherent descriptors of how successful leaders at all levels exercise leadership in a particular situation in order to execute a particular situational strategy. Chief staff executives use them to lead staff, and chief elected officers use them to lead the board. The board uses them to lead the organization, and the organization can use them to lead the profession, industry, or cause.

Effective selection of one of these portraits in a particular leadership situation requires competent diagnosis of the context, careful selection on a case-by-case basis, and common understanding of and commitment to the portrait chosen by the key leaders, so that their common language will facilitate their behavioral consistency.

A Portrait of Catalytic Leadership

Catalytic leadership means that the individual, group, or association as an enterprise is acting as an agent that, when mixed with others, causes things to occur that would not occur otherwise. Catalytic leadership tends to be most effective in professional, trade, philanthropic, or cause-related organizations that possess a strong volunteer culture and have a solid core of both members and values. In executing this kind of leadership strategy in governance restructuring, a cause-related organization might create a relatively small number of positions on the board for nonmembers who possess power or influence related to the work of the organization that is not naturally found in the membership.

Other examples of the use of this strategy can be found in associations that bring together many voices in a profession or industry to create a common understanding of an issue or to gain agreement on collaborative work among organizations for a common problem. One organization in the health care arena executed this strategy by acting as a "convener;" bringing many related organizations together to seek a common set of actions to address the industry-wide issue of staffing shortages in the profession.

A Portrait of Servant Leadership

Servant leadership appears to be most successful in cause-related or professional organizations that are stable, have a strong sense of community, are oriented toward human service, and have a solid core. Constituencies of the organization will value the act of serving. An example is a philanthropic organization that employs market research or anecdotal evidence gathered from the communities it is organized to serve as the primary rationale for executing a significant change in their program of work or focus. The act of serving is valued by constituencies of the organization. When they observe governance actively and visibly serving, they will extend to governance the opportunity to lead out of respect for that service. Robert Greenleaf, who originated the concept of servant leadership, defines it in his 1982 book, *Servant as Leader*, as "a practical philosophy that supports people who choose to serve first, and then lead as a way of expanding service to individuals and institutions. Servant leadership encourages collaboration, trust, foresight, listening, and the ethical use of power and empowerment." Servant leadership is leadership exercised by virtue of what the governing body does and how it executes its role. The work itself is the strategy it chooses to lead. For example, it is unlikely that people would agree to follow the lead of a governing board of a philanthropic organization if the behavior of the governance body was not reflective of the core values of the enterprise. One of the core values is commitment to serving others, so the leadership strategy here is to be the model of service to others, and as a result of being recognized as the model of service to others, others are willing to afford them the opportunity to lead.

A Portrait of Visionary Leadership

Visionary leadership involves clearly describing a set of conditions or attributes radically different from the current situation in meaningful and understandable terms that compel others to alter their own behavior willingly because they view that change as ultimately in their own self-interest. Visionary leadership appears to be most successful in trade and professional associations that require radical change and that have a solid core of change agents as well as a smaller but equally vociferous chorus of change resisters. For example, members in these organizations might be confronted with a choice between a very different future that is highly attractive and a very different future that is fundamentally unacceptable. A case in point might be a professional association representing a specialty that is rapidly being supplanted by competitors who are more attractive to the marketplace. The execution of a visionary leadership strategy might either describe the competing scenarios of dissolution or create a new vision in which the new entrants are embraced, with an attempt to persuade the traditional core membership that their long-term future interests would be best served by embracing their successful competitors rather than seeking to forestall them. Members look to their association to help them deal with what is coming in their industry or profession, and sometimes that means helping them see a new vision of their professional role, or even a way to transition out of the profession!

A Portrait of Expert Leadership

Expert leadership involves earning sufficient respect from a long and visible track record of relevant successes so that others defer to the leader's judgment. Expert leadership appears to be most successful in trade and professional associations that require evolutionary or continuous but well-managed change, that have a solid core attributed to the experts' track record for success, and that maintain a critical mass of activists who respect the leadership expertise sufficiently to commit their resources to supporting the leaders. An example might be the board of a trade association whose major business line is advocacy choosing to use an expert-leader strategy because it has earned sufficient respect to do so and effectively employs the intellectual and political interests of its members' companies to accomplish its work.

The use of these strategies must align with the situation addressed. We can apply these leadership strategies to the case study discussed earlier in this chapter that focused on an organizational change effort to win member acceptance of a new set of bylaws. If the board had used servant leadership, it would have been saying, "We're building this set of bylaws to change the organization to be of better service to you." It could have used catalytic leadership, saying, "We're building this change of bylaws to catalyze action, to initiate a large-scale change, after which we'll move out of the way." In this case, it probably would not have been advisable to use expert leadership, because having the board say, "We know what's best," would have seemed high-handed and would not have given governance the necessary credibility. In this case study, the board actually chose visionary leadership, painting a compelling, vivid portrait of how the organization would be better positioned as a result of changing structure to achieve vision. As a general rule, governance must select a leadership portrait that is closely aligned with the strategy it seeks to execute. We plan to research the application of these four strategies, within context, to more fully discover the subtleties of successful selection

A Call to Action

As we indicated in the beginning, it is no longer possible to generalize about the association community. Nevertheless, this book has provided a number of observations about the links between knowledge, trust, and nimbleness, and how together they can contribute to effective governance systems in the 21st century.

We believe that developing and sustaining the will to govern well will truly remain an imperative for all associations in the 21st century. It is the only thing that can ensure preservation of the uniqueness associations represent as enterprises. Associations function as a triple helix of organizational DNA, composed of three intertwined threads—with members as owners, as customers, and as workforce. Unraveling this balance would put at risk key competitive advantages that associations have in the 21st century—the aggregate intellectual capital of their membership, their energy as communities with common purpose, and their credibility as voluntary institutions. If associations are not able to create more effective systems of work and decision making, they will not be able to sustain these relationships.

We hope this book will be of value to association leaders. As we conclude it, we offer the following guideposts on the journey to developing and sustaining the will to govern well:

- Provide value—if you do not, you will not be able to do anything else.
- Enjoy your work—if you do not, your association's members, customers, clients, beneficiaries, and stakeholders will not get the quality they deserve.
- Do good things for good people, and don't kowtow to fools, charlatans, or liars.

Those who are successful will know it when people say about them in the future that they always took what they did seriously, but never took themselves too seriously. To make the choice of enjoying the experience of leadership without being "filled with themselves" is the kind of noble aspiration that has characterized the most successful association leaders.

APPENDIX

Using the Competencies of Collaborative Strategic Thinking

A "Real-Time" Mini-Case Study

Step 1 | Describe the Initiative

Step 2 | Author a Vision/Goal

Step 3 | Determine Key Stakeholders

Step 4 | Conduct Conditions Assessment

Step 5 | Identify Strategic Issues

Step 6 | Determine Key Factors

Step 7 | Develop Strategies

Step 8 | Assess Strategies

Step 9 | Select Strategies

Step 10 | Develop Action Plans

"Strategic thinking is a cognitive discipline that can be learned. Competency can increase with practice over time. Application will improve as insight is gleaned from experience."

–Glenn Tecker
Address to The Planning Forum, 1991

Step 1: Describe the Initiative

1.1 What do you want to accomplish?

_____

_____

1.2 Generally, how do you intend to accomplish this?

Step 2: Author a Vision/Goal

2.1 Who will benefit from this initiative?

2.2 What will be the benefit to <u>them?</u>

[Beneficiary(ies)] will [action verb] [condition or attribute to be attained]

Step 3: Determine the Stakeholders

Definitions: Stakeholder(s) - an individual or group with a significant interest in what you will do or what will be accomplished.

Key Stakeholder(s) - an individual or group who either (a) has a "right" to be involved or (b) is well positioned to be a significant supporter or opposer of the initiative.

Key Stakeholders	Interest/Concern	Implications for the Initiative

Step 4: Conduct Conditions Assessment

<u>"WOTS-UP?"</u>

<u>**STRENGTHS**</u> INTERNAL	<u>**OPPORTUNITIES**</u>
EXTERNAL	
<u>**WEAKNESSES**</u> INTERNAL	<u>**THREATS**</u>
EXTERNAL	

Step 5: Identify Strategic Issues

CRITERIA FOR IMPORTANCE

DEFINITIONS

Impact:

A measure of "breadth" of importance. How basic is the factor? How many other things depend on it or are related to it? A measure related to relationships.

Consequence:

A measure of "depth" of importance. How bad or good will it be? A measure related to intensity.

Immediacy:

A measure of the importance of opportunity and sequence. How much time is available? Is there a chronological order? A measure related to time.

Strategic issues that must be addressed:

- _____
- _____
- _____
- _____
- _____
- _____

Step 6: Determine Key Factors

What are the most important factors/forces that will need to be considered in addressing each strategic issue?

Example Strategic Issue: _____

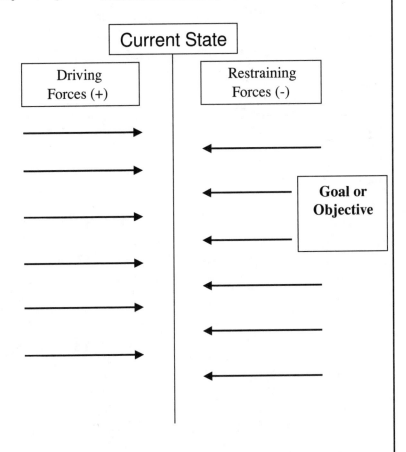

Current State

Driving
Forces (+)

Restraining
Forces (-)

**Goal or
Objective**

Step 7: Develop Strategies

7.1 What actions will be required to address the strategic issues?

7.2 How can the existing capabilities of the organization (assets, skills, technologies, relationships, expertise, etc.) be most effectively used?

7.3 What other capabilities will be required to succeed?

Example Strategic Issue: _____

Potential Strategies:

☐ • _____

☐ • _____

☐ • _____

☐ • _____

Step 8: Assess Strategies

CRITERIA TO ASSESS STRATEGIES

Is each strategy:

Necessary

...responsive to an area of strategic importance

Feasible

...will be able to make some progress toward achieving the objective

Appropriate

...for your organization
...related to mission of the organization

As a set of strategies, are they:

Sufficient

...all areas of strategic importance have been included

Step 9: Select Strategies

How do you want to (a) add to,(b) delete from, or (c) modify the "potential strategies" list?

_____

_____

_____

_____

_____

_____

Step 10: Develop Action Plans

Sample Strategy Selected: _____

Key Event	Responsibility	Target Date

Resources Required:

The Four Competencies of Leadership

- **Management of Attention**
- **Management of Meaning**
- **Management of Trust**
- **Management of Self**

The Management of Attention...

Communicate a compelling vision that brings others to a place they have not been before.

- A set of intentions or a vision
- A sense of outcome, goal, or direction

MANAGEMENT OF ATTENTION

WORKSHEET

Goal / Intent: _____

Key Stakeholders	Communication Opportunities		Primary Message(s)
	Formal	Informal	

The Management of Meaning...

Make ideas tangible and real to others.

- Use a metaphor, a word, or a model

- Integrate facts, concepts, and anecdotes into meaning for the public

- Get people to understand and support goals in a variety of ways

MANAGEMENT OF MEANING

WORKSHEET

Goal / Intent: _____

Stakeholder	Self-Interest(s)	Descriptive Aid (metaphor, word, analogy, etc.)	How They Are Affected	How They Can Support

The Management of Trust...

Reliability

■ Constancy

■ Focus

MANAGEMENT OF MEANING

WORKSHEET

Leader Behavior That Can Earn and Enhance Trust (+)

Leader Behavior That Can Inhibit or Diminish Trust (-)

Goal or Intent

The Management of Self...

Knowing one's skills —
Deploying them effectively.

- Know strengths and nurture them

- Failure is referred to as a mistake, error, false start, miss, etc.

- Concentrate on winning, not on "not losing."

MANAGEMENT OF MEANING

Self-Appraisal

Goal / Intent: _____

The primary strengths I bring to pursuit of this goal are:

1. _____

2. _____

3. _____

Other strengths (competencies, skills, abilities) we'll need to pursue this goal are:

<table>
<tr><td></td><td>Strength</td><td>Source</td></tr>
<tr><td>1.</td><td>_____</td><td>_____</td></tr>
<tr><td>2.</td><td>_____</td><td>_____</td></tr>
<tr><td>3.</td><td>_____</td><td>_____</td></tr>
</table>

About the Authors

Glenn H. Tecker is president and chief executive officer of Tecker Consultants LLC, Trenton, New Jersey, an international consulting firm specializing in management, education, and organization. He has served as an association executive and as a board member both for not-for-profit and private sector organizations. He has assisted a wide variety of trade, professional, and philanthropic organizations in the redesign of governance, program, and operations so that they might more effectively navigate through today's rapidly shifting environments. His other published works for ASAE include *Building a Knowledge-Based Culture* (co-authored with Jean S. Frankel and Kermit M. Eide), *Successful Association Leadership: Dimensions of 21st Century Competency for the CEO* (co-authored with Marybeth Fidler), and the *Association Education Handbook*.

Jean S. Frankel is a principal partner of Tecker Consultants LLC. She works with associations on strategic planning and thinking, organizational redesign, and leadership development initiatives. She has held management and consulting positions at major corporations such as American Express and AT&T and now focuses her practice primarily on strategic and organizational planning for associations. She is a frequent speaker on organizational strategy at association conferences and symposiums and is co-author with Glenn H. Tecker and Kermit M. Eide of *Building a Knowledge-Based Culture*.

Paul D. Meyer, CAE, is a principal partner of Tecker Consultants LLC. He works with both associations and corporations on strategic planning and thinking, governance redesign, research, program assessment, innovation training, and organizational change initiatives with a focus on implementation strategy. He has held a variety of positions with associations and corporations, all of which have contributed practical experience to his consulting engagements. Paul is a frequent speaker and writer on strategic thinking, organizational change, innovation, leadership development, technology strategy, and marketing.

The American Society of Association Executives Foundation

Vision Statement

The ASAE Foundation will be the global leader enabling associates, their executives, and their partners to prepare for the future.

Mission Statement

The ASAE Foundation, in partnership with ASAE, is dedicated to enhancing the association community's ability to anticipate and prepare for change through education and research, thereby maximizing the community's positive impact on society.

About the ASAE Foundation

Associations and the businesses that serve them need comprehensive, credible, and current information to make wise strategic decisions in our constantly changing world. The American Society of Association Executives Foundation has accepted the challenge of providing research to ensure that associations and their partners can face the future with confidence.

The Foundation forms partnerships with qualified researchers to use a range of methodologies, including environmental scanning, case studies, think tanks, focus groups, and extensive literature searches within and outside the association body of knowledge. The Foundation convenes the best thinkers and practitioners to shape and test its research; its work is not done until it has created tools to put its research findings into everyday practice.

Through the Endowing the Future and the Partners for the Future campaigns, the ASAE Foundation built a $10 million research endowment to provide an ongoing source of funding for this work. It also welcomes contributions through other development initiatives. For more information about the ASAE Foundation research and fundraising programs, visit www.asaefoundation.org